COLLECTIONS

Leveled Library Plus
Teacher's Guide

Grade 3

Harcourt

Orlando   Boston   Dallas   Chicago   San Diego

Visit *The Learning Site!*
www.harcourtschool.com

The Leveled Libraries Chart is intended to help Reading Recovery® teachers in purchasing leveled books from Harcourt. Please note the following:

(1) Reading Recovery® is a registered service mark of The Ohio State University.

(2) The complete Reading Recovery® book list, created by the Reading Recovery® Council of North America, includes books from numerous publishers since a premise of the program is that children be provided with a wide range of texts. One publisher's book list alone is not sufficient to implement a Reading Recovery® program.

(3) Levels are subject to change as they are periodically tested and reevaluated.

Printed in the United States of America

ISBN 0-15-322548-3

2 3 4 5 6 7 8 9 10   073   2003 2002 2001

Contents

Using Trade Books

> *"Children's literature lies at the heart of the elementary school curriculum; its use is informed by theory and research and based on sound practices that teachers and librarians have developed through experience."*
>
> **Beatrice E. Cullinan**
> ***Literature and the Child***

Literature in the Classroom

Guiding students to become effective, enthusiastic readers is a major goal for every teacher. Research confirms the experiences of many teachers who have found that creating a classroom environment that surrounds students with language in every form is an important step in achieving this goal. Students need to hear, read, and use both formal and informal language for a variety of purposes and in a variety of formats and settings.

A key ingredient in enriching students' experience with language is providing quality literature for them to read, discuss, and explore. The wider the selection of available reading materials, the more likely it is that a student will come upon that one special book that sparks a new interest, expands a horizon, or produces a significant insight. The discovery of a particular subject, author, genre, or style often motivates students to seek out similar works on their own and to share their enthusiasm, which may well be contagious, with classmates. Successful and rewarding reading experiences lead to increased motivation and a lifelong love of reading.

Using trade books, either in conjunction with *Collections* or in other ways, is an excellent method for exposing students to a wide variety of fine literature. Studies show also that using trade books to teach skills and strategies is very successful and that students do transfer this learning to their reading in other contexts.

About the Leveled Library Plus Teacher's Guide

The *Leveled Library Plus Teacher's Guide* provides inviting literacy activites for twenty-four diverse, high-quality trade books. Each trade book connects to a popular thematic unit and has a daily lesson plan that reinforces reading skills and strategies. These daily student-centered lessons make it easy to include trade books as part of a rich, well-balanced reading program.

Features of Lesson Plans

- reproducible pages for daily instruction

- focus skills and strategies that correlate with *Collections*

- theme connections that correlate with themes in *Collections*

- vocabulary study and Language Links

- Response Journal activities

- Book Talk questions for guided reading

- Wrap-Up Projects and Inquiry Projects

- writing activities that include narrative, informative, and persuasive writing

Additional Program Features

- bookmarks, role badges, and record-keeping instruments for Literature Circles

- The Traits of Good Writing and writing rubrics

- additional vocabulary activities

- reproducible student glossary

- learning contracts

Using the Leveled Library

Using the Leveled Library with *Collections*

There are a number of options for using the trade books in the Leveled Library and the accompanying lessons in the *Leveled Library Plus Teacher's Guide* to supplement, complement, or expand upon your students' reading in *Collections*. Because the trade books are theme-related, you can use them in conjunction with the anthology without interrupting your theme-based instruction.

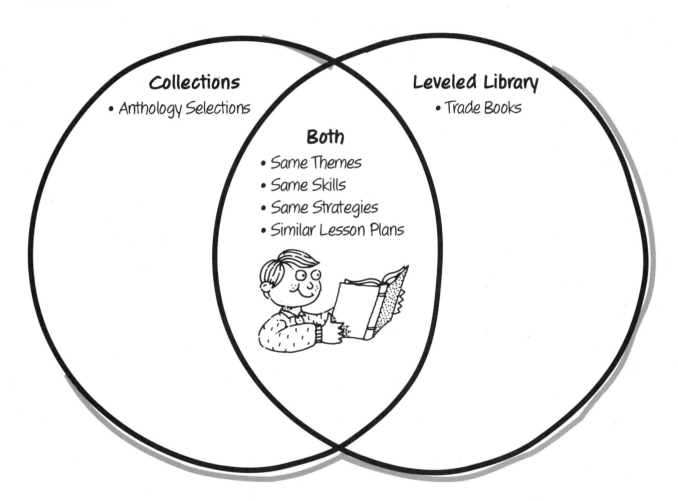

Collections
- Anthology Selections

Leveled Library
- Trade Books

Both
- Same Themes
- Same Skills
- Same Strategies
- Similar Lesson Plans

Leveled Library books that correlate with each *Collections* theme are listed on the Multi-Level Books pages in the *Teacher's Edition*. The Leveled Libraries Chart on pages 6 and 7 shows how the focus skills and strategies in the Leveled Library lesson plans match the focus skills and strategies for the *Collections* selections.

Skills and Strategies Chart

Each Leveled Library book is paired with a selection from the *Collections* Student Edition. Every trade book lesson teaches the same focus skill and strategy as the corresponding selection from *Collections*.

	Collections Selection	Leveled Library Book	Focus Skill	Focus Strategy
Book 1, Theme 1: Something Special!	Arthur Writes a Story	What Do Authors Do?	Prefixes and Suffixes	Make and Confirm Predictions
	Marta's Magnets		Word Identification Strategies	Use Prior Knowledge
	Ronald Morgan Goes to Camp	Ibis: A True Whale Story	Predict Outcomes	Reread
	Allie's Basketball Dream	Snowshoe Thompson	Multiple-Meaning Words	Summarize
	Water Woman	Making Friends	Elements of Nonfiction	Adjust Reading Rate
Book 1, Theme 2: What a Team!	Officer Buckle and Gloria	Two of Everything	Story Elements	Use Prior Knowledge
	Turtle Bay	The Wave	Drawing Conclusions	Use Context to Confirm Meaning
	Wild Shots, They're My Life	Dolphin Adventure: A True Story	Vocabulary in Context	Use Text Structure and Format
	Balto, the Dog Who Saved Nome		Make Inferences	Use Graphic Aids
	Little Grunt and the Big Egg	The Edible Pyramid: Good Eating Every day	Reality and Fantasy	Self-Question
Book 1, Theme 3: Friends to Grow With	The Stories Julian Tells	Julian's Glorious Summer	Synonyms and Antonyms	Read Ahead
	The Talent Show	Cam Jansen and the Triceratops Pops Mystery	Locating Information	Create Mental Images
	Rosie, a Visiting Dog's Story		Main Idea	Use Context to Confirm Meaning
	Centerfield Ballhawk	Ramona Quimby, Age 8	Homographs and Homophones	Use Reference Sources
	Ramona Forever	Willie's Not the Hugging Kind	Author's Purpose	Self-Question

	Collections Selection	Leveled Library Book	Focus Skill	Focus Strategy
Book 2, Theme 1: Tell Me a Story	Coyote Places the Stars	Coyote: A Trickster Tale from the American Southwest	Sequence	Self-Question
	Why Mosquitoes Buzz in People's Ears	Coyote and the Laughing Butterflies	Syllabication	Use Text Structure and Format
	A Bookworm Who Hatched	Booker T. Washington	Fact and Opinion	Summarize
	Cloudy With a Chance of Meatballs	The Chickenhouse House	Figurative Language	Make and Confirm Predictions
	The Crowded House		Skim and Scan	Create Mental Images
Book 2, Theme 2: Good Neighbors	Leah's Pony	Bonesy and Isabel	Characters' Feelings and Actions	Reread
	The Three Little Javelinas	Aldo Ice Cream	Compare and Contrast	Use Prior Knowledge
	Cocoa Ice	Horsepower: The Wonder of Draft Horses	Summarize	Use Reference Sources
	Yippee-Yay!	My Horse of the North	Study Strategies	Use Context to Confirm Meaning
	If You Made a Million		Paraphrase	Adjust Reading Rate
Book 2, Theme 3: Celebrate Our World	I'm in Charge of Celebrations	Frida María: A Story of the Old Southwest	Important Details	Create Mental Images
	Alejandro's Gift	Mama Provi and the Pot of Rice	Problem Solving	Read Ahead
	Rocking and Rolling	Jordi's Star	Cause and Effect	Use Graphic Aids
	The Armadillo from Amarillo	Earth: Our Planet in Space	Referents	Use Context to Confirm Meaning
	Visitors from Space		Note Taking	Use Text Structure and Format

Management Options

The Leveled Library books and lesson plans can be used in a variety of ways to fit your teaching style and the needs of your students. The Leveled Library books and the accompanying lessons in the *Leveled Library Plus Teacher's Guide* can be used with whole groups or small groups.

Whole Group

1. Use a Leveled Library book to apply and reinforce skills after reading the *Student Edition* selection.

2. Expand on a theme by having students read theme-related Leveled Library books in addition to *Student Edition* selections.

Small Groups

1. Have some groups read a *Student Edition* selection while others read a complementary Leveled Library book. Laminate lesson plans to be used in **learning centers**.

2. Use challenging books from the Leveled Library to allow **above-level readers** to proceed at their own pace or to pursue individual interests. You may want to establish a learning contract with the student if he or she will be completing the book and lesson plan independently. For more information and a sample learning contract, see pages 290–291.

3. Have **below-level readers** read a book at their reading level and complete the lesson plan with other students reading the same book. Student-centered lesson plans provide teachers with the opportunity to give additional support to those who need it.

4. Have small mixed groups of students read a Leveled Library book that interests them. Discussion groups and cooperative activities provide **below-level readers** with peer support while providing **above-level readers** with the opportunity to take part in thought-provoking discussions and hands-on activities.

5. Have students read in Literature Circles. See pages 10–11 for suggestions on using Literature Circles in the classroom.

Other Ways to Use the Leveled Library

In Leveled Order

- Students may read individually, with partners, or in small groups.
- For information and suggestions on providing students with appropriate texts and assessing their progress, see the Leveled Library Books and Benchmark Books section on page 16.

In Your Classroom Library

- Have Leveled Library books available for independent self-selected reading. Duplicate daily lessons for students to complete independently.
- Encourage groups of students to form informal book clubs based on shared interest in a self-selected book. Students meet on a regular basis to read and discuss the book they've chosen.

In Text Sets

- Integrate Leveled Library books into text sets for small group instruction. Text sets might be made up of different books on the same subject or theme, books by the same author, or books in the same genre.
- Including an Easy or Challenge level book in a text set with other books can help you accommodate the needs of all your students in the small group setting.

For Cross-Curricular Connections

- Choose Leveled Library books that you can link to units you are teaching in science, social studies, math, music, art, and other areas.
- Use Leveled Library books to introduce, support, and extend your teaching of content-area units.

> *"As proficiency develops, reading should be thought of not so much as a separate subject in school but as integral to learning literature, social studies, and science."*
>
> **The Commission on Reading**
> *Becoming a Nation of Readers*

Literature Circles

Literature Circles are small groups of students who come together to read and respond to a piece of literature of their choice. The Literature Circle approach is an excellent way to integrate quality trade books and collaborative learning into a classroom reading program.

◉ **Getting Started** Select trade books that reflect students' interests. Give a brief presentation to introduce each of the books. Use students' book choices as the basis for forming Literature Circles.

◉ **Scheduling Literature Circles** Set up a schedule for Literature Circles to meet on a regular basis. You might divide each session into periods for reading, writing, and discussion; or you may prefer to rotate sessions devoted to reading and writing with group meetings on alternate days.

◉ **Conducting Literature Circles** Students determine a reasonable number of pages to read for each session. After they read each day's portion, they write responses to what they have just read. Then they use their written responses to launch a discussion of the day's reading. The **Literature Circle Bookmarks** on pages 283–284 provide questions that students might ask themselves to guide their reading and discussion. When the group has finished their book, they decide on an interesting and creative way to share it with classmates and perhaps to interest others in reading it. Have students use the **Literature Circle Checklist** on page 289 to monitor their own participation in Literature Circles and to remind them of their responsibilities as members of the group.

◉ **Using Roles** When Literature Circles are relatively new, it is helpful to have students take turns assuming a variety of task roles to guide and focus their reading, writing, and discussion. You may assign roles or allow students to choose their own.

Literature Circle Role Badges can be found on pages 285–288. The badges show eight possible roles for both fiction and non-fiction, with a brief description of each role on the reverse side of the badge. After students complete their daily reading, have them make notes about the literature from the perspective of their role for that day. They can then bring their notes to contribute to the discussion.

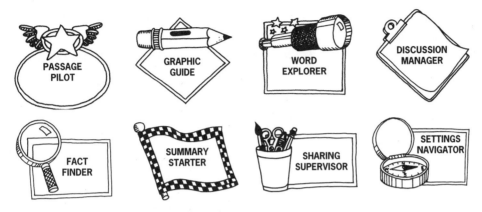

PASSAGE PILOT

GRAPHIC GUIDE

WORD EXPLORER

DISCUSSION MANAGER

FACT FINDER

SUMMARY STARTER

SHARING SUPERVISOR

SETTINGS NAVIGATOR

◎ **Using Journals** After students have become familiar with Literature Circles, you can eliminate the roles and instead have students write entries in their response journals to use as a springboard for discussion.

◎ **Promoting Free Discussion** Guide students to understand that their roles or journal notes are meant to provide a springboard for discussion rather than a formula that must be followed. Encourage group members to engage in conversations that allow for spontaneous observations and responses.

◎ **Introducing Procedures and Concepts** The ultimate goal is for students to conduct Literature Circles on their own. However, they may first require guidance and practice. One way to familiarize students with the concepts and practices is by using brief selections for practice sessions during which you model good discussion questions, responses that enrich the discussion, and effective group dynamics. Help students learn to use the roles by focusing on one role at a time.

◎ **Assessing Students' Progress** Literature Circles lend themselves to informal observation and assessment. The **Literature Circle Student Record Form** on page 282 provides a convenient means for assessing students' progress.

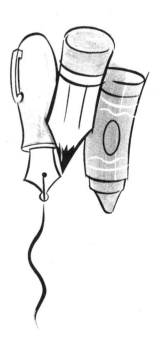

Journaling

How to Use Journals

Journaling has become a valuable tool widely used in today's classroom. The following chart shows how you might use some popular types of journals.

TYPE OF JOURNAL	HOW IT'S USED	POSSIBLE SCHEDULING
daily journal	Students record their experiences, feelings, and ideas.	at the beginning of the school day
learning log	Students write their reflections on content-area learning.	at the end of a class session or study unit
response journal (reading log, literature log)	Students write responses to what they are reading.	during/after each reading session

More About Response Journals

When writing in response journals, students should record the title of the book they are reading and their thoughts and feelings about what they have just read. It may be helpful to ask some guiding questions, such as:

 What did you like best and least about the part you just read, and why?

 What thoughts do you have about the characters and what they did?

 What questions did you ask yourself as you were reading?

 What did you picture in your mind as you were reading?

 What do you predict might happen next?

Journaling as a Springboard for Literature Circles

After students have become familiar with Literature Circles and comfortable with participating in them, role sheets can be replaced by personal response journals. During and after reading, students can record their responses and ideas for discussion topics in their journals to bring to the literature circle meeting.

Genre

Why is it important to learn about genre?

Students should know and understand that there are many genres and that each one offers different and exciting approaches to literature. Learning about genre helps students become more effective and successful readers. Knowing the characteristics of each genre improves students' comprehension by empowering them to set appropriate purposes for reading and to interpret information based on those purposes. When students understand that texts of different genres have different forms and functions, they are able to engage in reading and be active, knowledgeable readers.

What are the different types of genres?

Students should become familiar with the distinguishing characteristics of each major genre and the purposes, or goals, authors often associate with each one.

- ◎ **autobiography:** The story of a real person's life, told by that person. The author's purpose is usually to express thoughts and feelings, not just give information.

- ◎ **biography:** The story of a real person's life, told by someone else. The purpose is to inform, but the author may invent some details, such as dialogue, to bring the person to life.

- ◎ **fantasy:** A fanciful story about events that could not really happen. The purpose is to entertain, but the story may also have a message.

- ◎ **mystery:** A story in which the main character and the reader are challenged to solve a problem. The purpose is to entertain.

- ◎ **nonfiction:** Information about a particular topic which often includes photos, captions, or diagrams. The author's purpose is to give factual information.

- ◎ **realistic fiction:** A made-up story. The characters and events in the story often imitate real life.

- ◎ **science fiction:** A story based on ideas from science. The plot is unrealistic, and the story is usually set in the future.

You may choose to use titles from the Leveled Library to examine the nuances of the different genres with students. For example, students may be familiar with the character Ramona Quimby from Beverly Cleary's *Ramona Quimby, Age 8*. Knowing that the trade book is realistic fiction can help students understand Ramona's actions by comparing them to their own. Historical fiction such as *When Willard Met Babe Ruth* can be used to elicit from students that although Babe Ruth was a real person, the events in the story were invented by the author.

How can I use the Leveled Library books to teach about genre?

The chart on page 15 shows the genre designations for the trade books in the Leveled Library. You can integrate Leveled Library books into your teaching of genre in a number of ways. The graphic below shows some suggestions.

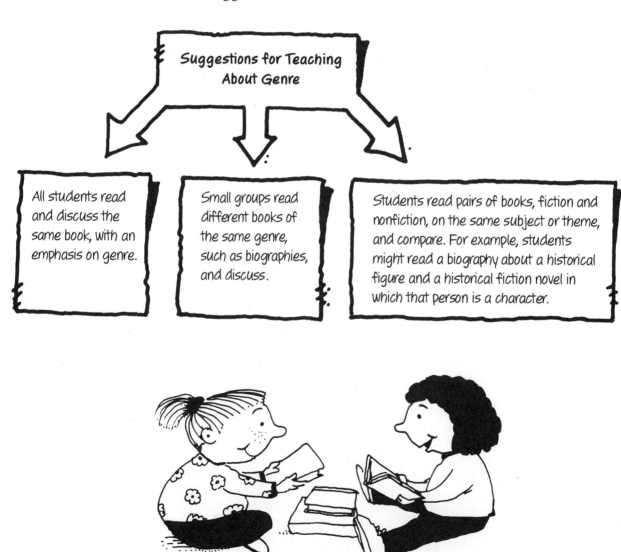

Suggestions for Teaching About Genre

All students read and discuss the same book, with an emphasis on genre.

Small groups read different books of the same genre, such as biographies, and discuss.

Students read pairs of books, fiction and nonfiction, on the same subject or theme, and compare. For example, students might read a biography about a historical figure and a historical fiction novel in which that person is a character.

Genre and Cross-Curricular Chart

Genre	Collections Themes						Cross-Curricular Connections					
	Self-Discovery	Working Together	Growth and Change	Creativity	Communities	Explorations	Science	Social Studies	Language Arts	Math	Health	The Arts
Realistic Fiction												
Willie's Not the Hugging Kind			•					•				
Frida María: A Story of the Old Southwest						•		•				
Jordi's Star						•	•					
Julian's Glorious Summer			•					•				
Aldo Ice Cream					•			•				
Ramona Quimby, Age 8			•					•				
Bonesy and Isabel					•			•				
Mama Provi and the Pot of Rice						•		•				
Nonfiction												
Making Friends	•							•				
My Horse of the North						•		•				
What Do Authors Do?	•								•			
Earth: Our Planet in Space						•	•					
Horsepower: The Wonder of Draft Horses						•		•				
Biography												
Booker T. Washington				•						•		
Historical Fiction												
Snowshoe Thompson	•							•				
The Chickenhouse House				•				•				
Mystery												
Cam Jansen and the Triceratops Pops Mystery			•									•
Folktales												
Coyote: A Trickster Tale from the American Southwest				•				•				
Two of Everything		•								•		
Coyote and the Laughing Butterflies				•				•				
The Wave		•						•				
Informational Narrative												
Ibis: A True Whale Story	•						•					
The Edible Pyramid		•									•	
Dolphin Adventure: A True Story		•					•					

Leveled Library Books

Leveled Library books are trade books that have been leveled using a consistent set of criteria. The library at each grade offers a range of difficulty from approximately one grade below level to two grades above. Leveled Library books make it possible to match students to texts with which they will be successful. Using the Leveled Library in leveled order gives all students the opportunity to progress, level by level, toward becoming fluent, lifelong readers.

Criteria Used in Leveling Process

PRIMARY LEVELS	PRIMARY AND INTERMEDIATE	INTERMEDIATE LEVELS
• illustrations • repetition of language patterns • language structures • text position	• content • vocabulary • prior knowledge • amount of text/length of book • narrative structure or text structure	• vocabulary concepts • genre • illustration or graphic support

Benchmark Books

The three Benchmark Books for each grade are Leveled Library books that represent specific levels of reading difficulty. **Individual Reading Inventory Forms** are provided for assessing students' reading progress at various times during the school year. More information about using the Individual Reading Inventory can be found on page 302.

- If you find that the student reads the indicated passage from the Benchmark Book with almost perfect accuracy, reassess him or her at a higher level and provide appropriate instruction with books from the Leveled Library.

- If the student meets the benchmark according to the criteria on page 302, he or she is ready to begin reading instruction at the indicated level.

- If the student makes too many errors, reassess him or her at a lower level and provide support through partner reading, teacher intervention, or other appropriate means.

Leveled Library Chart

Books in the Leveled Libraries overlap across the grade levels. The following chart shows the placement of the Leveled Library books for Grade 3.

Book Title	Leveled Library Level	Guided Reading Level	Lexile Level
Snowshoe Thompson	2.0–2.5	J–L	330
Coyote: A Trickster Tale from the American Southwest	2.0–2.5	J–L	360
Two of Everything	2.0–2.5	J–L	540
Booker T. Washington	2.5–3.0	L–M	350
Ibis: A True Whale Story	2.5–3.0	L–M	530
The Edible Pyramid: Good Eating Every Day	2.5–3.0	L–M	370
Making Friends	2.5–3.0	L–M	480
Willie's Not the Hugging Kind	*3.0	M–N	560
Frida María: A Story of the Old Southwest	3.0–3.5	N–O	620
Jordi's Star	3.0–3.5	N–O	780
Cam Jansen and the Triceratops Pops Mystery	3.0–3.5	N–O	490
Julian's Glorious Summer	3.0–3.5	N–O	480
Coyote and the Laughing Butterflies	*3.5	O	620
My Horse of the North	3.5–4.0	O–P	540
Mama Provi and the Pot of Rice	3.5–4.0	O–P	900
What Do Authors Do?	3.5–4.0	O–P	220
Earth: Our Planet in Space	3.5–4.0	O–P	620
The Chickenhouse House	*4.0	P–Q	610
Aldo Ice Cream	4.0–4.5	Q	770
The Wave	4.0–4.5	Q	700
Ramona Quimby, Age 8	4.0–4.5	Q	860
Bonesy and Isabel	4.5–5.0	R	920
Dolphin Adventure: A True Story	4.5–5.0	R	930
Horsepower: The Wonder of Draft Horses	4.5–5.0	R	930

* Benchmark Book

Snowshoe Thompson

by Nancy Smiler Levinson

Reading Level

▶ Theme Connection
Snowshoe Thompson echoes "Allie's Basketball Dream" in its presentation of a main character who does not give up. In both stories, the characters work hard to achieve something.

▶ Summary
John "Snowshoe" Thompson was a Scandinavian immigrant who introduced snow skis in California in the 1850s. In this story, Thompson crafts a pair of skis so he can transport a child's letter across the treacherous Sierra Nevada range to the boy's father, who is digging for gold. When Thompson returns, he has something for the boy—a letter from Pa!

▶ Building Background
Ask students what snowshoes are and how they are used. You or a volunteer might try drawing one on the board. Ask students to read to find out whether there is "something special" about Snowshoe Thompson. Explain that this is an informational story. It is based on the true story of a man named John Thompson, and it is set long ago, at a time when there were no easy ways to send mail to many areas of our country. Ask students for their ideas about how people got their words to one another across long distances.

Author Profile
Author of many well-crafted biographies, Nancy Smiler Levinson can make inspirational historical figures come alive for children. Levinson began writing for young readers when her own children were toddlers. "During the many hours I spent reading to them," she says, "I felt a growing urge to write for the young audience."

Additional Books by the Author
- *Thomas Alva Edison, Great Inventor*
- *Clara and the Bookwagon*
- *If You Lived in the Alaskan Territory*

Vocabulary

Have students use the vocabulary words to complete a diagram like the one below. See pages 296–299 for additional vocabulary activities. For definitions of the words, see the Glossary.

Day 1	Day 2	Day 3	Day 4
Nevada p. 9	skis p. 18	pole p. 34	mailbag p. 56
snow p. 11	snowshoes p. 21	boots p. 42	
mountains p. 12	glide p. 21	meadows p. 45	
	Norway p. 21	slopes p. 45	
	smooth p. 22		

© Harcourt

	Response	Strategies	Skill
Day 1 Chapter 1	**Book Talk** • Important Details • Retell • Make Predictions **Writing:** Express Personal Opinion	**SUMMARIZE** FOCUS STRATEGY *Hidden Surprises, p. T161	**MULTIPLE-MEANING WORDS** FOCUS SKILL *Hidden Surprises, pp. T160–T161
Day 2 Chapter 2	**Book Talk** • Draw Conclusions • Determine Author's Purpose • Determine Characters' Traits **Writing:** Make Judgments	Use Prior Knowledge *Hidden Surprises, p. T71	Make Inferences *Hidden Surprises, pp. T408–T409
Day 3 Chapters 3–4	**Book Talk** • Sequence • Generalize • Draw Conclusions/Classify **Writing:** Express Personal Opinion	Create Mental Images *Hidden Surprises, p. T567	Vocabulary in Context *Hidden Surprises, pp. T370–T371
Day 4 Chapter 5	**Book Talk** • Make Comparisons • Theme • Express Personal Opinion **Writing:** Express Personal Opinion	**SUMMARIZE** FOCUS STRATEGY *Hidden Surprises, p. T161	**MULTIPLE-MEANING WORDS** FOCUS SKILL *Hidden Surprises, pp. T160–T161
Day 5 Wrap-Up	**Project** ✓ Design and Create Awards • Inquiry Project **Writing** ✓ Personal Narrative *Hidden Surprises, pp. T54–T55 **Language Link** • Words That Imitate Sounds **Assessment** ✓ Comprehension Test		

*Additional support is provided in *Collections*.
✓ Options for Assessment

© Harcourt

Snowshoe Thompson

BOOK TALK

After you read Chapter 1, meet with your group to discuss and answer the following questions:

❶ Who is Danny, and what does he want?

❷ What is the problem to solve in this story?

❸ How will John Thompson try to solve the problem?

Strategies Good Readers Use

FOCUS STRATEGY **SUMMARIZE**

Summarize the first chapter. List all of the main characters and events so far.

RESPONSE JOURNAL

Do you feel sorry for Danny? Explain why or why not in your journal.

SKILLS IN CONTEXT

FOCUS SKILL **MULTIPLE-MEANING WORDS: MULTIPLE-MEANING CARD GAME** Some words, like *tank*, have more than one meaning. A tank can be a huge moving fighting machine. A tank can also be a container for gas or other liquids.

What You Need

- twelve to fifteen 3" x 5" index cards
- writing materials

What to Do

1. Work together with a small group of classmates. Find all the multiple-meaning words in the story so far.

2. Write each word on a separate index card. On any remaining cards, write other multiple-meaning words you know, such as *move*, *heart*, *hard*, and *top*.

3. Shuffle the cards, and then exchange your cards with another group.

4. Take turns drawing cards one at a time. Each time you draw, try to name two different meanings for the word. If you do so correctly, keep the card. If not, put it back, and reshuffle. See who gets the most cards.

Here are some words from the story to get you started: *coach, count, home*

Think Ahead What do you think John Thompson will show Danny?

© Harcourt

Snowshoe Thompson

BOOK TALK

After you read Chapter 2, meet with your group to discuss and answer the following questions:

1 How does Snowshoe Thompson know about skis?

2 Why do you think the author includes the part about making the skis?

3 What words would you use to describe Snowshoe Thompson?

RESPONSE JOURNAL

Do you think Snowshoe Thompson does a good job of showing Danny how to make skis? Why or why not?

> **Strategies Good Readers Use**
>
> **USE PRIOR KNOWLEDGE**
>
> *W*rite one or more reasons why skis are better than snowshoes for traveling long distances.

SKILLS IN CONTEXT

MAKE INFERENCES: MAKE A CHART Some things are not said in a book, but you can figure them out. You can use the information the author gives you to make guesses about characters and events. Create a chart that shows your guesses about Snowshoe.

What You Need

- poster board
- markers

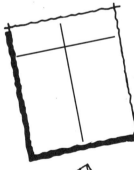

What to Do

1. Make a chart with two columns. Label one *What Snowshoe Says or Does* and the other *What This Shows About Him.*

2. In the first column, list some things that Snowshoe says and does. For example, he starts work right away. He does not stop until he is done.

3. In the second column, write next to each item in the first column what the words or actions tell about Snowshoe.

4. Hang your chart in the classroom.

Here is an example to get you started: *Snowshoe decides to cross the mountains. He is brave.*

Think Ahead *What do you think will happen next?*

© Harcourt

Snowshoe Thompson

BOOK TALK

After you read Chapters 3–4, meet with your group to discuss and answer the following questions:

❶ What does John (Snowshoe Thompson) do right after he makes the skis?

❷ How do others react to what John is doing?

❸ What dangers does John face crossing the mountains?

RESPONSE JOURNAL

Do you believe the part of the story in which the people make fun of John? Why or why not?

> **Strategies Good Readers Use**
>
> ### CREATE MENTAL IMAGES
>
> Imagine John alone at night in the mountains. Write one thing he sees, feels, or hears.

SKILLS IN CONTEXT

VOCABULARY IN CONTEXT: MAKE A DIAGRAM When you are reading and find a word you do not know, you can use the words before and after it to help you figure out its meaning. Make a diagram to show how you might do this.

What You Need

• colored markers
• paper

What to Do

1. Find an unfamiliar word in *Snowshoe Thompson*. Write on a sheet of paper the sentence that contains this word. Then write the sentences around it.

2. Use a red or blue marker to circle the word.

3. Use a different-colored marker to circle the clues around the word that helped you figure out the word's meaning. For example, you could write the sentence "He was gliding on the snow," and circle the word *gliding* in red or blue. You could circle *snow* in a different color. Then you could explain how you glide, or move, over something smooth like snow.

4. Explain your diagram to the class.

Here are some words you could show: *dash, foolhardy, deliver, howled*

Think Ahead How will the story end?

Snowshoe Thompson

BOOK TALK

After you read Chapter 5, meet with your group to discuss and answer the following questions:

1 *Snowshoe Thompson* is a story about someone working hard to meet a goal. What other stories have you read in *Hidden Surprises* about people who do not quit?

2 What message does this story send about trying out new ideas?

3 What else would you like to learn about Snowshoe Thompson and his travels?

> **Strategies Good Readers Use**
>
> **FOCUS STRATEGY SUMMARIZE**
>
> Summarize this book by writing sentences that tell the problem and how it is solved.

RESPONSE JOURNAL

What did you like best about this story?

SKILLS IN CONTEXT

FOCUS SKILL MULTIPLE-MEANING WORDS: MULTIPLE-MEANINGS BOOK When you are reading, you will often come across words with more than one meaning. Remember that the context will help you figure out which meaning the author intended.

What You Need

- writing materials
- paper
- construction paper
- stapler

What to Do

1. Make a page for a book of multiple-meaning words. Choose one word from *Snowshoe Thompson* with multiple meanings. Write the word and its meanings.

2. Use the word in sentences to show its different meanings. If possible, illustrate one or more of the meanings.

3. Add your page to those made by other students to form a book. Put the pages in alphabetical order. Staple the pages together to make a book.

Here are some multiple-meaning words from **Snowshoe Thompson:** *hand, fast, will, back, watch, dash, hit*

Wrap-Up

▶ **Project** DESIGN AND CREATE AWARDS Have students make two awards for Snowshoe Thompson: a medal of honor that he could wear and a certificate detailing his accomplishment.

- Organize students into groups, and have them discuss what medals and certificates usually show and tell.
- Ask students to complete the copying master on page 25 to plan their work. Students may wish to use software that creates certificates. They may create their medals in a variety of shapes from a variety of materials.
- Have groups post their certificates and display their medals.

▶ **Writing** PERSONAL NARRATIVE Have students respond to the following writing prompt: **Write a personal narrative about a time when you or someone you know solved a problem.** Have students use the copying master on page 26 to plan their personal narratives. Remind students to focus on creating a narrative voice. Use *Hidden Surprises* pages T54–T55 for additional support. Rubrics for evaluating student writing are provided on pages 292–295.

▶ **Language Link** WORDS THAT IMITATE SOUNDS Explain that some words sound like what they mean. For example, the word *buzz*, which describes the sound of a fly, sounds exactly like what the fly does. Have students list some words in this story that imitate sounds.

Inquiry Project

Ask students what questions their reading has left them with. Perhaps they would like to know about early travel on skis, how skis have changed over time, the Sierra Nevada, or people like Pa who looked for gold in California. Have students construct and complete the first two columns of a K-W-L chart to guide their research. When they are done, have them complete the last column.

K What I Know	W What I Want to Find Out	L What I Learned
The idea for skis came from Norway.	Were skis invented in Norway?	
Skis are made of wood.		

✔ **Comprehension Test** Test students' comprehension of *Snowshoe Thompson* by having them complete the copying master on page 27.

© Harcourt

Name _____

Project Planner

Snowshoe Thompson is a thoughtful and brave person.
It is your job to honor him with a medal and certificate.

☐ **Step 1.** Brainstorm ideas about what an award
for Snowshoe Thompson might say or
show.

Say   Show

_____   _____

_____   _____

_____   _____

_____   _____

What You Need
- paper
- writing materials
- materials to make a medal, such as cardboard and foil, or other items of your choice

☐ **Step 2.** Complete this organizer to show the details you learned about
Snowshoe Thompson.

Who:
What:
Where:
When:
Why:
How:

☐ **Step 3.** Choose a shape for the medal, such as a star, snowshoe, or diamond.
Use any materials you want to make it. Then put Snowshoe's name on it.

☐ **Step 4.** Make the certificate. Use a computer program to write what he did, or
print it neatly on heavy paper. Be sure the certificate gives all the facts.

☐ **Step 5.** Display your medal and certificate in the classroom.

Personal Narrative

Write a narrative about a time when you or someone you know solved a problem. Tell the events in the order they happened. Complete this graphic organizer to help you plan your narrative.

Prewriting Graphic Organizer

Who: _____

Where: _____

When: _____

Problem: _____

_____

_____

Steps to Solve Problem: _____

_____

_____

_____

Solution: _____

_____

_____

_____

Name _____

Comprehension Test

Read each question below. Then mark the letter for the answer you have chosen.

1. **Who is Danny?**
   - Ⓐ a skier
   - Ⓑ the son of Snowshoe Thompson
   - Ⓒ a boy whose father is away
   - Ⓓ a boy who wants to hunt gold

2. **Who is John?**
   - Ⓕ Danny's dad
   - Ⓖ Aunt Nan's husband
   - Ⓗ a gold miner
   - Ⓙ Snowshoe Thompson

3. **What does Danny want?**
   - Ⓐ his dad to find gold
   - Ⓑ his dad to come home for Christmas
   - Ⓒ a pair of skis
   - Ⓓ a dad like Snowshoe Thompson

4. **What is the first thing Snowshoe does to make skis?**
   - Ⓕ boils wood
   - Ⓖ chops a log
   - Ⓗ curves the tips
   - Ⓙ sands the skis

5. **How does Snowshoe Thompson know about skis?**
   - Ⓐ He invented them.
   - Ⓑ He learned from some miners.
   - Ⓒ He learned about them in Norway or from someone from Norway.
   - Ⓓ He made them by cutting down snowshoes.

6. **How long does it take Snowshoe to make skis?**
   - Ⓕ one day
   - Ⓗ more than a week
   - Ⓖ several days
   - Ⓙ months

7. **Why do the people who see the skis think they are silly?**
   - Ⓐ They are not smart people.
   - Ⓑ They do not like John.
   - Ⓒ They do not like new ideas.
   - Ⓓ They have never seen skis before.

8. **What does John bring for Danny?**
   - Ⓕ new skis
   - Ⓖ a letter from his pa
   - Ⓗ Danny's pa
   - Ⓙ an empty mailbag

9. **What do you think is most likely to happen in the future?**
   - Ⓐ Pa will give up his job mining.
   - Ⓑ Pa will not come home for Christmas.
   - Ⓒ More people will travel on skis.
   - Ⓓ Snowshoe will get into trouble crossing the mountains.

10. **Write a short answer in response to the question below.**
    Someday Danny will grow up and tell the story of Snowshoe Thompson to his children or to someone else. What will he say?

Coyote: A Trickster Tale from the American Southwest

Reading Level

by Gerald McDermott

▶ Theme Connection
In both "Coyote Places the Stars" and *Coyote: A Trickster Tale from the American Southwest*, students will learn about the adventures of the clever Coyote.

▶ Summary
Coyote is about a mischief-making and demanding creature. Insisting on flying with the crows, this endearing trickster fails to recognize his limits and ends up the victim of his own inquisitive nature. Illustrated in warm, southwestern hues, the book glows with images of Coyote, his crow playmates, and the desert panorama of the Southwest.

▶ Building Background
Tell students that *Coyote: A Trickster Tale from the American Southwest* is a folktale, the kind that explains how something in the natural world came to be the way it is. Point out that such tales often involve animals. Add that it is also a trickster tale in which a clever character outsmarts others. Encourage students to share what they recall about Coyote or other tricksters. Then have them read to find out why Coyote needs all his famous cleverness to help him stay out of trouble.

Author Profile

As a child, Gerald McDermott wandered the local museum with pad and paints in hand, yearning to be an artist. Now the award-winning author and illustrator studies myths and mythological characters to inspire many of his books' characters. His favorite is Coyote. "Coyote is such a loony, wonderful character . . . so foolish, so human," says McDermott. "I found myself very sad the day I finished the art work for that book . . . after months of working with Coyote, I was sorry to let him go."

Additional Books by the Author
- *Anansi the Spider*
- *Zomo the Rabbit*
- *Arrow to the Sun*

Vocabulary

Help students make a deck of Definition Password cards. Have them write each word on the front of a card and its definition on the back. Students can play Definition Password in pairs or small groups. After students have reviewed the words, one student draws a card from the deck and reads the definition. The person who is "it" must say the correct word. If the player does so, he or she draws the next card. See pages 296–299 for additional vocabulary activities. For definitions of the words, see the Glossary.

Definition Password Card

chanting | singing in a rhythm that repeats itself

Day 1	Day 2	Day 3	Day 4
flaming p. 4	winced p. 12	soared p. 16	leapt p. 22
crows p. 7	twitched p. 12	cringed p. 19	demanded p. 23
flock p. 7	chuckled p. 13	cackled p. 19	mesa p. 27
chanting p. 7		boastful p. 21	

© Harcourt

	Response	Strategies	Skill
Day 1 **Pages 2–9**	**Book Talk** • Figurative Language • Draw Conclusions • Determine Characters' Emotions **Writing:** Determine Characters' Traits	**SELF-QUESTION** FOCUS STRATEGY *Journeys of Wonder,* p. T21	**SEQUENCE** FOCUS SKILL *Journeys of Wonder,* pp. T20–T21
Day 2 **Pages 10–15**	**Book Talk** • Interpret Characters' Motivations • Draw Conclusions • Summarize **Writing:** Express Personal Opinion	Use Prior Knowledge *Hidden Surprises,* p. T71	Homographs and Homophones *Hidden Surprises,* pp. T656–T657
Day 3 **Pages 16–21**	**Book Talk** • Cause-Effect • Determine Characters' Emotions • Draw Conclusions **Writing:** Express Personal Opinion	Use Context to Confirm Meaning *Hidden Surprises,* p. T613	Multiple-Meaning Words *Hidden Surprises,* pp. T160–T161
Day 4 **Pages 22–30**	**Book Talk** • Summarize • Determine Characters' Traits • Make Comparisons **Writing:** Identify with Characters	**SELF-QUESTION** FOCUS STRATEGY *Journeys of Wonder,* p. T21	**SEQUENCE** FOCUS SKILL *Journeys of Wonder,* pp. T20–T21
Day 5 **Wrap-Up**	**Project** ✓ Illustrate Coyote's Next Adventure • Inquiry Project **Writing** ✓ Paragraph That Compares *Journeys of Wonder,* pp. T44–T45 **Language Link** • Dialogue and Narration **Assessment** ✓ Comprehension Test		

*Additional support is provided in *Collections.*
✓ Options for Assessment

© Harcourt

Coyote: A Trickster Tale from the American Southwest

BOOK TALK

After you read pages 2–9, meet with your group to discuss and answer the following questions:

1 What does the writer mean when he says that Coyote follows his nose?

2 Why do you think Coyote is so good at getting into trouble?

3 How do you think the other animals feel when they see Coyote coming?

RESPONSE JOURNAL

Do you think Coyote ever stops to think about what will happen next? Explain.

SKILLS IN CONTEXT

FOCUS SKILL **SEQUENCE: A STORY COMIC STRIP** Being able to remember events in the order they happen can help you better remember a story. Coyote visits three animals. What happens each time? What might those animals have said to Coyote when they saw him? Make a comic strip that shows each visit.

What You Need

- **three pieces of drawing paper**
- **drawing tools**
- **tape**

What to Do

1. On each piece of paper, draw a scene to show what happens during one of Coyote's visits.
2. Think about what each animal might have said to Coyote. Add those words.
3. Put the three scenes in the order they happened.
4. Tape the pictures together in that order.
5. Share your comic strip with a classmate.

Here's a scene to get you started:
Coyote follows his nose into Badger's hole.

Think Ahead
Do you think Coyote will get into trouble with the crows?

© Harcourt

Coyote: A Trickster Tale from the American Southwest

BOOK TALK

After you read pages 10–15, meet with your group to discuss and respond to the following questions or statements:

1 Why does Coyote want to fly?

2 How do you know that Old Man Crow does not like Coyote?

3 Describe how the crows get Coyote ready to fly.

RESPONSE JOURNAL

Old Man Crow calls Coyote foolish. Do you agree with him? Explain.

USE PRIOR KNOWLEDGE

Think about a time when you asked someone to teach you how to do something. How does this help you understand how Coyote feels?

SKILLS IN CONTEXT

HOMOGRAPHS AND HOMOPHONES: PLAY A GAME Homographs are words that have the same spellings but different pronunciations and meanings. Homophones are words that sound alike but are spelled differently. They also have different meanings. Invite several friends to play a word game with homophones.

What You Need

- **16 index cards**
- **pencil**
- **dictionary**

What to Do

1. Write *nose, where, threw, wood, some, soar, right, one* on one set of cards. Write *knows, wear, through, would, sum, sore, write, won* on the other.

2. Spread out one set of cards face up.

3. Put the other cards in a deck.

4. Draw one card from the deck. Then find the face-up card with that word's homophone. Say a sentence for each word.

5. If a player uses both words correctly, he or she can keep that pair of cards. The player with the most cards wins.

Here is a pair of sentences to get you started: *My nose itches. Who knows why?*

Think Ahead
Will Coyote be able to fly well?

© Harcourt

BOOK TALK

After you read pages 16–21, meet with your group to discuss and answer the following questions:

1 Why does Coyote tilt to one side as he flies?

2 How can you tell the crows are enjoying themselves at first?

3 Why do the crows stop having fun with Coyote?

RESPONSE JOURNAL

Coyote thinks he is perfect now. Do you agree? Explain.

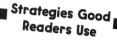
SKILLS IN CONTEXT

MULTIPLE-MEANING WORDS: DOUBLE PUZZLE Some words have more than one meaning. You can use context to help you decide which meaning of the word is being used. For example, you may *pat* your cat or put a *pat* of butter on a slice of bread. Make a puzzle that uses different meanings of the same word.

What You Need

- graph or puzzle paper
- pencil
- dictionary

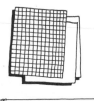

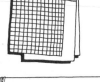

What to Do

1. In the middle of the paper, make a crossword puzzle with these five words: *fly, left, right, spread, stand.*

2. On the left side of the puzzle, write a set of across and down clues for one meaning of each word.

3. On the right side, write a set of across and down clues for another meaning of each word.

4. Use a dictionary to help you think of clues.

Here is a clue to get you started: *When something is correct, it is _____.*

Think Ahead

Do you believe Coyote will stay as perfect as he thinks he is?

© Harcourt

Coyote: A Trickster Tale from the American Southwest

BOOK TALK

After you read pages 22–30, meet with your group to discuss and answer the following questions:

1 How does this story explain why Coyote looks the way he does?

2 How can you tell that Coyote does not learn his lesson when he falls onto the mesa?

3 Which stories in *Journeys of Wonder* does *Coyote* remind you of?

RESPONSE JOURNAL

Imagine that you are one of the crows. How would you act the next time you saw Coyote?

Strategies Good Readers Use

FOCUS STRATEGY **SELF-QUESTION**

*W*hat is one question you asked yourself while reading? Explain how asking yourself this question helped you understand the story.

SKILLS IN CONTEXT

FOCUS SKILL **SEQUENCE: WHAT HAPPENS NEXT?** Knowing the sequence of events can help you understand why some things happen the way they do. For example, if you read that Coyote does a foolish thing, you can understand why someone gets angry with him.

What You Need

- small pieces of paper
- pencil
- a bowl or box

What to Do

1. Look through *Coyote* and find the important events. Write each event on one piece of paper.
2. Put all the pieces of paper in a bowl or box.
3. Ask each player to take one piece of paper, read it, and tell what happens next in the story.
4. Mix up the pieces of paper and play again.

Here is an event to get you started:
Coyote sticks his nose into Badger's hole.
What happens next? (He gets bitten.)

Wrap-Up

▶ **Project** ILLUSTRATE COYOTE'S NEXT ADVENTURE Remind students that knowing how characters usually behave can help readers predict how they will act in the future. Tell students that they will use what they know about Coyote to plan and illustrate a new adventure for him.

• Organize students into small groups.
• Ask students to complete the copying master on page 35 to plan their illustrations.
• Have each group share its illustration with the class.

▶ **Writing** PARAGRAPH THAT COMPARES Have students respond to the following writing prompt: **Compare Coyote in this folktale with an animal character you have read about in another story.** Have students use the copying master on page 36 to plan their paragraphs. Use *Journeys of Wonder* pages T44–T45 for additional support. Rubrics for evaluating student writing are provided on pages 292–295.

▶ **Language Link** DIALOGUE AND NARRATION Have students present pages 9–12 as a Readers Theatre. Remind them that the characters speak the dialogue, or words in quotation marks, and the narrator speaks the lines that are not in quotation marks. Tell them they can also leave out some words or sentences if they are not important to the story.

Inquiry Project

Coyote can be a springboard for inquiry into a variety of topics and ideas. Have students brainstorm topics they would like to know more about and organize their responses in a web. For example, they may wish to learn more about coyotes, such as where they live and what they eat. Students can use reference books and the Internet to begin their inquiry projects.

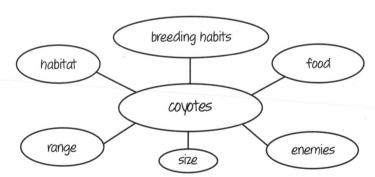

✔ **Comprehension Test** Test students' comprehension of *Coyote* by having them complete the copying master on page 37.

Name _____

Project Planner

In *Coyote*, you learned certain things about Coyote's character. Work in your group to plan Coyote's next adventure. Then illustrate Coyote's adventure.

What You Need
- paper
- pencils

☐ **Step 1.** Write Coyote's name in the center oval of the web below. Then use the ovals on the **left** side of the web to write three words that tell what Coyote is like. For example, suppose a character is always laughing and playing. You might write the word *playful* in one of the ovals on the left. Then talk about the kinds of adventures Coyote might have in the future because of the kind of character he is. In the ovals on the **right**, write the three ideas your group agrees are the best.

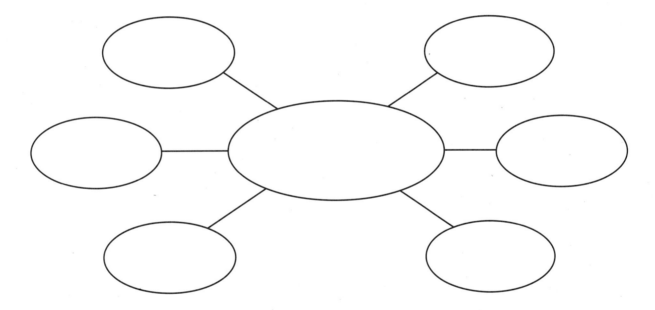

☐ **Step 2.** Work with your group to illustrate Coyote in one of the adventures from your character web.

☐ **Step 3.** Present your illustration to the class.

Paragraph That Compares

Write a paragraph that compares Coyote with an animal character you
have read about in another story. The graphic organizer below will help you plan
your writing. When you finish, use the completed graphic organizer to help you
write your paragraph.

Prewriting Graphic Organizer

Topic: _____   Audience: _____

_____   _____

Main Idea: _____

Likeness 1: _____

Details: _____

Likeness 2: _____

Details: _____

Likeness 3: _____

Details: _____

Main Point Summarized: _____

_____

_____

© Harcourt

Name _____

Comprehension Test

Read each question below. Then mark the letter for the answer you have chosen.

1. **Why is Coyote always in trouble?**
   - Ⓐ He is mean to other animals.
   - Ⓑ He is very curious about everything.
   - Ⓒ He likes to get into fights.
   - Ⓓ He is trying to make friends.

2. **What are the crows doing when Coyote first sees them?**
   - Ⓕ chanting and dancing
   - Ⓖ flying over the canyon
   - Ⓗ plucking feathers from their wings
   - Ⓙ laughing and talking

3. **Why does Coyote want to fly?**
   - Ⓐ so he can chase and eat birds
   - Ⓑ so he can escape from enemies
   - Ⓒ so he can cross the river
   - Ⓓ so he can be the best coyote

4. **Why does Old Man Crow think Coyote is foolish?**
   - Ⓕ He knows Coyote gets in trouble.
   - Ⓖ He knows coyotes can't dance.
   - Ⓗ He knows coyotes cannot be like crows.
   - Ⓙ He thinks only crows are wise.

5. **What is the first thing Old Man Crow says that Coyote can do?**
   - Ⓐ He can fly with them.
   - Ⓑ He can dance with the crows.
   - Ⓒ He can chant with them.
   - Ⓓ He can change color.

6. **How does getting feathers from the crows make Coyote feel?**
   - Ⓕ He does not feel a thing.
   - Ⓖ It makes him scream.
   - Ⓗ He laughs happily.
   - Ⓙ It makes him wince.

7. **Why is Coyote's flying off-balance at first?**
   - Ⓐ He is too heavy to fly.
   - Ⓑ He has only left wing feathers.
   - Ⓒ The crows push him.
   - Ⓓ He doesn't know how to fly.

8. **Which sentence shows that Coyote is boastful?**
   - Ⓕ "Don't leave me behind!"
   - Ⓖ "Oh, if only I could fly."
   - Ⓗ "Let me join you."
   - Ⓙ "Now I'm perfect!"

9. **What does Coyote demand the crows to do?**
   - Ⓐ take back their feathers
   - Ⓑ carry him
   - Ⓒ feed him
   - Ⓓ give him even more feathers

10. **Write a response to this question:**
    What makes Coyote an interesting character to read about?

© Harcourt

Two of Everything

by Lily Toy Hong

Reading Level

> ▶ **Theme Connection** In *Two of Everything*, a couple comes to accept the idea of having twice as much of everything. In "Officer Buckle and Gloria," characters learn that two really is better than one.

> ▶ **Summary** Mr. Haktak, a Chinese farmer of humble means, carries home to his wife an ancient brass pot he has found buried in the ground. Suddenly, something extraordinary happens. The pot doubles everything that's dropped into it . . . *everything!* This charmingly illustrated story, based on a Chinese folktale, entertains and surprises.

> ▶ **Building Background** Tell students that this is a folktale with elements of fantasy, set long ago and far away. Ask students to tell what they already know about this kind of story. Explain that people usually read these stories to be entertained. Ask students to write a question about the title or cover illustration. Have them read to find the answer.

Author Profile

Lily Toy Hong, whose parents emigrated from China only ten years before her birth, grew up in a large Chinese-American family. The idea for her first book, *How the Ox Star Fell from Heaven*, came to her while she studied art in college. "It has always been my secret desire to write and illustrate children's books," says Hong. "Now that I'm almost grown up, I can't believe my dream has come true."

Additional Books by the Author
• *How the Ox Star Fell from Heaven*
• *The Empress and the Silkworm*

Vocabulary

Have students make word maps like the one below to explore the meanings of each noun in the vocabulary list. See pages 296–299 for additional vocabulary activities. For definitions of the words, see the Glossary.

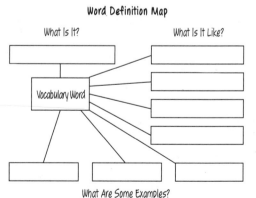

Word Definition Map

What Is It?   What Is It Like?

Vocabulary Word

What Are Some Examples?

Day 1	Day 2	Day 3	Day 4
hut p. 3	coins p. 8	twice p. 15	double p. 24
garden p. 3	wife p. 8	headfirst p. 18	
harvest p. 5	husband p. 8		
village p. 5	identical p. 10		
shovel p. 6			
pot p. 6			

	Response	Strategies	Skills
▶Day 1 **Pages 2–7**	**Book Talk** • Important Details • Important Details • Note Details **Writing:** Express Personal Opinion	**USE PRIOR KNOWLEDGE** [FOCUS STRATEGY] *Hidden Surprises*, p. T275	**STORY ELEMENTS** [FOCUS SKILL] *Hidden Surprises*, pp. T274–T275
▶Day 2 **Pages 8–13**	**Book Talk** • Fantasy and Reality • Generalize • Determine Characters' Emotions **Writing:** Express Personal Opinion	Use Context to Confirm Meaning *Hidden Surprises*, p. T323	Sequence *Journeys of Wonder*, pp. T20–T21
▶Day 3 **Pages 14–21**	**Book Talk** • Summarize • Cause-Effect • Identify with Characters **Writing:** Speculate	Make and Confirm Predictions *Hidden Surprises*, p. T21	Reality and Fantasy *Hidden Surprises*, pp. T452–T453
▶Day 4 **Pages 22–29**	**Book Talk** • Make Comparisons • Main Idea • Express Personal Opinions **Writing:** Express Personal Opinion	**USE PRIOR KNOWLEDGE** [FOCUS STRATEGY] *Hidden Surprises*, p. T275	**STORY ELEMENTS** [FOCUS SKILL] *Hidden Surprises*, pp. T274–T275
▶Day 5 **Wrap-Up**	**Project** ✓ Make a Book Cube • Inquiry Project **Writing** ✓ Friendly Letter *Journeys of Wonder*, pp. T652–T653 **Language Link** • Exclamations **Assessment** ✓ Comprehension Test		

*Additional support is provided in *Collections*.
✓ Options for Assessment

Two of Everything

BOOK TALK

After you read pages 2–7, meet with your group
to discuss and answer the following questions:

1 Who are the Haktaks?

2 Where does the story take place?

3 What is unusual about the pot?

RESPONSE JOURNAL

What do you like about this story so far?
Write your thoughts in your journal.

Strategies Good Readers Use

FOCUS STRATEGY USE PRIOR KNOWLEDGE

You are reading a folktale. It is set in a long ago and faraway place. Write two things you expect to happen in such a story.

SKILLS IN CONTEXT

FOCUS SKILL **STORY ELEMENTS: MAKE A STORY MOBILE** Key story elements include the *setting* (where and when), the *characters* (people or animals), and the *plot* (what happens). Create a mobile showing the three key story elements in *Two of Everything*.

What You Need

- **hanger**
- **string**
- **heavy paper**
- **hole punch**
- **writing tools and scissors**

What to Do

1. Make at least three paper cutouts to show the story elements you have read about so far: you need to show at least one character, one detail that suggests the setting, and one event that tells about the plot.

2. Punch a hole in each cutout and attach it with a piece of string to the hanger.

3. Hang your mobile in the classroom.

Here is an idea to get you started: The first event of the plot occurs when Mr. Haktak finds something. You might show what he finds or what he uses to find it.

Think Ahead What do you think this pot has to do with the title of the story?

© Harcourt

Two of Everything

BOOK TALK

After you read pages 8–13, meet with your group to discuss and answer the following questions:

❶ What is the first thing that happens that could not happen in real life?

❷ What is magical about the pot?

❸ How do the Haktaks feel about the pot?

RESPONSE JOURNAL

What would you have put into the pot? Explain your choice.

SKILLS IN CONTEXT

SEQUENCE: STORY STEPS When one event leads to the next in a plot, that is a sequence of events. In *Two of Everything*, the characters experience a sequence of events. The events act like a staircase, bringing the characters closer to the story's ending.

What You Need

- large, long sheet of cardboard or poster board
- markers

What to Do

1. Write the steps of the story so far on a sheet of paper. That is, list everything that has happened.

2. Count the number of steps you listed. Divide your cardboard or poster board into that many parts.

3. Make folds for each part.

4. Divide each folded part in half in the same direction as the folding, then fold again to form a staircase.

5. Write the steps of the story in order beginning at the bottom of the stairs.

6. Display your steps by leaning the staircase against a wall or window. If needed, place a weight at the bottom to hold the steps in place.

Mr. Haktak finds the pot.

Here are two steps: *Mr. Haktak finds the pot. Mr. Haktak brings the pot home.*

Think Ahead What do you think the Haktaks will put into the pot next?

© Harcourt

Two of Everything

BOOK TALK

After you read pages 14–21, meet with your group to discuss and answer the following questions:

❶ How does Mrs. Haktak fall into the pot?

❷ What happens as a result of Mrs. Haktak's fall?

❸ What do you suppose Mr. and Mrs. Haktak are feeling after they fall into the pot? How would you feel?

Strategies Good Readers Use

MAKE AND CONFIRM PREDICTIONS

Write what you think will happen to the Haktaks.

RESPONSE JOURNAL

What are some problems that could result from having two Mr. Haktaks and two Mrs. Haktaks? List them in your journal.

SKILLS IN CONTEXT

REALITY AND FANTASY: MAKE A FANTASY AND REAL CHART Many stories tell about things that could never happen in real life. Still, they contain some events, settings, and characters that could be real. Some aspects of *Two of Everything* are real. Other aspects are fantasy and could not happen in real life. Make a chart that shows which events, settings, and characters in the story are real and which are fantasy.

What You Need

- poster board
- writing tools
- stars, glitter, or other items to show fantasy

What to Do

1. List all the events that have happened in the story so far. Also, list the characters and settings.

2. Put everything you listed in one of two groups: those that could be real, or those that are fantasy.

3. Make a chart with two columns. Label them *Real* and *Fantasy*. List the events, settings, and characters in the correct columns.

4. Decorate the fantasy side of your chart with glitter, stars, or drawings, to show that it is fantasy.

Here are some ideas to get you started: *The farm is real. Digging is real.*

Think Ahead
Will there be a happy ending to this story? Why or why not?

© Harcourt

Two of Everything

BOOK TALK

After you read pages 22–29, meet with your group to discuss and answer the following questions:

❶ In *Two of Everything*, people learn to accept huge surprises. What selections in *Hidden Surprises* show people dealing with things that they never expected to happen?

❷ How do you think the people who first told this folktale felt about having more of everything?

❸ How would you rate this among other folktales you have read? Give it a letter grade or a thumbs up or down. Tell why you rated it as you did.

Strategies Good Readers Use

FOCUS STRATEGY **USE PRIOR KNOWLEDGE**

*W*rite a sentence telling why you expected this story to have a happy ending.

RESPONSE JOURNAL

How would you like having another person exactly like you in your school, house, and class? Describe your reaction to this idea in your journal.

SKILLS IN CONTEXT

FOCUS SKILL **STORY ELEMENTS: MAKE A STORY SCROLL** You have already explored some story elements. Now you know all the elements related to the story. Work with a small group to create a story scroll that shows all of the elements of *Two of Everything*, including the characters, setting, and plot.

What You Need

- several sheets of blank paper, taped, glued, or stapled end to end
- writing and drawing tools
- ribbon, string, or other material to tie your scroll

What to Do

1. Attach three or more sheets of paper end to end lengthwise to make one very long, thin scroll.
2. Decorate the paper with story elements. (If you want, work from right to left, just as in a real Chinese scroll.) Show the characters and the setting. Label them. Then show events of the plot in order. Label the problem. Label the ending or the solution.
3. Roll up your scroll and tie it with a ribbon.
4. Present the scroll to other groups.

Here is one plot event to show: *The hairpin falling into the pot, or two hairpins.*

Wrap-Up

▶ **Project** **MAKE A BOOK CUBE** Show students a book cube or a picture cube. Point out its six sides. Explain that book cubes use words and pictures to tell about a book.
- Organize students into groups.
- Ask them to begin planning their book cubes by completing the copying master on page 45.
- Provide an opportunity to discuss the book cubes that students create.

▶ **Writing** **FRIENDLY LETTER** Have students respond to the following writing prompt: **Imagine that you are Mrs. Haktak. Write a letter to a friend telling him or her how your life has changed.** Have students use the copying master on page 46 to plan a letter. Remind students to consider the conventions of a friendly letter. Use *Journeys of Wonder* pages T652–T653 for additional support. Rubrics for evaluating student writing are provided on pages 292–295.

▶ **Language Link** **EXCLAMATIONS** There are many exclamations in the story. Have students write at least five of them. Also have them find one exclamation that is also a command.

─────────── **Inquiry Project** ───────────

What would students like to learn more about after reading *Two of Everything*? Have students brainstorm a list of topics and organize their ideas in a web like the one below. Students can use reference sources and the Internet to begin their inquiry projects.

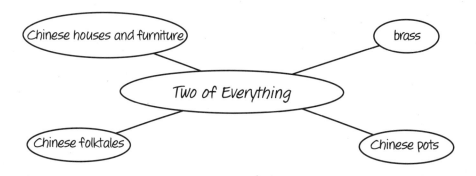

✔ **Comprehension Test** Test students' comprehension of *Two of Everything* by having them complete the copying master on page 47.

© Harcourt

Name _____

Project Planner

Two of Everything is a story that is full of surprises. Make a book cube that shows and tells about it.

☐ **Step 1.** Discuss with your group what you will show on each side of your book cube. Remember that you can show or write about characters, the setting, and important events. Be sure to use one side to write the title and author. Record your ideas on the lines below.

What You Need
- poster board or heavy cardboard
- tape or paste
- scissors
- writing and drawing materials

Side 1 Title and author

Side 2 _____

Side 3 _____

Side 4 _____

Side 5 _____

Side 6 _____

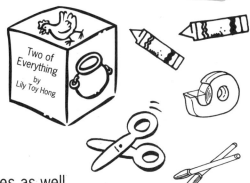

☐ **Step 2.** A book cube is best when it has pictures as well as words. With your group, brainstorm ideas to draw.

Two of Everything

☐ **Step 3.** Have your teacher show you how to make a book cube, or draw the outline that you must cut and fold. Write the title and author on one side and make the cube.

☐ **Step 4.** Work together to decorate the other sides with descriptions and pictures.

☐ **Step 5.** Display your cube in the classroom.

Name _____

Two of
Everything

Friendly Letter

Imagine that you are Mrs. Haktak. Write a letter to a friend telling him or
her how your life has changed. Complete the graphic organizer below to plan your letter.

Prewriting Graphic Organizer

Topic: _____

_____

Audience: _____

_____

Paragraph 1

Main Idea: _____

Details: _____

_____

Paragraph 2

Main Idea: _____

Details: _____

_____

Paragraph 3

Conclusion: _____

_____

_____

© Harcourt

46 • Leveled Library Plus Teacher's Guide

Name _____

Comprehension Test

Read each question below. Then mark the letter for the
answer you have chosen.

1. **Which words describe the Haktaks in the beginning?**
   - Ⓐ old and poor
   - Ⓑ old and angry
   - Ⓒ young and poor
   - Ⓓ young and angry

2. **Why does the pot change the Haktaks' lives?**
   - Ⓕ It is ancient.
   - Ⓖ It is brass.
   - Ⓗ It was under the ground.
   - Ⓙ It makes two of everything.

3. **How does Mr. Haktak discover the pot?**
   - Ⓐ He finds it in the village.
   - Ⓑ He trades turnips for it.
   - Ⓒ He finds it in his garden.
   - Ⓓ He trades five gold coins for it.

4. **Why does Mr. Haktak take the pot home?**
   - Ⓕ He knows it is magical.
   - Ⓖ He thinks Mrs. Haktak can use it.
   - Ⓗ He wants to get rich.
   - Ⓙ He wants to fix it.

5. **When do the Haktaks first discover that the pot is magical?**
   - Ⓐ when Mr. Haktak falls in
   - Ⓑ when Mrs. Haktak falls in
   - Ⓒ when the money falls in
   - Ⓓ when the hairpin falls in

6. **What is the Haktaks' favorite use for the pot?**
   - Ⓕ making more money
   - Ⓖ making more hairpins
   - Ⓗ making more people
   - Ⓙ making furniture and clothing

7. **Why are there two Mrs. Haktaks?**
   - Ⓐ Mr. Haktak gets married twice.
   - Ⓑ One is Mr. Haktak's wife, and one is his sister.
   - Ⓒ The pot makes a second Mrs. Haktak.
   - Ⓓ One Mrs. Haktak is a visitor.

8. **How do the Haktaks deal with having two of themselves?**
   - Ⓕ They accept it and do fine.
   - Ⓖ They smash the magical pot.
   - Ⓗ They make the second Haktaks leave.
   - Ⓙ They move away and do fine.

9. **Which sentence best states a main idea of the story?**
   - Ⓐ Never dig in your garden.
   - Ⓑ Always look for buried treasure.
   - Ⓒ Accept what happens to you.
   - Ⓓ Try to change what happens to you.

10. **Do you think the Haktaks are happier at the end of the story than they were at the beginning? Explain your answer.**

© Harcourt

Booker T. Washington

Reading Level

by Jan Gleiter and Kathleen Thompson

Theme Connection

As students read *Booker T. Washington*, they will learn about a real person whose determination to get an education parallels the strength of purpose of the resolute writer in "A Bookworm Who Hatched."

Summary

Born into slavery in 1856 and freed in 1865, Booker T. Washington worked hard at a number of jobs and went to school when he could. He finally received a formal education at Hampton Institute in Virginia and became a teacher there. Then, in 1881, he launched what was to become Tuskegee Institute.

Building Background

Tell students that *Booker T. Washington* is a biography, a book that tells the life of a real person. Ask them to recall other biographies they have read. Point out that biographers—authors who write about real people's lives—often write about people they admire. The authors of such books want to share with their readers the admirable qualities of their subjects. Have students read to find out what qualities Booker T. Washington had that helped him to reach his goals.

Author Profile

Jan Gleiter and Kathleen Thompson have collaborated on many books for young readers. They specialize in nonfiction series that are sold to elementary school libraries. Among their books are a series about each of the fifty states and another series of biographies of Hispanic, Native American, African American, and traditional American folk heroes.

Additional Books by the Authors
- *Pocahontas*
- *Daniel Boone*
- *Molly Pitcher*

Vocabulary

Have students use the vocabulary words to complete a chart like the following. See pages 296–299 for additional vocabulary activities. For definitions of the words, see the Glossary.

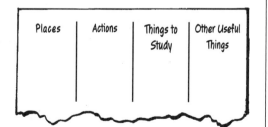

Places	Actions	Things to Study	Other Useful Things

Day 1	Day 2	Day 3	Day 4
boiled p. 6	mules p. 13	work lamp p. 19	handkerchief p. 28
burlap p. 6	salt mine p. 14	institute p. 20	history p. 30
mill p. 10	speller p. 16	shed p. 22	poured p. 31
		stagecoach p. 25	subjects p. 32
		loading p. 25	

© Harcourt

	Book Talk	Strategies	Skills
Day 1 Pages 1–11	**Book Talk** • Important Details • Make Comparisons • Synthesize **Writing:** Determine Characters' Emotions	**SUMMARIZE** FOCUS STRATEGY *Journeys of Wonder*, p. T113	**FACT AND OPINION** FOCUS SKILL *Journeys of Wonder*, pp. T112–T113
Day 2 Pages 12–18	**Book Talk** • Speculate • Draw Conclusions • Compare and Contrast **Writing:** Write from the Perspective of Character	Create Mental Images *Hidden Surprises*, p. T567	Sequence *Journeys of Wonder*, pp. T20–T21
Day 3 Pages 19–26	**Book Talk** • Interpret Characters' Motivations • Synthesize • Speculate **Writing:** Write a Letter	Use Graphic Aids *Hidden Surprises*, p. T409	Main Idea *Hidden Surprises*, pp. T612–T613
Day 4 Pages 27–32	**Book Talk** • Interpret Story Events • Synthesize • Express Personal Opinion **Writing:** Determine Characters' Motivations	**SUMMARIZE** FOCUS STRATEGY *Journeys of Wonder*, p. T113	**FACT AND OPINION** FOCUS SKILL *Journeys of Wonder*, pp. T112–T113
Day 5 Wrap-Up	**Project** ✓ Create a Mural • Inquiry Project **Writing** ✓ Paragraph That Classifies *Journeys of Wonder*, pp. T136–T137 **Language Link** • Adjectives That Describe Feelings **Assessment** ✓ Comprehension Test		

*Additional support is provided in *Collections*.
✓ Options for Assessment

Booker T. Washington

BOOK TALK

After you read pages 1–11, meet with your group to discuss and answer the following questions:

❶ Why was life on the plantation hard for Booker's family?

❷ In what ways was Booker's life different from that of the girls who lived in the big house?

❸ How can you tell that Booker's family was very poor?

RESPONSE JOURNAL

How do you think Booker felt when he saw the girls from the big house go into the school and knew he could not go in?

Strategies Good Readers Use

FOCUS STRATEGY SUMMARIZE

Make a list of the important events in this section. How does summarizing help you remember the important points?

SKILLS IN CONTEXT

FOCUS SKILL FACT AND OPINION: FACT AND OPINION "FISH" A biography gives facts about a person's life. It is important to be able to tell the difference between facts and the opinions the authors have about those facts. Play Fact and Opinion "Fish" with a friend to see if you can tell the difference between facts and opinions about the life of Booker T. Washington.

What You Need

- **10 index cards**
- **pencils**
- **empty fishbowl**

What to Do

1. On each card, write a sentence that contains a fact or an opinion from or about the story.

2. Place the cards in the fishbowl and mix them up.

3. Take turns drawing a card from the bowl. Read the sentence out loud, and say "Fact" or "Opinion."

4. Explain why you think as you do. For example, if you draw a fact, you might say, "This tells about an event that really happened." If it is an opinion, you might say, "This tells how someone feels about what happened."

Here's an opinion to get you started: *It was too hot in the cabin during the summer.*

Think Ahead
Do you think things will get better for Booker and his family?

© Harcourt

Booker T. Washington

BOOK TALK

After you read pages 12–18, meet with your group to discuss and answer the following questions:

1 Why do you think Booker said his last name was Washington?

2 Why did Booker's stepfather want him to work full time?

3 How did Booker's life change after he left the plantation? How did it stay the same?

> **Strategies Good Readers Use**
>
> ### CREATE MENTAL IMAGES
>
> Use what you have read and what you know to imagine what it was like to work in a salt mine. What do you see?

RESPONSE JOURNAL

What might Booker have said to his stepfather about his wish to go to school?

SKILLS IN CONTEXT

SEQUENCE: CHAIN OF EVENTS A biography usually tells about events as they happened in the subject's life. One reason for this is to show how each new event helped shape the character of the person. Each event described in *Booker T. Washington* helps the reader to understand Booker's life. Events that follow one after the other are called a chain of events. You can make a real chain of events by following these directions.

What You Need

- **strips of construction paper (about 8-1/2 inches long and 2 inches wide)**
- **writing materials**
- **tape**

What to Do

1. Use at least five strips of paper. On each strip, write a description of a major event in Booker's life.

2. Put the strips of paper in the order the events happened.

3. With the writing side showing, tape together the two ends of the strip with the first event on it.

4. Loop the strip with the second event into the first one. Make sure the writing shows. Then tape the second strip.

5. Continue until you have a whole chain of events. You can add to it as you read the rest of the book.

Here is an event to get you started:
In 1865, the slaves were freed.

Think Ahead
Do you think Booker will ever get to stay in a school?

Booker T. Washington

BOOK TALK

After you read pages 19–26, meet with your group to discuss and answer the following questions:

1 Why would Booker rather work for the hard-to-please Mrs. Ruffin than in the mine?

2 How can you tell that other people believed in Booker's dream of going to school?

3 Why do you think Miss Mackie was not sure at first about admitting Booker to the Institute?

RESPONSE JOURNAL

Imagine that you are Booker. Write a letter to Mrs. Ruffin telling her what you learned from her.

> **Strategies Good Readers Use**
>
> ### USE GRAPHIC AIDS
>
> Sometimes if you do not understand a word, you might find a picture that shows what it is. For example, the word *stagecoach* appears on page 25, and the picture on page 24 shows you what it might have looked like.

SKILLS IN CONTEXT

MAIN IDEA: THE PATH TO SUCCESS As you read, you can determine the main idea, or the most important point that an author is trying to tell you. Supporting details help to make the main idea clear. Make a road map to show how details support the main idea of the section you just read.

What You Need

- **drawing paper**
- **drawing tools**
- **ruler**

What to Do

1. Reread pages 19–26.

2. Decide what the main idea of this section is.

3. On a piece of drawing paper, carefully draw a main road. Label it with the main idea.

4. Decide what the supporting details of this section are. Draw and label each as a side road that connects to the main road.

Here is a hint to get you started:
What events in this section show how much Booker wants to carry out a certain plan?

Think Ahead Do you think Booker will succeed at Hampton Institute?

© Harcourt

Booker T. Washington

BOOK TALK

After you read pages 27–32, meet with your group to discuss and answer the following questions:

1 How did Booker's background help him develop Tuskegee Institute?

2 What did you learn about Booker as a child that explains his success as an adult?

3 Why is Booker T. Washington's life a good model for young readers?

RESPONSE JOURNAL

What do you think kept Booker T. Washington from giving up when things were hard for him?

Strategies Good Readers Use

FOCUS STRATEGY SUMMARIZE

Summarize the book in a sentence or two. How has summarizing helped you understand what you read?

SKILLS IN CONTEXT

FOCUS SKILL **FACT AND OPINION: COVER FOR A FAVORITE BOOK** We do not know exactly how Booker T. Washington felt about the events in his life. But we can tell from his actions that he loved books. You have read that at one time he owned only one book and read it over and over. Think about a book that you have enjoyed reading many times. Design a book cover for your favorite book.

What You Need

- **drawing paper**
- **scrap paper**
- **drawing tools**
- **samples of other book covers**

What to Do

1. Study the sample book covers. Look at the different parts: the book flaps, title, cover illustration, spine, and back cover.

2. Decide what information you will include on your book cover and where you will put it. Use facts and opinions to communicate ideas to readers.

3. Use scrap paper to design your cover. When you are satisfied with it, make the cover itself.

4. Share your book cover with the class. Also, tell your classmates a little about why the book is your favorite.

Here is an idea to get you started: *The front cover illustration should give readers an idea of what the whole book is about.*

© Harcourt

Wrap-Up

▶ **Project** **CREATE A MURAL** Remind students that in *Booker T. Washington*, Booker had to walk a long way to reach Hampton Institute. Explain that along the way he may have seen some milestones. These were stones that marked the miles between towns. Then explain that the word *milestones* can also mean important times in a person's life.

- Organize students into groups, and have them discuss the important times in Booker T. Washington's life.
- Ask students to complete the copying master on page 55 to design a mural that illustrates the milestones in Booker T. Washington's life.
- Have each group present its finished mural to the class.

▶ **Writing** **PARAGRAPH THAT CLASSIFIES** Have students respond to the following writing prompt: **Write a paragraph that classifies Booker T. Washington's work: what did he not want to do as an adult, and what work was he determined to do?** Have students use the copying master on page 56 to plan their paragraphs. Remind students to focus on organization. For more support, use *Journeys of Wonder*, pages T136–T137. Rubrics for evaluating student writing are provided on pages 292–295.

▶ **Language Link** **ADJECTIVES THAT DESCRIBE FEELINGS** Have students reread pages 26–28. Explain that these pages describe an important moment in Booker T. Washington's life, one that would change it forever. Suggest that students work together in small groups to generate a word web of adjectives that describe how Booker felt at this time.

Inquiry Project

Booker T. Washington can be a springboard for inquiry into a variety of topics. For example, recalling Booker T. Washington's experience working in mines, students might research what modern coal mining is like. Have students brainstorm topics they would like to know more about and organize their responses in the following K-W-L chart. Students can use reference books and the Internet to begin their inquiry projects.

K What I Know	W What I Want to Find Out	L What I Learned
Booker T. Washington worked in a coal mine.	What is modern coal mining like?	

✔ **Comprehension Test** Test students' comprehension of *Booker T. Washington* by having them complete the copying master on page 57.

© Harcourt

Name _____

Project Planner

Milestones are important times in a person's life. Work with a group to design a mural that illustrates the milestones in Booker T. Washington's life. To decide which events to show, try putting yourself in Booker's place as he thinks about the events that changed his life.

☐ **Step 1.** Discuss with your group some of the milestones in Booker T. Washington's life. Make a list of the group's ideas. Narrow the list down to six events.

What You Need
- long pieces of drawing paper
- writing and drawing materials

_____ _____

_____ _____

_____ _____

☐ **Step 2.** As a group, decide how you will show the events you have chosen. Ask yourselves, "What should we show in each picture?"

☐ **Step 3.** Decide who will draw each picture. Then use the box below to plan your part of the mural.

☐ **Step 4.** When everyone has agreed on what to show, section off the drawing paper, and work on your part. Share the whole mural with the class.

© Harcourt

Name _____

Paragraph That Classifies

Over the course of his life, Booker T. Washington did a variety of work, and some of it was very hard. Write a paragraph that classifies Booker's work: what did he not want to do as an adult, and what work was he determined to do? The graphic organizer below will help you plan your paragraph. Write down your main idea and the examples that support it. When you finish, use the completed chart to write your paragraph.

Prewriting Graphic Organizer

Topic: _____

_____

Audience: _____

_____

Main Idea: _____

_____

Likes/Advantages	Dislikes/Disadvantages
_____	_____
_____	_____
_____	_____
_____	_____
_____	_____

Main Idea Restated: _____

_____

© Harcourt

Name _____

Comprehension Test Test Prep

Read each question below. Then mark the letter for the answer you have chosen.

1. **Where did Booker T. Washington live right after he was born?**
   - Ⓐ with his stepfather in Virginia
   - Ⓑ on a plantation in Virginia
   - Ⓒ in a big house in Alabama
   - Ⓓ on a farm in West Virginia

2. **Which of the following was Booker not able to do as a child?**
   - Ⓕ wear a burlap shirt
   - Ⓖ take corn to the mill
   - Ⓗ go inside the school
   - Ⓙ carry the girls' books

3. **How did Booker feel about reading?**
   - Ⓐ He made up his mind to do it.
   - Ⓑ He did not want to learn to read.
   - Ⓒ He did not feel it made any difference in people's lives.
   - Ⓓ He wondered why it was important.

4. **Why did Booker leave school?**
   - Ⓕ He decided to be a coal miner.
   - Ⓖ He thought he knew enough.
   - Ⓗ He could not tell anyone his last name.
   - Ⓙ He had to work full time.

5. **Which sentence describes what working for Mrs. Ruffin was like?**
   - Ⓐ He worked in an unsafe place.
   - Ⓑ He had no time to go to school.
   - Ⓒ He did jobs over and over.
   - Ⓓ He found Mrs. Ruffin easy to please.

6. **Which sentence is true of how Booker got to Hampton Institute?**
   - Ⓕ His neighbors helped pay for his trip.
   - Ⓖ He rode there in a stagecoach.
   - Ⓗ He had enough to pay for school.
   - Ⓙ He walked the whole way.

7. **How did Miss Mackie test Booker?**
   - Ⓐ She asked him to prepare a meal.
   - Ⓑ She had him clean a room.
   - Ⓒ She had him write a letter.
   - Ⓓ She made him write a speech.

8. **Which sentence shows how well Booker did at Hampton Institute?**
   - Ⓕ He was asked to be its principal.
   - Ⓖ He was asked to get more students.
   - Ⓗ He wrote a book for the students.
   - Ⓙ He came back as a teacher.

9. **What happened at the school Booker started in Tuskegee?**
   - Ⓐ He built it with his own hands.
   - Ⓑ He had to find a principal.
   - Ⓒ There were many students and few teachers.
   - Ⓓ He had to find students for the school.

10. **Write a response to the following question:**
    How did Booker achieve his goals? Explain.

© Harcourt

Ibis: A True Whale Story

Reading Level

by John Himmelman

> ### Theme Connection
> In *Ibis: A True Whale Story*, not only does one whale help another, but people pitch in as well to save a whale. Like "Ronald Morgan Goes to Camp," this book features characters helping others.

> ### Summary
> Ibis the whale grows up in a bay surrounded by boats and people. Her natural curiosity draws her to the surface, until one day she is caught in a fishing net. Tangled in the net, Ibis struggles into the deep ocean. She is too weak to join the other whales in migration, but finally humans rescue her. Ibis is then able to join the other whales in their migration to warmer waters.

> ### Building Background
> Tell students that *Ibis: A True Whale Story* is a realistic fiction story about a whale. It is based on a true story, but some of it is made up, such as the ideas about the whale's feelings and friendships. Ask students what they already know about whales. Explain that sometimes people can read for more than one purpose, such as to be entertained and informed. Tell students to read to be entertained by Ibis's story and to learn more about whales.

Author Profile

Author and illustrator John Himmelman is known primarily for his nature books, many of which are part of a series called Nature Upclose. He heard Ibis's story from a marine scientist aboard a whale-watching ship. After seeing the real Ibis, Himmelman was inspired to write her story.

Additional Books by the Author
- *The Animal Rescue Club*
- *A Dandelion's Life*
- *The Great Leaf Blast-Off!*

Vocabulary

Have students make a chart like the one below and sort the vocabulary words into categories. See pages 296–299 for additional vocabulary activities. For definitions of the words, see the Glossary.

Words That Name		
Places	Animals	Actions

Day 1	Day 2	Day 3	Day 4
bay p. 1	sea p. 9	journey p. 16	panic p. 22
whales p. 1	fishing p. 12	breathe p. 18	tugging p. 24
curious p. 2	tangled p. 12	engines p. 19	
ocean p. 2			
surface p. 6			

© Harcourt

	Response	Strategies	Skills
Day 1 **Pages 1–7**	**Book Talk** • Draw Conclusions • Important Details • Determine Characters' Emotions **Writing:** Write Advice for a Character	**REREAD** `FOCUS STRATEGY` *Hidden Surprises,* p. T119	**PREDICT OUTCOMES** `FOCUS SKILL` *Hidden Surprises,* pp. T118–T119
Day 2 **Pages 8–14**	**Book Talk** • Determine Characters' Traits • Draw Conclusions • Make Predictions **Writing:** Generalize	Self-Question *Journeys of Wonder,* p. T21	Sequence *Journeys of Wonder,* pp. T20–T21
Day 3 **Pages 15–21**	**Book Talk** • Sequence • Summarize • Determine Characters' Emotions **Writing:** Personal Response	Read Ahead *Hidden Surprises,* p. T525	Story Elements *Hidden Surprises,* pp. T274–T275
Day 4 **Pages 22–28**	**Book Talk** • Make Comparisons • Main Idea • Express Personal Opinion **Writing:** Distinguish Between Reality and Fantasy	**REREAD** `FOCUS STRATEGY` *Hidden Surprises,* p. T119	**PREDICT OUTCOMES** `FOCUS SKILL` *Hidden Surprises,* pp. T118–T119

Day 5
Wrap-Up

Project
✓ Make a Flyer
• Inquiry Project

Writing
✓ Story
Hidden Surprises,
pp. T144–T145

Language Link
• Compound Words

Assessment
✓ Comprehension Test

*Additional support is provided in *Collections*.
✓ Options for Assessment

Ibis: A True Whale Story

BOOK TALK

After you read pages 1–7, meet with your group to discuss and answer the following questions:

1 Ibis is a whale calf. What does this mean?

2 What do the young whales have to learn to get used to?

3 How do Ibis's feelings about the boats change?

Strategies Good Readers Use

FOCUS STRATEGY **REREAD**

*R*eread the first seven pages. Did you find any important information that you missed the first time?

RESPONSE JOURNAL

What advice would you like to give Ibis about people and boats? Write it in your journal.

SKILLS IN CONTEXT

FOCUS SKILL **PREDICT OUTCOMES: MAKE A TAPE** When you predict outcomes, you tell how you think a story will end. How do you think *Ibis: A True Whale Story* will end? With a small group of classmates, make a cassette tape of your predictions about the story to share with the rest of your class.

What You Need

- tape recorder
- blank audiotape

What to Do

1. Make predictions with your group. Decide what will happen next and how the story will end.

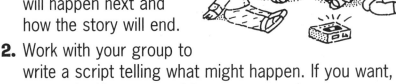

2. Work with your group to write a script telling what might happen. If you want, write it as if you were Ibis.

3. Practice reading the script before you record it.

4. Play your recording for the class.

Here is a sentence to get you started: Ibis saw more and more boats. Then one day . . .

Think Ahead What do you think will happen with the people in the boats?

© Harcourt

Ibis: A True Whale Story

BOOK TALK

After you read pages 8–14, meet with your group to discuss and answer the following questions:

1 Ibis is no longer a baby. How would you describe her now?

2 Why is it bad for Ibis to get caught in a net?

3 What do you think will happen to Ibis?

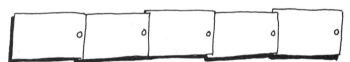

> **Strategies Good Readers Use**
>
> **SELF-QUESTION**
>
> Write a question you could ask yourself about how Ibis got caught in the net.

RESPONSE JOURNAL

Do you think what happened to Ibis could happen to other whales? Why?

SKILLS IN CONTEXT

SEQUENCE: MAKE A SEQUENCE CHAIN The things that happen in a story are events. When one event leads to the next, that is a sequence. Create a sequence chain to show what has happened so far in *Ibis: A True Whale Story*.

What You Need

- sheets of colored paper
- markers
- paper fasteners

What to Do

1. Notice that Ibis's bad luck begins when she gets used to boats. Begin a sequence chain by writing *Ibis gets used to boats* on one sheet of paper.

2. Use a separate sheet of colored paper to write each event that happens after. End with what Blizzard does.

3. Attach your sheets in order using paper fasteners. You may make your chain read from top to bottom or left to right.

4. Hang your chain in the classroom.

Here is another event:

Blizzard and Ibis see lots of fish.

Think Ahead
Will Blizzard be able to help Ibis?

Ibis: A True Whale Story

BOOK TALK

After you read pages 15–21, meet with your group to discuss and answer the following questions:

❶ What does Ibis do after she gets caught in the net?

❷ How would you describe Ibis's condition before Blizzard pushes her to the surface?

❸ Put yourself in Ibis's place. How do you think she feels when she is being tied to the floats?

Strategies Good Readers Use

READ AHEAD

If you don't understand something you just read, try reading ahead to see if the next part of the story clears up your confusion.

RESPONSE JOURNAL

Tell about a friend, adult, or other person who might help you if you were in trouble.

SKILLS IN CONTEXT

STORY ELEMENTS: STORY ELEMENT ROLE-PLAY Story elements tell *who* (the characters), *where* and *when* (the setting), and *what* happens (the plot). Work in a group to discuss and demonstrate how the story elements come together in *Ibis: A True Whale Story.*

What You Need

- **writing materials**
- **paper**

What to Do

1. Work together to make a list of the characters, setting, and events in this part of the book (pages 15–21).

2. One group member should "be" the setting, another should "be" the characters, and the rest of the group should "be" the plot.

3. Have the setting person tell who he or she is, what he or she adds, and why this is important to the story. The character person and events people should do the same.

4. Put your ideas together. Practice presenting them, and then perform a role-play for the class.

Here is one idea to get you started:

Plot: I am the plot. I tell what happens to Ibis. Ibis is in trouble when . . .

Think Ahead
What are the people going to do?

© Harcourt

Ibis: A True Whale Story

BOOK TALK

After you read pages 22–28, meet with your group to discuss and answer the following questions:

❶ *Ibis: A True Whale Story* shows friendship between two whales. What other selections in *Hidden Surprises* are about friendship?

❷ What do you think is the most important idea about whales and people in this book?

❸ What did you like best about this story? Is there anything you would change?

> **Strategies Good Readers Use**
>
> **FOCUS STRATEGY REREAD**
>
> *W*rite a sentence telling one part of the story you might reread and why.

RESPONSE JOURNAL

In this story, Ibis thinks just like a person. Do you think that's really how whales act? Why or why not?

SKILLS IN CONTEXT

FOCUS SKILL PREDICT OUTCOMES: PANEL DISCUSSION When you predict outcomes, you should always think later about how many of your predictions were correct. Now that you have finished the story, you can use the tape you created during Day 1 to guide your discussion of how you make predictions as you read.

What You Need

- the tape you made on Day 1

What to Do

1. With your group, listen to the tape you made. Talk about whether your predictions turned out to be right.

2. Discuss whether the predictions were good ones. Remember: a prediction does not have to be correct to be a good prediction!

3. Plan a panel discussion about how to predict outcomes. Each person in the group should speak at least twice. Use *Ibis: A True Whale Story* as an example of how you can predict outcomes.

4. Present your discussion.

Here is an idea to get you started: *Look for clues the author gives about what will happen.*

Wrap-Up

▶ **Project** **MAKE A FLYER** One way to help animals in danger is to learn about them. Show students a six-page, trifold flyer. Point out its cover, its "inside," and its two other pages. Tell students they will be creating flyers to educate others about whales. Organize students into groups, and ask them to complete the copying master on page 65. Encourage students to present or display their flyers.

▶ **Writing** **STORY** Have students respond to the following writing prompt: **Write a story about a whale or some other animal in danger.** Have students use the copying master on page 66 to plan their stories. Remind students to focus on their story's organization. Use *Hidden Surprises* pages T144–T145 for additional support. Rubrics for evaluating student writing are provided on pages 292–295.

▶ **Language Link** **COMPOUND WORDS** Point out that there are some words in *Ibis: A True Whale Story* that are made of two words put together. These are compound words. Have students list the compound words from the story and draw a line between the two words that make up each longer word. *(hump/back, every/thing, star/fish, some/thing, over/head, an/other, her/self)*

Inquiry Project

What questions do students still have about whales? Students might enjoy learning more about the humpback whale or about groups that help and study whales. Remind students that a good way to begin is by doing research and taking notes. Have students use a web like the one below to organize their information about whales.

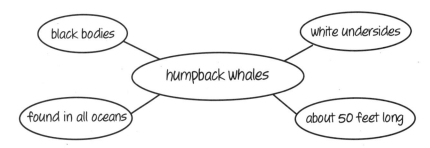

✔ **Comprehension Test** Test students' comprehension of *Ibis: A True Whale Story* by having them complete the copying master on page 67.

Name _____

Project Planner

Ibis: A True Whale Story shows how people can both hurt and help whales. Sometimes, the difference between hurting and helping is a matter of knowing. Work with a group to make a flyer that gives information about whales.

☐ **Step 1.** Ask questions to help you think of ideas to write about and show. Complete this organizer by writing one question about whales that begins with each of the following words.

What You Need

- paper
- writing and drawing materials
- research materials, such as books, CD-ROMs, and magazines

Who	
What	
Where	
When	
Why	
How	

☐ **Step 2.** Discuss with your group what you will show on each part of your flyer.

Front cover _____

Inside of flyer _____

_____

Back side _____

☐ **Step 3.** Make a plan with the other members of your group for writing and illustrating your flyer. You can draw the pictures, photocopy them, cut them from old magazines, or print them from software or online sources.

☐ **Step 4.** Present your flyer to the class.

Name _____

Story

Write a story about a whale or some other animal in danger. Complete the story map below to plan your story.

Prewriting Graphic Organizer

Characters: _____ _____

_____ _____

_____ _____

Setting: _____

Problem: _____

_____

Important Events: _____

_____

_____

_____

_____

_____

_____

Solution: _____

_____

© Harcourt

Name _____

Comprehension Test

Read each question below. Then mark the letter for the answer you have chosen.

1. **When does this story begin?**
   - Ⓐ before Ibis is born
   - Ⓑ on the day Ibis is born
   - Ⓒ when Ibis is very young
   - Ⓓ when Ibis is full grown

2. **What does Ibis like to look at on the bottom of the sea?**
   - Ⓕ starfish
   - Ⓗ colored rocks
   - Ⓖ coral
   - Ⓙ parts of old ships

3. **What is the first thing that scares Ibis?**
   - Ⓐ sharks
   - Ⓒ people
   - Ⓑ bigger fish
   - Ⓓ boats

4. **After she meets them the first time, how does Ibis feel about people?**
   - Ⓕ She is scared of them.
   - Ⓖ She likes them.
   - Ⓗ She warns other whales about them.
   - Ⓙ She tries to avoid them.

5. **How does Ibis get caught in the fishing net?**
   - Ⓐ Fishing boats try to catch her.
   - Ⓑ Small fish trick her into swimming into the net.
   - Ⓒ She swims into the net when looking for something to eat.
   - Ⓓ Blizzard leads her into the net by mistake.

6. **What part does Blizzard play in this story?**
   - Ⓕ He is Ibis's friend and helper.
   - Ⓖ He is the opposite of Ibis.
   - Ⓗ He shows the difference between a grown whale and a young whale.
   - Ⓙ He is Ibis's father and helper.

7. **How do the people who help Ibis get her to stay still?**
   - Ⓐ They attach a raft to her blowhole.
   - Ⓑ They attach a raft to her tail.
   - Ⓒ They attach floats to her body.
   - Ⓓ They attach floats to parts of the net.

8. **What does the story seem to say about Ibis's future?**
   - Ⓕ She will get caught in another net.
   - Ⓖ She will be safe and happy now.
   - Ⓗ She will always come back to the same bay.
   - Ⓙ She will leave Blizzard behind.

9. **What message might the author be sending about whales and fishing nets?**
   - Ⓐ Whales cannot be harmed by the nets.
   - Ⓑ Whales can get trapped in the nets.
   - Ⓒ There should be no more fishing.
   - Ⓓ People who use the nets are cruel.

10. **Write a response to this question:**
    How does the author help you like Ibis and care about what happens to her?

The Edible Pyramid

Reading Level

by Loreen Leedy

▶ Theme Connection

As in "Little Grunt and the Big Egg," the animals in *The Edible Pyramid* do unexpected things and play unusual roles.

▶ Summary

Several animals enjoy the grand opening celebration at The Edible Pyramid restaurant. The owner and maitre d', a tuxedo-clad cat, explains the benefits of eating the recommended daily servings of foods from each level of the Food Guide Pyramid.

▶ Building Background

First, read the title and explain the word *edible* to students. Build background by asking students to tell what pyramid they think this book is about. Find out what they already know about the food pyramid. Then ask students to give examples of their favorite foods. Help students determine where the foods they listed would be located on the Food Guide Pyramid. Explain that this story is written to inform and entertain. Have students write a question that they hope the book will answer.

Author Profile

For as long as she can remember, Loreen Leedy has loved to draw. When she was thirteen years old, a national magazine published her drawing of a horse. After graduating from college with a degree in art, she became a designer of jewelry. At 25, she wrote and published her first picture book, *A Number of Dragons*. Since then, she has written and illustrated more than twenty books.

Additional Books by the Author
- *Blast Off to Earth*
- *Monster Money Book*
- *Tracks in the Sand*

Vocabulary

Have students sort the vocabulary words into the categories in the chart. See pages 296–299 for additional vocabulary activities. For definitions of the words, see the Glossary.

Types of Food	Words About Healthy Eating

Day 1	Day 2	Day 3	Day 4
pyramid p. 2	raisin p. 14	chicken p. 19	estimate p. 26
menu p. 4	kiwi p. 14	seed p. 21	order p. 28
meals p. 4		butter p. 22	
variety p. 4		margarine p. 22	
servings p. 4			

© Harcourt

	Response	Strategies	Skills
Day 1 **Pages 2–7**	**Book Talk** • Note Details • Synthesize • Important Details **Writing:** Express Personal Opinion	**SELF-QUESTION** **FOCUS STRATEGY** *Hidden Surprises,* p. T453	**REALITY AND FANTASY** **FOCUS SKILL** *Hidden Surprises,* pp. T452–T453
Day 2 **Pages 8–15**	**Book Talk** • Classify • Generalize • Compare and Contrast **Writing:** Personal Response	Use Graphic Aids *Hidden Surprises,* p. T409	Important Details *Journeys of Wonder,* pp. T536–T537
Day 3 **Pages 16–23**	**Book Talk** • Important Details • Classify • Author's Purpose **Writing:** Express Personal Opinion	Summarize *Hidden Surprises,* p. T161	Main Idea *Hidden Surprises,* pp. T612–T613
Day 4 **Pages 24–30**	**Book Talk** • Make Comparisons • Author's Purpose • Express Personal Opinion **Writing:** Make Connections	**SELF-QUESTION** **FOCUS STRATEGY** *Hidden Surprises,* p. T453	**REALITY AND FANTASY** **FOCUS SKILL** *Hidden Surprises,* pp. T452–T453

Day 5
Wrap-Up

Project
✓ Make a Menu
• Inquiry Project

Writing
✓ Persuasive Paragraph
Hidden Surprises,
pp. T550–T551

Language Link
• Compound Words

Assessment
✓ Comprehension Test

© Harcourt

*Additional support is provided in *Collections.*
✓ Options for Assessment

The Edible Pyramid

BOOK TALK

After you read pages 2–7, meet with your group to discuss and answer the following questions:

1 What is the name of the restaurant in this story?

2 What do the restaurant and the Food Guide Pyramid have to do with each other?

3 Who is the spokesperson for the restaurant, and who are the customers?

RESPONSE JOURNAL

Would you like to go to this restaurant? Why or why not?

Strategies Good Readers Use

FOCUS STRATEGY **SELF-QUESTION**

Good readers think of questions as they read. List one or more questions you have about this book so far.

SKILLS IN CONTEXT

FOCUS SKILL **REALITY AND FANTASY: MAKE A CHART** Some events in a story could never happen in real life. They are fantasy. Other events could happen in real life. Some events in *The Edible Pyramid* could happen in real life. Other events are fantasy and could not happen. Create a chart that shows which parts of the story are real and which parts are fantasy.

What You Need

- **paper**
- **writing tools**

What to Do

1. Look back over pages 2–7 of *The Edible Pyramid*. What do you find that is real, and what do you find that is not real?

2. Make a two-column chart. Label the columns *Reality* and *Fantasy*.

3. Write as many items as you can in each column of the chart.

4. Compare your completed chart with one of your class-mates' charts.

Here are some ideas for the fantasy column: a cat in a tuxedo, a cat standing up straight like a person

Think Ahead
What do you think the cat will do next?

© Harcourt

The Edible Pyramid

BOOK TALK

After you read pages 8–15, meet with your group to discuss and answer the following questions:

1 What are some foods in the bottom row of the pyramid?

2 What are the rows of the pyramid?

3 How does the bottom row differ from the second row?

Strategies Good Readers Use

USE GRAPHIC AIDS

Write meanings for the words *tortellini* and *ramen noodle*. Use the pictures as well as the context to guide you.

RESPONSE JOURNAL

What have you learned about the food pyramid so far? Write in your journal about what you have learned.

SKILLS IN CONTEXT

IMPORTANT DETAILS: CREATE A POSTCARD When you read, be sure you note the most important details in the story. Imagine that you have just visited The Edible Pyramid restaurant. You want to tell a friend about the experience. Make a postcard that will use details to show and tell your friend what the restaurant is like.

What You Need

- **an unlined index card, or a small piece of poster board**
- **writing and art materials**

What to Do

1. Make a drawing on the front of the card.
2. Divide the back of your postcard into two parts. One part, on the right, is for the address. The other part is for the message.
3. Write a message. Include important details about The Edible Pyramid restaurant. Address your postcard to a friend.
4. Display your postcard in the classroom.

Here are some ideas: For the picture, show the restaurant or the food pyramid. For the message, tell about the food groups you have learned about so far.

Think Ahead What parts of the pyramid are left to learn about?

© Harcourt

The Edible Pyramid • 71

The Edible Pyramid

BOOK TALK

After you read pages 16–23, meet with your group to discuss and answer the following questions:

1 What do you find on the second smallest row of the pyramid?

2 What group is chicken in?

3 Why do you think there are so many pictures of so many kinds of foods?

RESPONSE JOURNAL

Think about who is eating what at The Edible Pyramid restaurant. Which illustration do you like best or find funniest? Tell why.

SKILLS IN CONTEXT

MAIN IDEA: WRITE A NEWSPAPER AD The main idea is the most important idea in a paragraph, chapter, or book. All the other details support that one main idea. A newspaper ad expresses a main idea with a few words and pictures that catch the reader's eye. Write and illustrate an ad for The Edible Pyramid restaurant.

What You Need

- **newspapers**
- **writing and drawing tools**
- **paper**

What to Do

1. Look at ads in old newspapers. Then write a newspaper ad for The Edible Pyramid restaurant.

2. Include at least one picture, or illustration, in your ad. Also, include the name of the restaurant. Make sure that your ad expresses one main idea about the restaurant.

3. Post your ad in the classroom.

Here are some ideas for illustrations:
Show the food pyramid, or make a border of art that shows examples of all the food groups.

Think Ahead
What is left to tell readers about the food pyramid?

© Harcourt

The Edible Pyramid

BOOK TALK

After you read pages 24–30, meet with your group to discuss and answer the following questions:

❶ In *The Edible Pyramid*, animals run the show. What other unusual pets or friends have you read about in *Hidden Surprises*?

❷ What do you think the author wants you to learn from this book?

❸ What do you like best about this book?

> **Strategies Good Readers Use**
>
> **FOCUS STRATEGY** **SELF-QUESTION**
>
> *W*rite a question you have about servings or serving sizes.

RESPONSE JOURNAL

How can you use the information in this book in your own life?

SKILLS IN CONTEXT

FOCUS SKILL **REALITY AND FANTASY: CONDUCT AN INTERVIEW** Ideas that are not real often work together with facts and real events to add interest to a book. Since an interview is a good way to find out more information about something, work in pairs to role-play an interview with the author of *The Edible Pyramid*. Ask and answer questions about why the author uses reality and fantasy in the book.

What You Need

- **writing tools**
- **paper**

What to Do

1. Work with a partner. Talk about the way the author uses animals and fantastic actions to show something real: the food pyramid.

2. Write four or more questions that you would like to ask the author about the real and unreal things in this book. Then write the answers that the author might give.

3. Decide which role you will take in the interview. One partner will be the interviewer, and the other will pretend to be the author. Practice saying the parts out loud. Edit your interview as needed.

4. Perform the interview for the class.

   Here is a question you might ask: *Why did you decide to make the restaurant owner a cat?*

Wrap-Up

▶ **Project** **MAKE A MENU** Explain that a menu can be a list of meals with prices in a restaurant. It can also be a list of what is to be eaten at any given meal.

- Organize students into groups.
- Tell them they are going to plan a menu for three meals they would like to eat.
- Ask groups to begin planning by completing the copying master on page 75.
- Provide an opportunity to discuss the menus that students create.

▶ **Writing** **PERSUASIVE PARAGRAPH** Have students respond to the following writing prompt: **Write a paragraph urging your classmates to eat right.** Have students use the copying master on page 76 to plan a persuasive paragraph. Remind them to use special care when choosing words. Use *Hidden Surprises* pages T550–T551 for additional support. Rubrics for evaluating student writing are provided on pages 292–295.

▶ **Language Link** **COMPOUND WORDS** There are many compound words in this book that name foods. How many can students find? Ask students to list them, draw a line between the words that make them up, and compare their finished work.

Inquiry Project

Students can now be food investigators. Do people follow the Food Guide Pyramid in everyday life? Maybe students would like to determine what servings school lunches and homemade lunches contain. Maybe they would like to keep track of their own eating for a full day. Maybe they would like to learn more about serving sizes. If students track the contents of meals they eat or observe, they might use a form like the one below.

	Number of Servings
Bread Group	
Vegetable Group	
Fruit Group	
Meat Group	
Milk Group	
Fats/Sweets	

© Harcourt

✔ **Comprehension Test** Test students' comprehension of *The Edible Pyramid* by having them complete the copying master on page 77.

Name _____

Project Planner

The Edible Pyramid is a feast of information! You can put this information to work to plan meals for one day's menu.

☐ **Step 1.** With your group, discuss things you would like to eat for breakfast, lunch, and dinner that contain lots of servings from the bread and pasta group and the fruit and vegetable groups. List them.

What You Need

- poster board, heavy cardboard, or construction paper
- tape or paste
- scissors
- writing and drawing materials

Breakfast	Lunch	Dinner
_____	_____	_____
_____	_____	_____
_____	_____	_____
_____	_____	_____

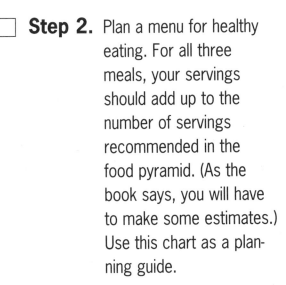

☐ **Step 2.** Plan a menu for healthy eating. For all three meals, your servings should add up to the number of servings recommended in the food pyramid. (As the book says, you will have to make some estimates.) Use this chart as a planning guide.

Bread Group	Fruit Group	Vegetable Group
Total: 6–11	Total: 2–4	Total: 3–5
Milk Group	Meat Group	Fats/Sweets
Total: 2–3	Total: 2–3	Total: Very Little

☐ **Step 3.** Choose three meals and write them out. Paste the menu to a large piece of poster board, cardboard, or construction paper. Cut out or draw pictures of the foods you need most and put them around your menu.

☐ **Step 4.** Display your menu in the classroom.

Name _____

Persuasive Paragraph

Write a paragraph urging your classmates to eat right. Back up your
opinion with facts and examples you have learned by reading *The Edible Pyramid*.
Plan your paragraph by completing this organizer.

Prewriting Graphic Organizer

Topic: _____ **Audience:** _____

Opinion: _____

Reason 1: _____

Details: _____

_____

Reason 2: _____

Details: _____

_____

Reason 3: _____

Details: _____

_____

Opinion Restated/Action Requested: _____

_____

_____

© Harcourt

Comprehension Test   Test Prep

Read each question below. Then mark the letter for the answer you have chosen.

1. **Who greets the customers at The Edible Pyramid restaurant?**
   - Ⓐ a cat
   - Ⓑ a rabbit
   - Ⓒ a pelican
   - Ⓓ a man in a tuxedo

2. **What is the pyramid in this book?**
   - Ⓕ a restaurant
   - Ⓖ a food guide
   - Ⓗ a group of animals
   - Ⓙ both a restaurant and a food guide

3. **Which food group should you eat the most servings from?**
   - Ⓐ vegetable
   - Ⓑ fruit
   - Ⓒ bread and cereal
   - Ⓓ meat

4. **Which food groups is macaroni and cheese in?**
   - Ⓕ bread and milk
   - Ⓖ meat and milk
   - Ⓗ bread and vegetable
   - Ⓙ bread and meat

5. **Of these groups, which should you have the most servings of each day?**
   - Ⓐ fruit
   - Ⓑ meat
   - Ⓒ milk
   - Ⓓ vegetable

6. **If you eat an egg, what group are you eating from?**
   - Ⓕ bread
   - Ⓖ meat
   - Ⓗ milk
   - Ⓙ fats/sweets

7. **Which food is in the same group as peanuts?**
   - Ⓐ pineapple
   - Ⓒ cheese
   - Ⓑ chicken
   - Ⓓ spinach

8. **What is true of many things you eat, such as a slice of pizza?**
   - Ⓕ They are mostly meat.
   - Ⓖ They are mostly bread.
   - Ⓗ They give you servings from more than one food group.
   - Ⓙ They give you servings from just one food group.

9. **What is the most unusual thing about this story?**
   - Ⓐ It recommends healthful eating.
   - Ⓑ It shows a restaurant that only animals go to.
   - Ⓒ It includes facts and examples.
   - Ⓓ It has helpful illustrations.

10. **Explain the Food Guide Pyramid. Tell about its shape and rows. Use the words *base* (of the pyramid) and *top* (of the pyramid) in your answer.**

Making Friends

by Sarah Levete

Reading Level

► Theme Connection
Making Friends and "Water Woman" share the theme of doing what must be done, even when it is tough. A person needs to get through tough and lonely times in friendship as well as in sports.

► Summary
Josh, Elly, Amy, and Kev share their feelings and experiences about making and keeping friends. Students will read about the difference between being alone and feeling lonely. They will learn strategies that help when making new friends and strategies to use during the ups and downs of friendship.

► Building Background
Tell students the title, *Making Friends*, and explain that this nonfiction book gives advice. Ask students to make predictions about the kinds of advice the book will give them, and tell them to read to confirm their predictions. To build background, students might talk about some problems they have had or seen others have in making or keeping friends.

Author Profile
Sarah Levete is the author of several books in the How Do I Feel About series from Copper Beech Books.

Additional Books by the Author
- *(How Do I Feel About) Being Jealous*
- *(How Do I Feel About) Looking After Myself*

Vocabulary

Have students sort some of the vocabulary words into these two categories: *Things Friends Do* and *Feelings*. To use more of the words, students might discuss ways to be yourself in a group, in an argument, or in a friendship. Students might also discuss how being yourself is the same or different from being honest. See pages 296–299 for additional vocabulary activities. For definitions of the words, see the Glossary.

Things Friends Do	Feelings

Day 1	Day 2	Day 3	Day 4
friends p. 3	honest p. 9	groups p. 14	forgive p. 21
trust p. 3	happy p. 9	arguments p. 16	
share p. 3	threats p. 13	change p. 17	
lonely p. 4			
feelings p. 6			
shy p. 7			

© Harcourt

	Response	Strategies	Skills
Day 1 **Pages 3–7**	**Book Talk** • Compare and Contrast • Summarize • Cause-Effect **Writing:** Personal Response	**ADJUST READING RATE** `FOCUS STRATEGY` *Hidden Surprises, p. T209	**ELEMENTS OF NONFICTION** `FOCUS SKILL` *Hidden Surprises, pp. T208–T209
Day 2 **Pages 8–13**	**Book Talk** • Important Details • Summarize • Recognize Author's Purpose **Writing:** Express Personal Opinion	Use Text Structure and Format *Hidden Surprises, p. T371	Skim and Scan *Journeys of Wonder, pp. T196–T197
Day 3 **Pages 14–19**	**Book Talk** • Classify • Classify • Cause-Effect **Writing:** Personal Response	Use Graphic Aids *Hidden Surprises, p. T409	Compare and Contrast *Journeys of Wonder, pp. T304–T305
Day 4 **Pages 20–23**	**Book Talk** • Make Comparisons • Main Idea • Make Judgments **Writing:** Express Personal Opinion	**ADJUST READING RATE** `FOCUS STRATEGY` *Hidden Surprises, p. T209	**ELEMENTS OF NONFICTION** `FOCUS SKILL` *Hidden Surprises, pp. T208–T209
Day 5 **Wrap-Up**	**Project** ✓ Make a Friendship Board Game • Inquiry Project **Writing** ✓ Paragraph That Compares or Contrasts *Journeys of Wonder, pp. T44–T45, T96–T97 **Language Link** • Compound Words **Assessment** ✓ Comprehension Test		

*Additional support is provided in *Collections*.
✓ Options for Assessment

Making Friends

BOOK TALK

After you read pages 3–7, meet with your group to discuss and answer the following questions:

1 What is the difference between being alone and being lonely?

2 What happens to Chaz?

3 Feeling lonely can cause other feelings. What are some of them?

RESPONSE JOURNAL

In your journal, write about a time when you felt lonely.

> **Strategies Good Readers Use**
>
> **FOCUS STRATEGY ADJUST READING RATE**
>
> *R*eaders often have to slow down when they read nonfiction. Tell one place where you slowed down and why.

SKILLS IN CONTEXT

FOCUS SKILL **ELEMENTS OF NONFICTION: MAKE A PARTS POSTER** Books that give information on a topic often have sections with headings. They divide the information so you can read and find it easily. Make a poster to show the book parts in *Making Friends*.

What You Need

- cardboard or poster board
- writing and drawing materials

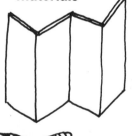

What to Do

1. In a group, discuss the parts that make up this book: a table of contents, chapters, headings, photos, art, and an index. Talk about what each part adds to the book.

2. Using cardboard or poster board, make an accordion-fold poster that stands up by itself and has sections created by the folds. Make the same number of sections as book parts.

3. Have each person in the group choose one book part to illustrate and explain on one section of the poster.

4. Display your poster in the classroom.

Here is an idea to get you started:
The table of contents shows all the main parts of the book.

Think Ahead
What other problems happen in friendships besides feeling lonely?

© Harcourt

Making Friends

BOOK TALK

After you read pages 8–13, meet with your group to discuss and answer the following questions:

❶ What are some things friends share?

❷ What does the author say about ways to make friends?

❸ Why do you think the author keeps giving examples of real children like Amy?

RESPONSE JOURNAL

What do you think is the best way to make friends? Write about it in your journal.

Strategies Good Readers Use

USE TEXT STRUCTURE AND FORMAT

Write the two chapter titles in this section of the book. Then write the main idea of each.

SKILLS IN CONTEXT

SKIM AND SCAN: TEACHER FOR A DAY   Sometimes you do not read every word on a page. Instead, you might scan the page to find a particular heading or key word, or you might skim the words to get the main idea but not all the details.

What You Need

- **paper and pencil**
- **chalkboard and chalk**

What to Do

1. Prepare to teach a lesson to the class on how to skim and scan. To do this, choose one or two pages from the book.

2. Jot down notes about what you might skim and scan. Think about reasons for doing each. Then think about how these strategies help you understand, organize, and get the most out of what you read.

3. Present your ideas to the class. Point out parts of the page as you tell what you do and why you do it. List key points on the board.

Here are some questions you should answer: Why do you skim? What do you skim? How do you skim?

Think Ahead
What do you think the next part will be about?

© Harcourt

Making Friends

BOOK TALK

After you read pages 14–19, meet with your group to discuss and answer the following questions:

1 What are some different kinds of friends?

2 What kinds of problems can come up in a friendship?

3 What makes Ashika angry?

RESPONSE JOURNAL

Write about the different kinds of friends you have.

> **Strategies Good Readers Use**
>
> ### USE GRAPHIC AIDS
>
> *L*ist the parts of page 18 in the order you should read them or study them. Begin with the title.

SKILLS IN CONTEXT

COMPARE AND CONTRAST: MAKE A FRIENDSHIP POSTER When you compare and contrast, you tell how two or more things are alike and different. Create a poster to compare and contrast different kinds of friendship in *Making Friends*.

What You Need

- **poster board**
- **writing materials**

What to Do

1. Decide on two or more kinds of friendship to show.
2. Make a chart or Venn diagram to show how two kinds of friendship are alike and different.
3. Copy your ideas neatly on a sheet of poster board. Give your poster a title.
4. Display your poster in the classroom.

Here is one comparison to get you started: *Best friends are different from friends you write to because you see a best friend often. Best friends and friends you write to are alike because you can share your feelings with both.*

Best Friends / share feelings / Friends You Write To / see often / don't see very often

Think Ahead How do you think this book will end?

© Harcourt

Making Friends

BOOK TALK

After you read pages 20–23, meet with your group to discuss and answer the following questions:

1 *Making Friends* helps kids make choices in their own lives. What other selections in *Hidden Surprises* are about real life?

2 What is one main idea you think the author wants you to understand about making friends?

3 What did you like best about the way this book is written or the way the pages look?

RESPONSE JOURNAL

What would you add to this book? What would you change?

Strategies Good Readers Use

FOCUS STRATEGY **ADJUST READING RATE** Find two places in this book where you changed your reading rate. With a partner, discuss how you changed your reading rate and why.

SKILLS IN CONTEXT

FOCUS SKILL **ELEMENTS OF NONFICTION: PRIZE PARTS** Nonfiction presents facts and information. Any part of the book that gives facts or helps you find or use information is an element of nonfiction. This includes the index, photographs, captions, and other features. With a group of classmates, create awards for the most useful elements of *Making Friends*.

What You Need

- red and blue ribbons, or paper cut to look like ribbons
- writing materials

What to Do

1. With your group, talk about the element of nonfiction that most helped you understand and enjoy this book.

2. Make a blue ribbon for first place. Make a red ribbon for second place.

3. Find the folding poster you made on Day 1 that shows the elements of nonfiction. Place the blue ribbon on the element that helped you most. Place the red ribbon on the second most helpful element.

4. Explain your choices to the class.

Here are ideas to get you started: Did you use the index often? How helpful were the photographs? Did you think the words in the speech balloons told you some of the real feelings of friendship?

Wrap-Up

▶ **Project**   MAKE A FRIENDSHIP BOARD GAME In *Making Friends*, students learn a great deal about the ups and downs of friendships. Explain that they will now create a friendship board game.

- Organize students into groups, and ask them to discuss the kinds of events in friendship that could be worked into a board game.
- Have students complete the copying master on page 85.
- After students have designed and created their games, have them play them with other group members and classmates.

▶ **Writing**   PARAGRAPH THAT COMPARES OR CONTRASTS Have students respond to the following writing prompt: **Write a paragraph that compares or contrasts a friendship you have experienced with one in the book.** Have students use the copying master on page 86 to plan the paragraph. Remind students to focus on paragraph organization. Use *Journeys of Wonder* pages T44–T45 and T96–T97 for additional support. Rubrics for evaluating student writing are provided on pages 292–295.

▶ **Language Link**   COMPOUND WORDS Have students find and list ten compound words that appear in *Making Friends*. Ask them to draw a line between the two words that make up each compound word.

Inquiry Project

Making Friends can lead students to make inquiries into a variety of topics and ideas. Brainstorm with students related subjects, and help them organize their responses in a web like the one below. Students can use reference sources or the Internet to begin their inquiry projects.

✔ **Comprehension Test** Test students' comprehension of *Making Friends* by having them complete the copying master on page 87.

Name _____

Project Planner

Making Friends tells how friends have their ups and downs. Make a board game that shows the ups and downs of friendship.

☐ **Step 1.** Brainstorm with your group ideas of friendship from this book that you want to put in your game. Use this web to list ideas.

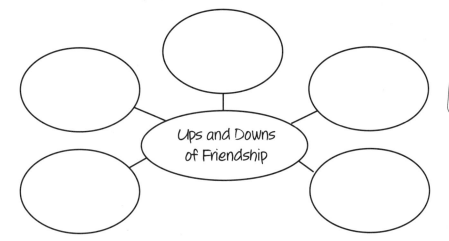

Ups and Downs of Friendship

What You Need
- large sheet of poster board
- writing and drawing materials
- game board pieces
- index cards

☐ **Step 2.** Organize your ideas into ups and downs. List the same number of each. When a player draws a down card, he or she will move back spaces. When a player draws an up card, he or she will move ahead.

☐ **Step 3.** Plan your board game on paper. Make cards for moving ahead and back.

☐ **Step 4.** Draw your game on the board. Make it colorful and easy to follow.

☐ **Step 5.** Play the game with classmates.

© Harcourt

Paragraph That Compares or Contrasts

Write a paragraph that compares or contrasts an experience you have had with friendship with one in the book. Complete the chart below to plan your story.

Prewriting Graphic Organizer

Topic: _____

_____

Audience: _____

_____

Main Idea: _____

_____

Likeness or Difference 1: _____

Details: _____

_____

Likeness or Difference 2: _____

Details: _____

_____

Likeness or Difference 3: _____

Details: _____

_____

Main Idea Summarized: _____

_____

© Harcourt

Name _____

Comprehension Test

Read each question below. Then mark the letter for the answer you have chosen.

1. **What does the book say about being alone?**
   - Ⓐ It is worse than being lonely.
   - Ⓑ No one should choose it.
   - Ⓒ It is better than being lonely.
   - Ⓓ It is for people without friends.

2. **What problem did Amy have?**
   - Ⓕ She was angry at her dad.
   - Ⓖ She was nasty to kids.
   - Ⓗ She did not have any toys.
   - Ⓙ She felt lonely.

3. **What does the author say about silent friends, like pets?**
   - Ⓐ People should not have them.
   - Ⓑ They can be friends, too.
   - Ⓒ They are better than real friends.
   - Ⓓ They can be difficult.

4. **Which of these ways of making friends works best in this story?**
   - Ⓕ making an extra effort to be friendly
   - Ⓖ ignoring friends who are not nice
   - Ⓗ pushing in
   - Ⓙ giving away candy

5. **What should you do if a friend makes you feel uneasy?**
   - Ⓐ Tell a grown-up.
   - Ⓑ Be careful with that person.
   - Ⓒ Be friends with that person.
   - Ⓓ Make an effort to be a better friend.

6. **What should you do if you are left out or not invited?**
   - Ⓕ complain
   - Ⓗ don't worry
   - Ⓖ act upset
   - Ⓙ find new friends

7. **When should you say *no* to friends?**
   - Ⓐ when they do not invite you to their parties
   - Ⓑ whenever they make you feel unhappy
   - Ⓒ when they have other friends
   - Ⓓ when they dare you to do something wrong

8. **What tips does Elly have for staying friends?**
   - Ⓕ Sit back and wait.
   - Ⓖ Buy the right games and clothes.
   - Ⓗ Get angry whenever you need to.
   - Ⓙ Talk to friends about feelings.

9. **According to this book, is it possible to make sure that no one is lonely?**
   - Ⓐ Yes, but you have to make an effort.
   - Ⓑ Yes, if everyone has friends.
   - Ⓒ No, some people like to be lonely.
   - Ⓓ No, being lonely happens to everyone sometimes.

10. **Write three things you should do to be a good friend. Then write three things you should *not* do to make friends.**

© Harcourt

Willie's Not the Hugging Kind

Reading Level

by Joyce Durham Barrett

Theme Connection
Like "Ramona Forever," *Willie's Not the Hugging Kind* spotlights growing up, school situations, friendships, and family relationships.

Summary
When Willie's friend Jo-Jo teases him about hugging people, Willie decides that he no longer wants to hug or be hugged. However, secretly he misses the hugs. All around him, he sees people expressing love and friendship through hugs. Finally, Willie admits that he is "the hugging kind" after all.

Building Background
Ask students to tell what they think it means when someone is "not the hugging kind." Tell students that the main character in this story stops hugging his family after his friend tells him that hugging is silly. Ask students if they have ever changed something about themselves so that someone would like them. Then ask them if they think it is a good idea to change so that others will like you. Have students read to be entertained and to learn about Willie's feelings.

Author Profile
Author and elementary school teacher Joyce Durham Barrett grew up in Homer, Georgia, with ten brothers and sisters. She has worked as an editor, reporter, and freelance writer, and along with *Willie's Not the Hugging Kind,* she has written and published many short stories and articles in the United States and England.

Additional Books by the Author
- *Jimmy Lee Did It*
- *C.L.O.U.D.S.*

Vocabulary

Have students explore the meanings of the vocabulary words by writing all the words that name actions in a chart like the one below. See pages 296–299 for additional vocabulary activities. For definitions of the words, see the Glossary.

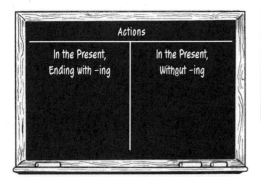

Actions	
In the Present, Ending with –ing	In the Present, Without –ing

Day 1
feel p. 9
hugging p. 9
safe p. 13
squeezing p. 13

Day 2
warm p. 17
hoping p. 19
watching p. 19
laughing p. 19

Day 3
mugging p. 21
greet p. 21
running p. 23

Day 4
burying p. 29

© Harcourt

	Response	Strategies	Skills
▶Day 1 **Pages 7–13**	**Book Talk** • Cause-Effect • Speculate • Compare and Contrast **Writing:** Personal Response	**SELF-QUESTION** FOCUS STRATEGY *Hidden Surprises*, p. T703	**AUTHOR'S PURPOSE** FOCUS SKILL *Hidden Surprises*, pp. T702–T703
▶Day 2 **Pages 14–19**	**Book Talk** • Interpret Characters' Motivations • Summarize • Important Details **Writing:** Express Personal Opinion	Read Ahead *Hidden Surprises*, p. T525	Story Elements *Hidden Surprises*, pp. T274–T275
▶Day 3 **Pages 20–25**	**Book Talk** • Draw Conclusions • Determine Characters' Emotions • Author's Viewpoint **Writing:** Identify with Characters	Create Mental Images *Hidden Surprises*, p. T567	Compare and Contrast *Journeys of Wonder*, pp. T304–T305
▶Day 4 **Pages 26–32**	**Book Talk** • Make Comparisons • Theme • Express Personal Opinion **Writing:** Write a Note	**SELF-QUESTION** FOCUS STRATEGY *Hidden Surprises*, p. T703	**AUTHOR'S PURPOSE** FOCUS SKILL *Hidden Surprises*, pp. T702–T703

▶Day 5
Wrap-Up

Project
✓ Perform a Puppet Show
• Inquiry Project

Writing
✓ Description
Hidden Surprises, pp. T102–T103

Language Link
• Adjectives

Assessment
✓ Comprehension Test

*Additional support is provided in *Collections.*
✓ Options for Assessment

Willie's Not the Hugging Kind

BOOK TALK

After you read pages 7–13, meet with your group to discuss and answer the following questions:

1 Why has Willie given up hugging?

2 Why do you think Jo-Jo is so against hugging?

3 How are Rose and Willie alike and different?

RESPONSE JOURNAL

Do you know any grown-up or child like Jo-Jo? Write about that person in your journal.

Strategies Good Readers Use

FOCUS STRATEGY SELF-QUESTION

Write down a question you asked yourself as you read the first pages of the book. Then write the answer.

SKILLS IN CONTEXT

FOCUS SKILL **AUTHOR'S PURPOSE: MAKE A WORD CROSS** One purpose for writing is to express, or tell, feelings about a topic. In this book, the author expresses feelings about hugging. You can make a word cross to show these feelings. Work with a partner to make a word cross with words that tell how hugging makes people feel.

What You Need

- **paper**
- **writing tools**

What to Do

1. Make a list of all the ways people feel about hugs.
2. Write the word *HUGS* in big, bold letters down a sheet of paper.
3. Write words across the paper that have an *H*, *U*, *G*, or *S* in them and that tell something about hugs or how they make people feel.
4. Compare your word cross with another pair's word cross.

Here is one word for the word cross: Secure. *A hug makes you feel secure. It has a letter* u, *and so does the word* hugs.

Think Ahead How will Willie solve his problem?

© Harcourt

Willie's Not the Hugging Kind

BOOK TALK

After you read pages 14–19, meet with your group to discuss and answer the following questions:

❶ If Willie wants to be hugged so much, why does he hide it?

❷ What does Willie remember as wonderful?

❸ What does Willie say that shows he is beginning to change?

Strategies Good Readers Use

READ AHEAD

*W*rite one reason why it makes sense to read ahead from page 15, even if you are not sure about what is happening.

RESPONSE JOURNAL

Do you think that Willie has a problem that only boys have?

SKILLS IN CONTEXT

STORY ELEMENTS: MAKE A STORY MAP Story elements include the characters, the setting, and the plot, or what happens in the story. A story map can help you understand and remember the story elements. Think about the characters, the settings, and the plot of this story. Work with a partner to make a story map for *Willie's Not the Hugging Kind.*

What You Need

- **large paper or poster board**
- **writing and art materials**

What to Do

1. Create the story map with your partner. Include a place to write the names of the characters, the settings (there is more than one in this story), the problem, and the main events so far.

2. Fill in each section of the story map based upon what you have read so far.

3. Share your story map with another pair. Talk about what is the same and different. Also, talk about how Willie might solve his problem.

Here are some characters to list:

Willie, Willie's mom, Willie's dad, Rose, and Jo-Jo

Think Ahead
Do you think that Rose will help Willie solve his problem? Why or why not?

Willie's Not the Hugging Kind

BOOK TALK

After you read pages 20–25, meet with your group to discuss and answer the following questions:

1 What does Jo-Jo mean when he talks about people being mugged?

2 How do you think Willie feels when he hugs the stop sign?

3 What do you think the author is saying about life without hugs?

RESPONSE JOURNAL

How do you think you would feel if you were Willie?

Strategies Good Readers Use

CREATE MENTAL IMAGES

Imagine Willie in his bed hugging a towel. Write five words that tell about how he feels and the look on his face.

SKILLS IN CONTEXT

COMPARE AND CONTRAST: MAKE A VENN DIAGRAM You can think about how the characters in a story are the same and different in order to understand them better. Jo-Jo and Willie are the same in some ways, but they are also very different. Work with a partner, and make a Venn diagram that shows how Jo-Jo and Willie are the same and different.

What You Need

- paper or poster board
- writing materials

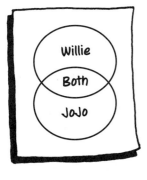

What to Do

1. Create a Venn diagram with your partner. Label one circle *Willie*, the other *Jo-Jo*, and the overlapping area *Both*.

2. List words and ideas that tell about how each character is different in the *Willie* and *Jo-Jo* circles. List what is alike about them in the overlapping area. For example, Willie and Jo-Jo are in the same grade and are both boys.

3. Share your Venn diagram with other classmates. Talk about what is the same and what is different about the information you listed in the diagram.

Here are some differences to help you get started: *Willie rides with his dad to school; Jo-Jo rides with someone else's dad to school.*

Think Ahead How will the story end?

© Harcourt

Willie's Not the Hugging Kind

BOOK TALK

After you read pages 26–32, meet with your group to discuss and answer the following questions:

1 *Willie's Not the Hugging Kind* is about family relationships. What stories in *Hidden Surprises* are also about families?

2 What do you think the author wants the reader to think about?

3 What did you like best about this book?

RESPONSE JOURNAL

In your journal, write a short note to Willie telling him what you think about how he has changed.

SKILLS IN CONTEXT

FOCUS SKILL **AUTHOR'S PURPOSE: PUZZLE IT OUT** Sometimes the details in a story are like pieces of a puzzle. When you put them together, you understand the author's purpose. In this story, the author's purpose is to express, or tell, feelings about a topic. Make a puzzle with a partner that shows how the author expresses her feelings about hugging.

What You Need

- paper
- writing tools and crayons

What to Do

1. Draw a puzzle with less than ten pieces on scrap paper. Make sure the puzzle has a center piece.

2. Make the center piece different by coloring, shading, striping, or decorating it in some way.

3. Write the word *express* in the center piece.

4. Think about what the story shows and how it ends. Then, on the other puzzle pieces, write details from the story that show how the author tells her feelings about hugging. Cut out the puzzle pieces.

5. Trade puzzles with another group and see if you can put together each other's puzzles.

Here are ideas for puzzle pieces to get you started: *Willie is sad when he does not hug. Willie secretly hugs a towel.*

© Harcourt

Wrap-Up

▶ **Project** **PERFORM A PUPPET SHOW** Tell students that *Willie's Not the Hugging Kind* would make a good puppet show. Then tell them that they will be acting out part of the story or a few main events by using puppets.

- Organize students into groups.
- Ask groups to begin planning their puppet shows by completing the copying master on page 95.
- Provide time for students to practice and perform their puppet shows.

▶ **Writing** **DESCRIPTION** Have students respond to the following writing prompt: **Write a descriptive paragraph about hugging. Use the example of hugging a parent, a pet, a favorite stuffed animal, or another favorite person or thing. Describe what you see, smell, feel, or hear as you hug.** Have students use the copying master on page 96 to plan their descriptive paragraphs. Remind them to be sure that each of their sentences leads smoothly to the next. Use *Hidden Surprises* pages T102–T103 for additional support. Rubrics for evaluating student writing are provided on pages 292–295.

▶ **Language Link** **ADJECTIVES** Have students list five or more adjectives that they find in this story. Also ask them to list the noun that each adjective describes.

Inquiry Project

Willie's Not the Hugging Kind can be a springboard for inquiry into a variety of topics and ideas. Have students brainstorm topics they would like to know more about and organize their responses in a web. Students can use reference sources and the Internet to begin their inquiry projects.

✔ **Comprehension Test** Test students' comprehension of *Willie's Not the Hugging Kind* by having them complete the copying master on page 97.

© Harcourt

Name _____

Project Planner

You can act out some or all of the main events in *Willie's Not the Hugging Kind*. All you need are some puppets and a plan.

☐ **Step 1.** Decide with your group about two or more characters that you will show and what you will show them doing. You can show part or all of the story. Make a list of the characters that you will use and what you will show about them.

What You Need
- small brown lunch bag or old socks
- construction paper and scissors
- tape or glue stick
- writing and drawing materials

☐ **Step 2.** Use the sequence chain below to plan your puppet show. Write the events that happen to the characters in the order in which they take place.

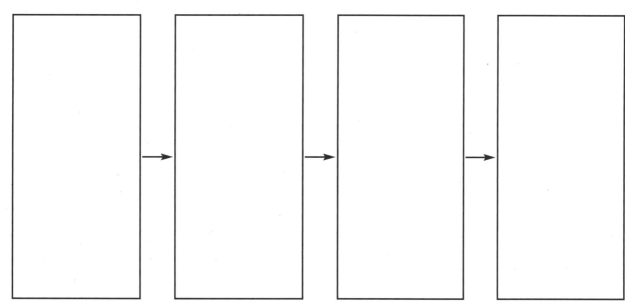

☐ **Step 3.** Make the puppets. Use lunch bags or socks and draw faces on them.

☐ **Step 4.** Use the puppets to practice your puppet show. Speak just as you think the characters in the book would speak. Figure out how you will show hugging and being afraid to hug.

☐ **Step 5.** Perform your puppet show for the class.

Name _____

Description

Write a descriptive paragraph about hugging. Use the example of hugging a parent, a pet, a favorite stuffed animal, or another favorite person or thing. Describe what you see, smell, hear, or feel as you hug. Use the graphic organizer below to help you plan your paragraph.

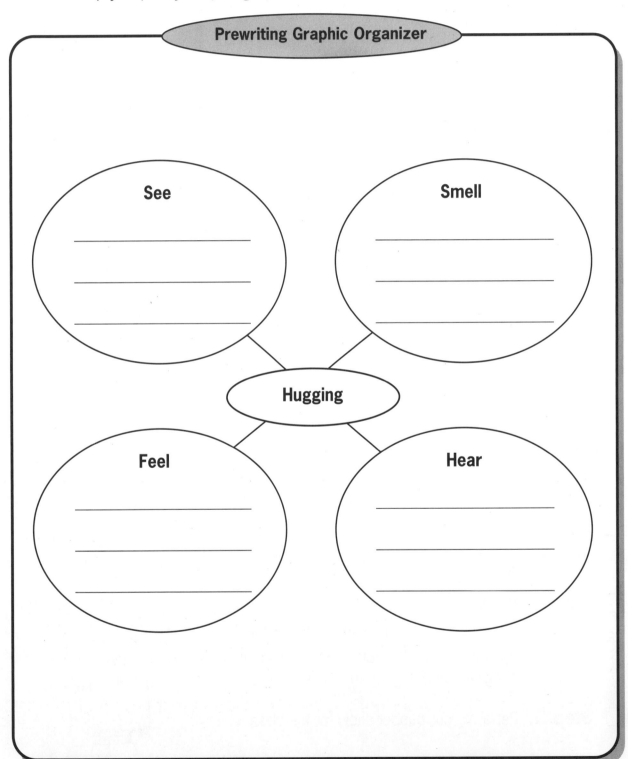

Prewriting Graphic Organizer

See

Smell

Hugging

Feel

Hear

© Harcourt

Name _____

Comprehension Test

Test Prep

Read each question below. Then mark the letter for the answer you have chosen.

1. **Who is against hugging?**
   - Ⓐ Willie
   - Ⓒ Rose
   - Ⓑ Willie's dad
   - Ⓓ Jo-Jo

2. **Who wants to be hugged but is not?**
   - Ⓕ Willie
   - Ⓗ Rose
   - Ⓖ Willie's dad
   - Ⓙ Jo-Jo

3. **What does Jo-Jo do when Miss Mary tries to hug him?**
   - Ⓐ He tries to get away.
   - Ⓑ He gets Willie to help him.
   - Ⓒ He laughs.
   - Ⓓ He hugs back.

4. **What does Willie feel when he sees Rose hugging her teddy bear?**
   - Ⓕ He is happy.
   - Ⓖ He is jealous.
   - Ⓗ He is angry.
   - Ⓙ He feels more grown-up than Rose.

5. **What is true of Willie's parents?**
   - Ⓐ They make him hug them.
   - Ⓑ They want to hug him, but they wait for him to hug them.
   - Ⓒ They think hugging is silly.
   - Ⓓ They do not want to hug him, but they change their minds.

6. **The day Willie walks home alone from school, what does he see?**
   - Ⓕ He sees how lonely Jo-Jo is.
   - Ⓖ He sees lots of people hugging.
   - Ⓗ He sees Miss Mary.
   - Ⓙ He sees his parents hugging.

7. **Why does Willie hug his bike?**
   - Ⓐ He loves his new bike.
   - Ⓑ He thinks this is what tough boys do.
   - Ⓒ He wants to hug so much, he even hugs his bike.
   - Ⓓ His parents will not hug him.

8. **How do Willie's parents act when he finally hugs them?**
   - Ⓕ They hug him back.
   - Ⓖ They make fun of him.
   - Ⓗ They tell him he is cute.
   - Ⓙ They tell him he was being dumb.

9. **What does "the hugging kind" mean?**
   - Ⓐ someone who doesn't like hugs
   - Ⓑ someone who hugs anything
   - Ⓒ someone who enjoys hugging
   - Ⓓ someone who hugs stop signs

10. **Write a response to the following question:**
    Will Jo-Jo and Willie still be friends? Explain.

Frida María

Reading Level

by Deborah Nourse Lattimore

Theme Connection
In "I'm in Charge of Celebrations," the natural wonders of an American Southwest desert inspire a young girl's personal celebrations. A traditional Southwestern celebration, a *fiesta*, is the setting of *Frida María*.

Summary
Frida María is hoping to ride in the horse race during Fiesta, her family's party, but her mother feels she should act more ladylike. On the day of Fiesta, Frida María makes a decision that leads her mother to realize that Frida María is special in her own way.

Building Background
Tell students that *Frida María* is historical fiction and is set in the old Southwest—southern California during the 1800s. Look at some illustrations together. Explain to students that the characters are preparing for a celebration called a *fiesta*. Suggest that students read this story to be informed and entertained. Have students read to find out what Frida María does at the celebration.

Author Profile
Deborah Nourse Lattimore became familiar with the culture of the Old Southwest from stories her grandmother told her. Lattimore graduated from UCLA with a degree in art history. She is a three-time winner of the Notable Social Studies Trade Book for Young People award.

Additional Books by the Author
- *The Flame of Peace: A Tale of the Aztecs*
- *The Fool and the Phoenix: A Tale of Ancient Japan.*

Vocabulary

Have students work in teams to group the vocabulary words. A sample grouping is shown. See pages 296–299 for additional vocabulary activities. For definitions of the words, see the Glossary.

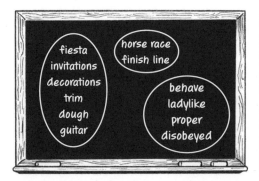

Day 1	Day 2	Day 3	Day 4
fiesta p. 3	dough p. 10	wrenched p. 22	finish line p. 25
invitations p. 4	ladylike p. 12	cactus p. 23	disobeyed p. 26
decorations p. 4	guitar p. 14		
horse race p. 5			
trim p. 7			
behave p. 9			
proper p. 9			

© Harcourt

	Response	**Strategies**	**Skills**
Day 1 **Pages 2–9**	**Book Talk** • Important Details • Determine Characters' Traits • Generalize **Writing:** Express Personal Opinion	**CREATE MENTAL IMAGES** FOCUS STRATEGY *Journeys of Wonder*, p. T537	**IMPORTANT DETAILS** FOCUS SKILL *Journeys of Wonder*, pp. T536–T537
Day 2 **Pages 10–15**	**Book Talk** • Draw Conclusions • Cause-Effect • Determine Characters' Emotions **Writing:** Express Personal Opinion	Use Prior Knowledge *Hidden Surprises*, p. T71	Characters' Feelings and Actions *Journeys of Wonder*, pp. T262–T263
Day 3 **Pages 16–23**	**Book Talk** • Determine Characters' Emotions • Cause-Effect • Speculate **Writing:** Express Personal Opinion/ Personal Narrative	Use Text Structure and Format *Hidden Surprises*, p. T371	Reality and Fantasy *Hidden Surprises*, pp. T452–T453
Day 4 **Pages 24–31**	**Book Talk** • Make Comparisons • Determine Theme • Make Judgments **Writing:** Express Personal Opinion	**CREATE MENTAL IMAGES** FOCUS STRATEGY *Journeys of Wonder*, p. T537	**IMPORTANT DETAILS** FOCUS SKILL *Journeys of Wonder*, pp. T536–T537
Day 5 **Wrap-Up**	**Project** ✓ Make a Set of Dioramas • Inquiry Project **Writing** ✓ Unrhymed Poem *Journeys of Wonder*, pp. T564–T565 **Language Link** • Dialogue **Assessment** ✓ Comprehension Test		

© Harcourt

*Additional support is provided in *Collections*.
✓ Options for Assessment

Frida María

BOOK TALK

After you read pages 2–9, meet with your group to discuss and answer the following questions:

1 Where and when does this story take place? How do you know?

2 What are some words that describe Frida María? Support your ideas with examples from the story.

3 What is the conflict between Frida María and Mamá?

RESPONSE JOURNAL

If you were Frida's mother, would you let Frida ride in the race? Explain why or why not.

Strategies Good Readers Use

FOCUS STRATEGY CREATE MENTAL IMAGES

What parts of this story can you see in your mind? How does the author help you see these images, or pictures?

SKILLS IN CONTEXT

FOCUS SKILL **IMPORTANT DETAILS: FIESTA INVITATION** Noticing details can help you understand what you read. Details help you answer important questions about a story, such as: *Who is the main character? Where and when does the story take place? What happens?* Use details in the story to make an invitation to the Fiesta.

What You Need

- **paper**
- **drawing paper**
- **ruler**
- **writing and drawing tools**
- **sample invitations**

What to Do

1. Look at some sample invitations for ideas.
2. Plan what you will write. Find as many details as you can in the story and the pictures. Make up any other details you need. Be sure to include information about *who, what, where, when,* and *why*. Decide what order the details should be in.
3. Fold or cut the drawing paper to make a card the size you want.
4. Write your invitation inside the card.
5. Draw a fiesta picture on the cover.

Here is a detail to get you started:

"On the last day of Fiesta there was to be a great horse race."

Think Ahead What will Frida do in the kitchen?

© Harcourt

Frida María

BOOK TALK

After you read pages 10–15, meet with your group to discuss and answer the following questions:

1 How do you know Cook is pleased with Frida? How do you know Mamá is not?

2 Why is Mamá worried about Frida? How does she think Frida should behave?

3 How do you think Frida feels as she sits on the patio? What clues tell you this?

RESPONSE JOURNAL

Do you think Frida María should try to please Mamá? How would you handle this situation?

SKILLS IN CONTEXT

CHARACTERS' FEELINGS AND ACTIONS: CHARACTER CUBE Being able to identify characters' feelings and actions helps you understand what kind of people they are. Make a character cube that shows what Frida María is like.

What You Need

- **construction paper**
- **scissors**
- **writing and drawing tools**
- **glue stick**

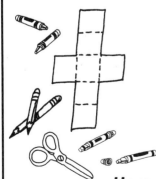

What to Do

1. Draw a cube pattern like the one below on the paper. Write something that Frida María does in each square of the cube pattern. On one square, write the title and author of the story.

2. Cut out the cube pattern. Cut only along outside lines.

3. Fold the paper into a cube. Make sure you fold it so that the words are on the outside of the cube. Glue the flaps to hold it together.

4. Take turns rolling the cube with a partner. Take turns explaining what you can learn about Frida from the action that shows on the side facing you.

Here is an idea to get you started:
Frida learns quickly how to make the dough.

Think Ahead
What will happen when Fiesta comes?

Frida María

BOOK TALK

Read pages 16–23. Then meet with your group to discuss and answer the following questions:

1 How does Frida feel when she is being ladylike? Why?

2 Why doesn't Frida enjoy Fiesta?

3 Why do you think Frida leaps onto Diablo?

RESPONSE JOURNAL

How do you think Frida's mother feels? Write your thoughts. Then write about a time when you surprised someone else.

> **Strategies Good Readers Use**
>
> ## USE TEXT STRUCTURE AND FORMAT
>
> How do the pictures help you understand what is happening on pages 18–19?

SKILLS IN CONTEXT

REALITY AND FANTASY: FOLDER BOOKMARK Historical fiction combines factual information with imaginary elements. Finding out which elements are historical and which are fictional helps readers learn from historical fiction. Make a folder bookmark that identifies the historical and fictional parts of *Frida María*.

What You Need

- **drawing paper**
- **scissors**
- **writing and drawing tools**

What to Do

1. Create a folder by folding your paper in half, long side to long side.

2. Write the title and author, and draw a scene from the story on the front of the paper.

3. Open the folder. On one side of the fold, write *Historical Elements*. On the other side, write *Fictional Elements*.

4. Think about the story's setting, characters, and events. Decide what is historical and what is fictional, and list each detail in the column that fits it.

5. Add historical and fictional items to your folder bookmark as you continue reading this book.

> ***Here are some ideas to get you started:*** *Historical Elements: the hacienda setting; Fictional Elements: Frida María.*

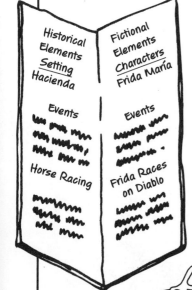

Think Ahead
What do you think will happen after the race?

© Harcourt

Frida María

BOOK TALK

Read pages 24–31 and meet with your group to discuss and answer the following questions:

1 Which characters from *Journeys of Wonder* does Frida Maria remind you of? How do they remind you of her?

2 What are some themes, or main ideas, in *Frida María*?

3 What is Frida María's most important success? Why?

RESPONSE JOURNAL

What is your opinion of the story's ending? Would you change it in any way? If so, how?

Strategies Good Readers Use

FOCUS STRATEGY CREATE MENTAL IMAGES

The words "proper señorita" appear three times. What is your mental image of a "proper señorita"? How does this image compare with your image of Frida María?

SKILLS IN CONTEXT

FOCUS SKILL **IMPORTANT DETAILS: DETAILS GAME** Details can help you understand a main idea and share a character's experience. Pay attention to the main idea and important details about the horse race in *Frida María*. Use these details to write a series of questions for a game.

What You Need

- index cards
- writing materials

What to Do

1. Work in a small group. Find details about the horse race in *Frida María*. Then work together to think of six questions about the race. The questions should ask *who, what, where, when, why,* and *how.*

2. Write each question on one side of an index card. Write the answer on the other.

3. Take turns asking your questions with other groups.

Here is a question to get you started: Who wins the horse race?

© Harcourt

Wrap-Up

> **Project** **MAKE A SET OF DIORAMAS** Point out that students learn a lot about life in the Old Southwest by reading *Frida María*. Read the Author's Note to students. Talk about the details and images she uses in her story. Tell students they will be creating a set of dioramas to show the different scenes from *Frida María*.
>
> - Organize students into small groups.
> - Ask students to complete the copying master on page 105 to plan their scenes.
> - Have each group present its finished set of dioramas to the class.

> **Writing** **UNRHYMED POEM** Have students respond to the following writing prompt: **Write an unrhymed poem about a celebration that is special to you.** Have students use the copying master on page 106 to brainstorm images and descriptive words. Remind students to focus on ideas. Use *Journeys of Wonder* pages T564–T565 for additional support. Rubrics for evaluating student writing are provided on pages 292–295.

> **Language Link** **DIALOGUE** Tell students that conversations among the characters convey their ideas and feelings. Have students identify important conversations in *Frida María*. Then have volunteers take characters' parts and perform the dialogue. Have students make notes of the main ideas and details presented in each conversation.

Inquiry Project

Frida María can be a springboard for inquiry into a variety of topics and ideas. Have students brainstorm topics they would like to know more about and organize their responses in a web. Students can use reference books and the Internet to begin their inquiry projects. They may also be able to use community resources.

✔ **Comprehension Test** Test students' comprehension of *Frida María* by having them complete the copying master on page 107.

Name _____

Project Planner

Frida María tells you a lot about life in the Old Southwest. In the Author's Note, you learn more about the details and images the author chose for her book. Choose four scenes from the book and make a diorama for each. Group the dioramas together to form a type of cube.

☐ **Step 1.** Decide with your group what scenes you will make. List your ideas on the lines below.

_____

_____

_____

_____

What You Need

- four shoe boxes
- large sheets of drawing paper
- scissors
- writing and drawing tools
- construction paper
- optional three-dimensional objects

☐ **Step 2.** Brainstorm with your group details from the story to include in each scene. Decide how you will create each scene.
You should discuss the following questions:

- What will the background look like?
- Who will be in the scene?
- Where will people and objects be placed?
- How will you label the scene?

☐ **Step 3.** Work together to create the dioramas. Use construction paper to make stand-up figures. Label each diorama. Tape the back side edges together to form a cube shape.

☐ **Step 4.** As a group, present your project to the class.

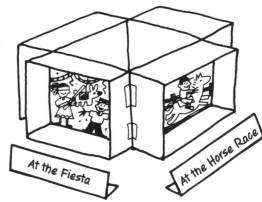

© Harcourt

Unrhymed Poem

Write an unrhymed poem about a celebration that is special to you.
Complete the web below to help you plan your poem.

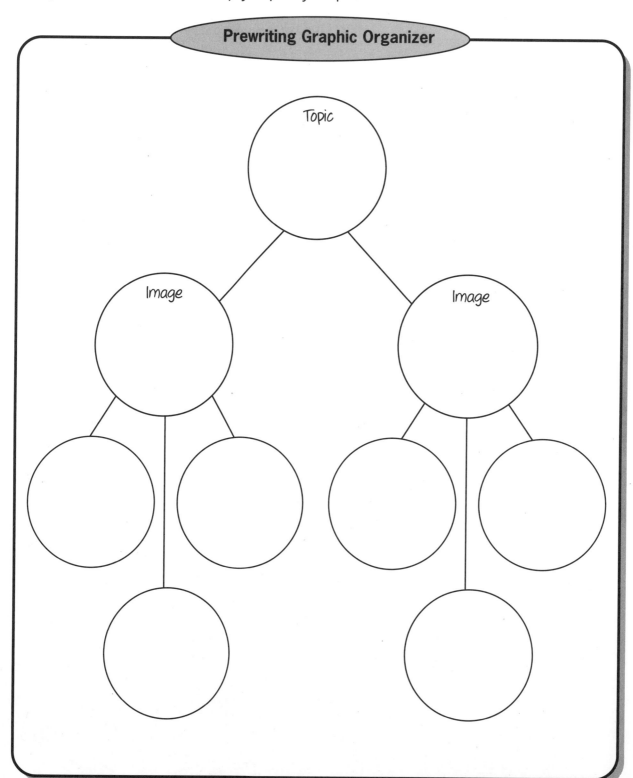

© Harcourt

Name _____

Comprehension Test Test Prep

Read each question below. Then mark the letter for the answer you have chosen.

1. **What is Fiesta?**
   - Ⓐ a celebration
   - Ⓑ a horse race
   - Ⓒ a horse
   - Ⓓ a large house

2. **When does this story take place?**
   - Ⓕ in the future
   - Ⓖ in the present
   - Ⓗ about ten years ago
   - Ⓙ about one hundred years ago

3. **What does Frida want to do most at Fiesta?**
   - Ⓐ eat wonderful food
   - Ⓑ play the guitar
   - Ⓒ ride in a horse race
   - Ⓓ dance and sing

4. **Why does Mamá say Frida cannot race?**
   - Ⓕ because the race is too far away
   - Ⓖ because proper señoritas do not ride in races
   - Ⓗ because Frida does not ride well
   - Ⓙ because Tío Narizo wants to race Diablo

5. **What does Frida do after Mamá says no?**
   - Ⓐ She tries to behave like a lady.
   - Ⓑ She talks to Tío Narizo herself.
   - Ⓒ She complains about everything.
   - Ⓓ She runs away from the hacienda.

6. **How does Frida feel when Fiesta starts?**
   - Ⓕ excited
   - Ⓗ nervous
   - Ⓖ afraid
   - Ⓙ unhappy

7. **What is the big surprise at Fiesta?**
   - Ⓐ Frida wins the race.
   - Ⓑ Diablo is hurt in the race.
   - Ⓒ Tío Narizo gives Diablo to Frida.
   - Ⓓ Mamá decides that Frida can race Diablo.

8. **What does Mamá say after the race?**
   - Ⓕ Frida María has become a proper señorita.
   - Ⓖ She is proud of Frida.
   - Ⓗ Frida must never ride Diablo again.
   - Ⓙ Frida was right to disobey this time.

9. **Which is a main idea in *Frida María*?**
   - Ⓐ Frida shows she is special in her own way.
   - Ⓑ Frida spoils Fiesta for everyone.
   - Ⓒ Frida learns to ride a horse.
   - Ⓓ Frida learns how to behave properly.

10. **On a separate sheet of paper, write a short answer in response to the question below.**
    How and why does Mamá's opinion of Frida change?

© Harcourt

Jordi's Star

by Alma Flor Ada

Reading Level

▶ Theme Connection
As students read *Jordi's Star*, they will learn about Jordi, a character who lives a hard life on hills left barren and dry by deforestation and erosion. When Jordi finds a puddle left after a rainstorm, he creates windbreaks and gardens that preserve the water and eventually transform the landscape. As in "Rocking and Rolling," this story explores how Earth changes.

▶ Summary
After a violent thunderstorm, goatherd Jordi finds a pool of water on his dry, rocky hillside. In the pool, he sees a reflection of a star, which he mistakenly thinks has fallen in. He puts newfound energy into making the pool beautiful for his new friend, the star, bringing moss and rocks and planting flowers and trees. Over time, his desolate hillside blooms, and Jordi blooms with it.

▶ Building Background
Tell students that *Jordi's Star* is a fictional story. Look at the book covers and some illustrations. Discuss where the setting of the story might be. Suggest that students read to be informed about the setting as well as to be entertained. Have them read to find out why Jordi has a star and how the star is important to him.

Author Profile
An accomplished translator of children's books from English to Spanish, Alma Flor Ada was born in Cuba and has lived in Spain, Peru, and the United States. Her original fiction often introduces children to Central and South American landscapes and cultures.

Additional Books by the Author
- *Dear Peter Rabbit*
- *Gathering the Sun: An Alphabet in Spanish and English*
- *The Lizard and the Sun/La Lagartija Y El Sol: A Folktale in English and Spanish*

Vocabulary

Have students work as a group or in teams to answer the questions below that use the vocabulary words. See pages 296–299 for additional vocabulary activities. For definitions of the words, see the Glossary.

1. Why would someone want a <u>well</u> near a <u>hut</u>?
2. What might you see in the <u>aftermath</u> of an <u>immense</u> storm?
3. What might you see <u>reflecting</u> in the surface of a pool?
4. What sort of treasures could be carried in a <u>kerchief</u>?
5. How could <u>quartz</u> pebbles cause the <u>water level</u> to rise in a pool?
6. What would a goatherd sell to <u>clients</u>?
7. What does <u>moisture</u> do for <u>seedlings</u> and <u>blossoms</u>?
8. Why would a pond be <u>surrounded</u> by <u>greenery</u>?

Day 1	Day 2	Day 3	Day 4
well p. 2	aftermath p. 8	quartz p. 17	blossoms p. 27
hut p. 2	immense p. 8	kerchief p. 17	greenery p. 27
	reflecting p. 11	water level p. 21	
		clients p. 23	
		seedlings p. 23	
		moisture p. 24	
		surrounded p. 24	

© Harcourt

	Response	Strategies	Skills
Day 1 **Pages 1–5**	**Book Talk** • Note Details • Cause-Effect • Draw Conclusions **Writing:** Express Personal Opinion	**USE GRAPHIC AIDS** FOCUS STRATEGY *Journeys of Wonder*, p. T625	**CAUSE AND EFFECT** FOCUS SKILL *Journeys of Wonder*, pp. T624–T625
Day 2 **Pages 6–15**	**Book Talk** • Compare and Contrast • Draw Conclusions • Determine Characters' Emotions **Writing:** Author's Craft	Use Prior Knowledge *Journeys of Wonder*, p. T305	Characters' Feelings and Actions *Journeys of Wonder*, pp. T262–T263
Day 3 **Pages 16–25**	**Book Talk** • Cause-Effect • Important Details • Generalize **Writing:** Determine Characters' Emotions	Create Mental Images *Journeys of Wonder*, p. T197	Sequence *Journeys of Wonder*, pp. T20–T21
Day 4 **Pages 26–30**	**Book Talk** • Make Comparisons • Theme • Express Personal Opinion/ Author's Craft **Writing:** Synthesize	**USE GRAPHIC AIDS** FOCUS STRATEGY *Journeys of Wonder*, p. T625	**CAUSE AND EFFECT** FOCUS SKILL *Journeys of Wonder*, pp. T624–T625
Day 5 **Wrap-Up**	**Project** ✓ Before-and-After Diorama • Inquiry Project **Writing** ✓ Friendly Letter *Journeys of Wonder*, pp. T652–T653 **Language Link** • Using Details **Assessment** ✓ Comprehension Test		

© Harcourt

*Additional support is provided in *Collections*.
✓ Options for Assessment

Jordi's Star

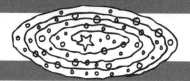

BOOK TALK

After you read pages 1–5, meet with your group to discuss and answer the following questions:

1 How does the author describe the place where Jordi lives?

2 Why does Jordi dig the hole? Does it work?

3 How is the storm helpful?

RESPONSE JOURNAL

What do you think about Jordi's life?
Would you like to be Jordi? Why or why not?

Strategies Good Readers Use

 FOCUS STRATEGY USE GRAPHIC AIDS

Graphic aids, such as maps, and pictures, help readers understand what they read. How do the pictures in *Jordi's Star* help you?

SKILLS IN CONTEXT

FOCUS SKILL **CAUSE AND EFFECT: CAUSE-AND-EFFECT FLAP CHART** Cause-and-effect relationships show how an event (a cause) makes something happen (an effect). Jordi has a hard life because of where he lives. Make some notes about events or situations and their causes in the story. Then make a flap chart to show cause-and-effect relationships in the story.

What You Need

- **drawing paper**
- **writing and drawing tools**
- **scissors**

What to Do

1. Fold a piece of drawing paper in half the long way. Then fold it in quarters. Then fold it in eighths. Now, open the paper up.

2. Cut along each fold line on one long side, from the edge to the center fold. You should end up with four flaps that fold down over the uncut half of your paper.

3. Draw and write an event or situation on the front of each flap. Write *because* as the last word on each flap.

4. Write the cause of the event or situation under each flap.

Here is an idea to get you started:
Jordi's hillside is bare and rocky because . . . woodcutters cut down the trees and rain washed away everything but weeds.

Think Ahead What could happen to make Jordi's life easier or more enjoyable?

© Harcourt

Jordi's Star

BOOK TALK

After you read pages 6–15, meet with your group to discuss and answer the following questions:

1 Reread page 8. How does Jordi feel before he looks into the pool? How does he feel when he sees the star?

2 What is Jordi doing with the rocks and moss? Why?

3 Is Jordi upset when he sees the star at night but not in the morning? Why?

RESPONSE JOURNAL

How does the author show you how Jordi feels?

SKILLS IN CONTEXT

CHARACTERS' FEELINGS AND ACTIONS: JORDI'S FEELINGS AND ACTIONS FOLDER

Characters' feelings and actions can help you understand what they are like. Thinking about a character's actions can help you understand the character's feelings. Create a folder that describes Jordi's feelings and actions. The folder can be displayed or used as a bookmark.

What You Need

- drawing paper
- writing and drawing tools

What to Do

1. Fold the paper in half the long way.

2. Draw Jordi at the top on the outside. You might cut the top of the folder around the shape of your picture.

3. Draw Jordi's star at the bottom. Write the title and author between your drawings.

4. Open the folder. Write *Jordi's Actions* on one side of the folder. List the things Jordi does on pages 8–15.

5. Write *Jordi's Feelings* on the other side of the folder. List the feelings Jordi has on pages 8–15, after he sees the star. Copy the author's words that show Jordi's feelings. Then add words of your own.

Here is a sentence to get you started:
"Jordi felt an immense joy." In your folder, under Jordi's Feelings, *write* immense joy.

Think Ahead
What do you think will happen the next day?

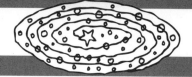

BOOK TALK

After you read pages 16–25, meet with your group to discuss and answer the following questions:

1 What happens to the little pool after the rain? Why?

2 What does Jordi do in town?

3 What is happening to Jordi as he works on his garden?

RESPONSE JOURNAL

Why is Jordi becoming a happier person?

> **Strategies Good Readers Use**
>
> ## CREATE MENTAL IMAGES
>
> Good readers create mental images, or pictures in their heads. Think back over *Jordi's Star* and describe the images you see in your mind.

SKILLS IN CONTEXT

SEQUENCE: SEQUENCE SPIRAL Sequence is the order of events or ideas. Understanding sequence is an important part of understanding what you read. On a paper spiral, write in sequence the things that Jordi gathers to create a garden around his pool. Use pages 12–25.

What You Need

- large paper circle
- scrap of paper for star
- writing and drawing tools
- glue

What to Do

1. Draw a spiral from the center of the paper to the edge. Give yourself room to write between your lines.

2. Make a small paper star and glue it in the center.

3. Start from the star. Write each thing that Jordi brings to make his garden. Use pages 12–25, and write each new thing he adds in sequence.

4. Illustrate the words on the spiral.

Here are details from page 12 to get you started: *two large rocks and a bit of moss*

Think Ahead What do you think will happen as time goes on?

© Harcourt

BOOK TALK

After you read pages 26–30, meet with your group to discuss and answer the following questions:

❶ What stories in *Journeys of Wonder* remind you of *Jordi's Star?*

❷ What are some themes in *Jordi's Star?*

❸ What do you like about this story? What does the author do well?

RESPONSE JOURNAL

What can you learn from this story about taking care of the earth?

Strategies Good Readers Use

FOCUS STRATEGY **USE GRAPHIC AIDS**

*W*hat are your favorite pictures in *Jordi's Star?* How do they add to your under-standing or enjoy-ment of the story?

SKILLS IN CONTEXT

FOCUS SKILL **CAUSE AND EFFECT: CAUSE-AND-EFFECT WEB** Cause-and-effect relationships help readers understand how events are related. A situation can have several causes and several effects. Build a web that shows the events that lead to Jordi finding his star and those that happen because Jordi finds the star.

What You Need

- **drawing paper**
- **writing and drawing tools**

What to Do

1. Write *Jordi finds the star* in the center of your paper.
2. Above that, write events that cause Jordi to find the star. Above those events, write their causes. Draw lines in one bright color to show how the causes are connected.
3. Below *Jordi finds the star*, write events that happen because he finds it. Below those events, write events that they cause. Use a second bright color to draw lines to show how the effects are connected.
4. Display your web on a bulletin board.

Here are some ideas to get you started:

Two events that cause Jordi to find the star are: Jordi digs a hole and rain fills the hole.

© Harcourt

Wrap-Up

▶ **Project** **BEFORE-AND-AFTER DIORAMA** Talk with students about the changes Jordi makes on his hillside. Compare the text on page 1 and the early pictures with the text on page 27 and the pictures on pages 26 and 28. Then have students make a two-part diorama that shows the two scenes. Ask students to complete the copying master on page 115 to plan their scenes. Have each group share its diorama with the class.

▶ **Writing** **FRIENDLY LETTER** Have students respond to the following writing prompt: **Write a letter that Jordi might send to one of his clients. Tell him or her how the hillside is changing.** Have students use the copying master on page 116 to brainstorm ideas and details. Remind students to focus on organization. Use *Journeys of Wonder* pages T652–T653 for additional support. Rubrics for evaluating student writing are provided on pages 292–295.

▶ **Language Link** **USING DETAILS** Explain to students that the author provides many details to support the main ideas. Have students identify some main ideas and list the details. For example, have them look at page 23. Talk about the effects of the details. Then have students write their own paragraphs using details to describe a place they want to write about.

Inquiry Project

Jordi's Star can be a springboard for inquiry into a variety of topics and ideas. Have students brainstorm topics they would like to know more about and organize their responses in a web. Students can use reference books and the Internet to begin their inquiry projects. They may also be able to use community resources.

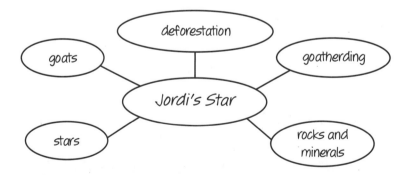

✔ **Comprehension Test** Test students' comprehension of *Jordi's Star* by having them complete the copying master on page 117.

Name _____

Project Planner

How does the author describe the hillside in the beginning of the story? How does she describe it at the end? Make a two-part diorama to compare the two scenes.

☐ **Step 1.** Make webs with your group to plan what you will include in each scene. Decide who will work on each scene.

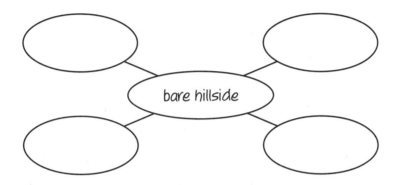

bare hillside

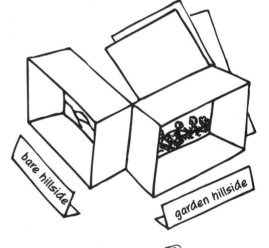

What You Need
- two shoe boxes
- construction paper
- drawing paper
- writing and drawing tools
- scissors
- glue
- optional objects to put in scenes

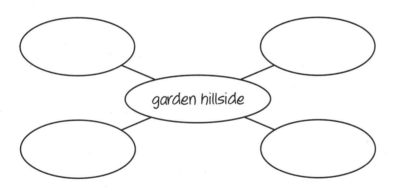

garden hillside

bare hillside

garden hillside

☐ **Step 2.** Make the dioramas. You may put the boxes on their sides and design backgrounds and pop-up figures. You may also leave the boxes flat and fill them with your details.

☐ **Step 3.** Write a label for each scene. Include a description and the names of the people who worked on it.

☐ **Step 4.** Display the scenes side by side and present them to the class.

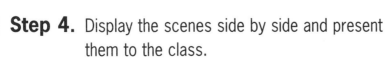

© Harcourt

Friendly Letter

Write a letter that Jordi might send to one of his clients. Tell him or her how the hillside is changing. Use the graphic organizer below to plan your letter. Use details from the book and add your own ideas as needed. Then draft your letter.

Prewriting Graphic Organizer

Topic: _____

Audience: _____

_____

_____

Paragraph 1

Main Idea: _____

Details: _____

_____

Paragraph 2

Main Idea: _____

Details: _____

_____

Paragraph 3

Main Idea: _____

Details: _____

_____

© Harcourt

Comprehension Test

Read each question below. Then mark the letter for the answer you have chosen.

1. **How does Jordi make his living?**
   - Ⓐ as a gardener
   - Ⓑ as a shop owner
   - Ⓒ as a mountain climber
   - Ⓓ as a goatherd

2. **Where does Jordi live when the story begins?**
   - Ⓕ on a bare hillside
   - Ⓖ in a large cave
   - Ⓗ in a small village
   - Ⓙ in a lovely garden

3. **When the story begins, how does Jordi get water when he needs it?**
   - Ⓐ He dips a bucket into his well.
   - Ⓑ He walks a long way to the river.
   - Ⓒ He turns on a faucet in his sink.
   - Ⓓ He borrows it from a neighbor.

4. **Which words best describe Jordi's life before the star?**
   - Ⓕ difficult and lonely
   - Ⓖ fun and exciting
   - Ⓗ comfortable but dull
   - Ⓙ busy but satisfying

5. **Where does Jordi find his star?**
   - Ⓐ in a shop in the village
   - Ⓑ in the river
   - Ⓒ in a pool that forms after a rainstorm
   - Ⓓ in the sky over his hillside

6. **Why does Jordi collect rocks, moss, and flowers?**
   - Ⓕ He wants to study nature.
   - Ⓖ He hopes to sell them to his clients.
   - Ⓗ They are presents from his clients.
   - Ⓙ They are gifts for the star.

7. **How does Jordi's land change?**
   - Ⓐ It becomes bare and rocky.
   - Ⓑ It becomes a mountain with a cave.
   - Ⓒ It becomes a garden with a pond.
   - Ⓓ It becomes a town.

8. **Why do people visit Jordi?**
   - Ⓕ to see his star
   - Ⓖ to bring seeds and share his fruit
   - Ⓗ to play with his goats
   - Ⓙ to ask him for advice on gardening

9. **Which is a theme in *Jordi's Star*?**
   - Ⓐ Finding something to love can change a person's life.
   - Ⓑ People can replant a forest.
   - Ⓒ A star can live in a pool.
   - Ⓓ People who live alone cannot get along with other people.

10. **On a separate sheet of paper, write a response to this question:**
    Why does finding the star change Jordi's life? Give as many reasons from the story as you can.

© Harcourt

Cam Jansen and the Triceratops Pops Mystery

Reading Level

by David A. Adler

▶ Theme Connection
Like many selections in "Friends to Grow With," *Cam Jansen and the Triceratops Pops Mystery* showcases a spunky character using her talents to do good deeds.

▶ Summary
Cam Jansen has a photographic memory, a trait that enables her to picture and remember details. Her skill comes in handy when she and Eric find all the new Triceratops Pops CDs missing from the music store. By clicking through her memories of whom and what she saw at the store, Cam identifies the crook. As a reward, the store guard gives Cam a Triceratops Pops CD for free.

▶ Building Background
Display the book cover, read the title, and tell students that a purpose for reading a mystery story is to be entertained. To build background, students might volunteer information about what happened in other Cam Jansen mysteries they have read. Ask students to make a prediction about what the mystery is in this book and how it will be solved.

Author Profile
David A. Adler has written biographies and books on a variety of scientific subjects, but his best-loved books are the Cam Jansen mysteries, which he began writing more than twenty years ago. *Cam Jansen and the Triceratops Pops Mystery* is number fifteen in the series.

Additional Books by the Author
- *Cam Jansen and the Mystery of the Stolen Corn Popper*
- *Cam Jansen and the Mystery of Flight 54*
- *Cam Jansen and the Catnapping Mystery*

Vocabulary

Have students use the vocabulary words to complete a chart like below. See pages 296–299 for additional vocabulary activities. For definitions of the words, see the Glossary.

Words About Shopping	Words About Crime	Compound Words

Day 1	Day 2	Day 3	Day 4
flyer p. 1	alarm p. 8	security p. 20	mystery p. 22
mall p. 2	departments p. 9		register p. 23
store p. 4	displayed p. 9		thief p. 24
	aisle p. 10		

Day 5	Day 6	Day 7	Day 8
guard p. 27	knapsack p. 34	sunglasses p. 40	private p. 47
watermelon p. 28			evidence p. 54
raincoat p. 31			crime p. 54

© Harcourt

		Response	Strategies	Skill
Day 1 Chapter 1		**Book Talk** • Important Details • Author's Purpose • Make Predictions **Writing:** Write a Description	**CREATE MENTAL IMAGES** FOCUS STRATEGY *Hidden Surprises, p. T567	**LOCATING INFORMATION** FOCUS SKILL *Hidden Surprises, pp. T566–T567
Day 2 Chapter 2		**Book Talk** • Synthesize • Note Details • Summarize **Writing:** Personal Response	Adjust Reading Rate *Hidden Surprises, p. T209	Problem Solving *Journeys of Wonder, pp. T580–T581
Day 3 Chapter 3		**Book Talk** • Determine Characters' Traits • Retell • Speculate **Writing:** Advice for a Character	Self-Question *Hidden Surprises, p. T453	Story Elements *Hidden Surprises, pp. T274–T275
Day 4 Chapter 4		**Book Talk** • Cause-Effect • Author's Craft/Appreciate Language • Identify with Characters **Writing:** Express Personal Opinion	**CREATE MENTAL IMAGES** FOCUS STRATEGY *Hidden Surprises, p. T567	**LOCATING INFORMATION** FOCUS SKILL *Hidden Surprises, pp. T566–T567
Day 5 Chapter 5		**Book Talk** • Draw Conclusions • Interpret Characters' Motivations • Make Inferences **Writing:** Express Personal Opinion	**USE CONTEXT TO CONFIRM MEANING** FOCUS STRATEGY *Hidden Surprises, p. T613	**MAIN IDEA** FOCUS SKILL *Hidden Surprises, pp. T612–T613
Day 6 Chapter 6		**Book Talk** • Author's Craft/Interpret Imagery • Summarize • Classify **Writing:** Express Personal Opinion	Summarize *Hidden Surprises, p. T161	Author's Purpose *Hidden Surprises, pp. T702–T703
Day 7 Chapter 7		**Book Talk** • Generalize • Make Judgments • Make Comparisons **Writing:** Make Judgments	Make and Confirm Predictions *Hidden Surprises, p. T21	Homographs and Homophones *Hidden Surprises, pp. T656–T657
Day 8 Chapters 8–9		**Book Talk** • Make Comparisons • Author's Perspective • Make Judgments **Writing:** Express Personal Opinion	**USE CONTEXT TO CONFIRM MEANING** FOCUS STRATEGY * Hidden Surprises, p. T613	**MAIN IDEA** FOCUS SKILL *Hidden Surprises, pp. T612–T613

Days 9–10 Wrap-Up	**Project** ✓ Create a Television News Segment • Inquiry Project	**Writing** ✓ News Story *Hidden Surprises, pp. T392–T393	**Language Link** • Irregular Verbs **Assessment** ✓ Comprehension Test

*Additional support is provided in *Collections.*
✓ Options for Assessment

Cam Jansen and the Triceratops Pops Mystery

BOOK TALK

After you read pages 1–7, meet with your group to discuss and answer the following questions:

❶ Why is Jennifer Jansen called Cam?

❷ Why does the author include the information about the birthday card?

❸ What do you think will happen in the music store?

RESPONSE JOURNAL

Use your journal to describe a music store or another store in a shopping mall you have visited.

Strategies Good Readers Use

FOCUS STRATEGY **CREATE MENTAL IMAGES**

As you read, try to create a mental image of the shopping mall and people in it. With a partner, discuss the mental image you have of Cam so far.

SKILLS IN CONTEXT

FOCUS SKILL **LOCATING INFORMATION: GO FISH FOR INFORMATION** You can find information when it is organized. One way to organize information is by making categories. Cam uses a variety of sources to find information. Play a card game to match the different kinds of information with where they can be found.

What You Need

- **24 index cards**
- **writing materials**

What to Do

1. With a partner, think of three kinds of information each of the following usually contains: a sale flyer, a birthday card, a music store, a map of a shopping mall, a photograph of a person, and a CD.

2. Write the name of each item listed above on a separate card. For each item, write three types of information contained in it on three separate cards. You will end up with six sets of four cards.

3. Mix up the cards and exchange them with another pair.

4. Play Go Fish with the set of cards by dealing seven cards to each player and asking for cards to make sets of four (the place or thing and the three kinds of information).

Here is an example to get you started: *A photograph of a person contains information about hair color, eye color, and shape of the face. A set of four cards might say* photograph of a person, eye color, hair color, *and* shape of face.

Think Ahead Will Cam Jansen solve a mystery in this story?

© Harcourt

Day 2 Chapter 2, pages 8–14

BOOK TALK

After you read pages 8–14, meet with your group to discuss and answer the following questions:

1 What do you think it would be like to shop in Ernie's Everything in Music and Video store?

ADJUST READING RATE

*T*alk with a partner about where you should slow down while reading this chapter and why.

2 What does Cam memorize about the store?

3 What do Cam and Eric do to try to find the Triceratops Pops CD?

RESPONSE JOURNAL

If you had a photographic memory, how would you use it?

SKILLS IN CONTEXT

PROBLEM SOLVING: PROBLEM AND SOLUTIONS WEB The music store faces the problem of stealing. Make a web to show the options the store has in solving this problem.

What You Need

- drawing and writing tools
- paper or poster board

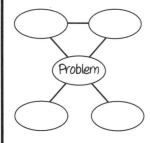

Problem

What to Do

1. The music store has many solutions to the problem of stealing. For example, some stores put strips on CDs and tapes, and they also put a machine at the exit that beeps when it "reads" those strips.

2. Make a web that shows the problem of stealing and some solutions or steps in the solutions.

3. Put the problem in the center and the solutions around the problem. Use lines to connect the solutions to the problem. Also connect any solutions that go together.

4. Explain your web.

Here is an idea to get you started:

Step in a solution: The music store puts a magnetic strip on each CD and tape.

Think Ahead
Will Cam find the Triceratops Pops CD? If so, where? If not, why not?

BOOK TALK

After you read pages 15–20, meet with your group to discuss and answer the following questions:

1 How would you describe Jordan?

2 What does Jordan think happened to the CDs?

3 What do you think happened to the CDs? Why?

Strategies Good Readers Use

SELF-QUESTION

*W*rite one question you asked yourself about this part of the story.

RESPONSE JOURNAL

What advice would you like to give Jordan about working in a store?

SKILLS IN CONTEXT

STORY ELEMENTS: MAKE A STORY MAP The main story elements are the characters (who is in the story), the setting (where and when the story takes place), and the plot (what happens, or the events). Create a map to show the different story elements.

What You Need

- **writing tools and paper**

What to Do

1. On a sheet of scrap paper, plan a story map like the one below. It should show the main characters, the setting, and the main events in the story so far.

2. Copy your story map onto a clean sheet of paper. Make it neat and colorful. Leave room to add new information.

3. Add to your story map as you gain more information.

Here is an event to get you started:
Cam and Eric go to the mall.

Characters Setting
Problem
Main Events
Solution

Think Ahead
What could have happened to the CDs?

© Harcourt

BOOK TALK

After you read pages 21–26, meet with your group to discuss and answer the following questions:

❶ What would make it difficult for a thief to steal CDs?

❷ Why do you think the author includes references to the Ripe Bananas?

❸ What would you do in this situation?

RESPONSE JOURNAL

Would you like to be involved in a mystery? Why or why not?

SKILLS IN CONTEXT

FOCUS SKILL **LOCATING INFORMATION: MAKE A MAP** You can use a map to help you understand a setting and what is happening in it. Understanding the way the music store looks can help you to better understand some key events in the book. Use details from the book to make a map of the music store.

What You Need

- **writing tools and paper**
- **straight edge or ruler**

What to Do

1. Work with a small group. Find all the details you can about the music store in Chapters 3 and 4.

2. On scrap paper, make a rough sketch. Show the aisles, the front and back of the store, the machine that beeps, and the back door.

3. Make a neat map showing how you think the store probably looks.

4. Hang your map in the classroom.

Here are some things to show on your map: *There are at least seven aisles and ten different music sections.*

Think Ahead
What will happen next? Has the thief been caught at the beeper?

© Harcourt

BOOK TALK

After you read pages 27–33, meet with your group to discuss and answer the following questions:

1 What is strange about the bag with the watermelon in it?

2 Why is Cam so interested in the back door?

3 What does the woman in the raincoat have to do with the story?

RESPONSE JOURNAL

Would you be suspicious of the woman in the raincoat? Explain your reasons.

> **Strategies Good Readers Use**
>
> **FOCUS STRATEGY** **USE CONTEXT TO CONFIRM MEANING**
>
> Find the word *handcart* on page 30. Explain how the words in the same paragraph with *handcart* help you understand its meaning.

SKILLS IN CONTEXT

FOCUS SKILL **MAIN IDEA: MAKE A MAIN IDEA TICKER TAPE** As you read about a topic, details that you learn help you to determine the main idea. Create ticker tape describing main ideas you have found in the book.

What You Need

- large continuous sheets or rolls of paper, or pieces of paper taped end to end
- writing and coloring materials

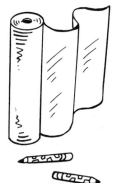

What to Do

1. With a small group, write main ideas you have learned so far about one of the following: how music stores are organized; how stores prevent the theft of CDs; the role of a security guard in a store; what a photographic memory is.

2. Once you have written the main ideas, display them on long sheets of paper you can put up in the room. Make each idea look like a news flash or a computer readout. Think about the way news is flashed across your television screen.

3. Use color and designs to separate your main ideas.

4. Hang up your ticker tape.

Here is a main idea sentence to start with: *Music stores use separate aisles and cases for different kinds of music.*

Think Ahead Where do you think Cam will find the answer to this mystery?

© Harcourt

Cam Jansen and the Triceratops Pops Mystery

BOOK TALK

After you read pages 34–39, meet with your group to discuss and answer the following questions:

1 What is happening each time the word *Click* appears?

2 How do Cam and Eric get locked out of the music store?

3 What kind of clue does Cam discover at the end of the chapter?

RESPONSE JOURNAL

Would you like to visit a shopping mall with Cam? Tell why in your journal.

SKILLS IN CONTEXT

AUTHOR'S PURPOSE: MAKE A CHART The author is writing to entertain. How does he do that? Create a chart showing the ways the author entertains you in this book.

What You Need

- notebook paper
- large sheet of paper
- writing materials

What to Do

1. Plan ideas for your chart. List the kinds of things the author does to entertain you. Group your ideas into categories.
2. Divide your chart into columns to show each group of ideas. Give each column a heading or title.
3. List ideas under each column.
4. Display your chart in the classroom.

Here are ideas to get you started: *One column heading could be* Several Suspects. *Under that, you could list anyone suspicious. Another column heading could be* Interesting Main Character.

Think Ahead
What is Cam pointing to on the floor, and what does it mean?

© Harcourt

BOOK TALK

After you read pages 40–45, meet with your group to discuss and answer the following questions:

1 Why doesn't Barry pay attention to Cam and Eric at first?

2 Does Cam's explanation of what happened make sense? Why or why not?

3 Who is doing a better job of solving the crime: Cam and Eric or the security guard? Why?

RESPONSE JOURNAL

What do you think is the smartest thing Cam has done yet? Write about it in your journal.

> **Strategies Good Readers Use**
>
> ### MAKE AND CONFIRM PREDICTIONS
>
> Write down your ideas about who the thief is, how the thief will be caught, and who will do the catching.

SKILLS IN CONTEXT

HOMOGRAPHS AND HOMOPHONES: MAKE FLASH CARDS Homographs are words that have the same spelling but different pronunciations and meanings. Homophones are words that sound alike but have different spellings and meanings, such as *knew* and *new*. Use flash cards to identify the different meanings of homophones.

What You Need

- **22 index cards**
- **writing and drawing materials**

What to Do

1. Write these words on cards: *hare, blew, four, to, tolled, you're, due, hear, gait, threw, hole.*

2. In Chapter 7, find the homophone for each word you wrote. Write the homophone on a separate card.

3. Make pairs of homophones. On the back of each card, either draw a picture or write a meaning for the word.

4. Use the backs of the cards as flash cards. Hold up the two cards in each pair at the same time. Have a partner use the clues to tell each word and its spelling.

Here is an idea for a drawing:
For hare, *draw an animal that looks like a rabbit.*

Think Ahead
Do you think Cam, Eric, and Barry will catch the thief by getting his address? Why or why not?

© Harcourt

Cam Jansen and the Triceratops Pops Mystery

BOOK TALK

After you read pages 46–56, meet with your group to discuss and answer the following questions:

1 Cam uses her talents to help others. What selections in *Hidden Surprises* also show people using their talents to help others?

2 What do you think is the author's opinion of Cam?

3 What did you like best about this story?

RESPONSE JOURNAL

Do you like the way this book ends? Tell why or why not.

Strategies Good Readers Use

FOCUS STRATEGY USE CONTEXT TO CONFIRM MEANING

Find the word *private* on page 47. Write the context clues that help you understand the meaning of the word.

SKILLS IN CONTEXT

FOCUS SKILL **MAIN IDEA: MAKE AN AWARD** The main idea is the most important idea in a paragraph or book. Sometimes, the main idea is stated. Sometimes you have to come up with the main idea by thinking about what you already know. Cam has solved a mystery and deserves an award. Make an award to present to Cam to recognize her good work.

What You Need

- cardboard, foil, ribbons, or other materials to make a medal, trophy, or award
- writing tools

What to Do

1. Make a medal, trophy, or other award for Cam.

2. Write two main idea sentences: one that tells the main idea about the crime and one that tells the main idea about how Cam solved the crime.

3. Write your main idea sentences somewhere on the trophy, award, or medal.

4. Display your work in the classroom.

Try answering this question to come up with a main idea statement about the crime: *What kind of thief does Cam catch?*

© Harcourt

Wrap-Up

▶ **Project** **CREATE A TELEVISION NEWS SEGMENT** Explain that students will create a TV news story about Eric, Cam, and the mystery they solved at the mall. Have students form small groups and complete the Project Planner on page 129. Then have each group perform its segment for the class.

▶ **Writing** **NEWS STORY** Have students respond to the following writing prompt: **Write a news story about what happened at the mall.** Have students use the copying master on page 130 to plan a news story. Encourage students to organize their ideas. Use *Hidden Surprises* pages T392–T393 for additional support. Writing rubrics for evaluating student writing can be found on pages 292–295.

▶ **Language Link** **IRREGULAR VERBS** When the author writes "Eric held her hand," he uses the irregular verb *held*. Have students find other past-tense verbs not ending in *-ed* and make a list.

Inquiry Project

Have students brainstorm topics they would like to know more about. Students can use reference sources or the Internet to begin their inquiry projects. If students enjoyed reading about Cam Jansen, they may want to read another book about her adventures.

✔ **Comprehension Test** Test students' comprehension of *Cam Jansen and the Triceratops Pops Mystery* by having them complete the copying master on page 131.

Name _____

Project Planner

What happened at the shopping mall makes a great news story. For this project, you will plan an introduction to the story. Then you will interview people who took part in the events.

☐ **Step 1.** Begin by thinking of who needs to be in your show. Be sure to include the anchorperson who will introduce the story. List all the parts. As a group, decide who will play each role.

_____

_____

_____

_____

What You Need
- writing materials
- materials to suggest a microphone
- video recorder (optional)

☐ **Step 2.** As a group, discuss, plan, and write ideas, questions, and possible answers for each part. Use the organizer below to plan your news story.

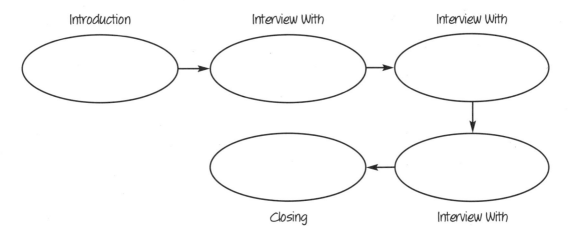

Introduction   Interview With   Interview With

Closing   Interview With

☐ **Step 3.** Make a pretend microphone. Practice performing the news story.

☐ **Step 4.** Videotape your news story and play it for the class or perform it for the class.

Name _____

News Story

What would a newspaper reporter write about what happened at the mall?
Use this graphic organizer to plan a news story. Then draft your news story.

Prewriting Graphic Organizer

Topic: _____

Headline: _____

Topic Sentence: _____

Who? _____

Details: _____

What? _____

Details: _____

When? _____

Details: _____

Where? _____

Details: _____

Why? _____

Details: _____

© Harcourt

Name _____

Comprehension Test Test Prep

Read each question below. Then mark the letter for the answer you have chosen.

1. Who is Eric Shelton?
- Ⓐ Cam's friend
- Ⓑ a robber
- Ⓒ a security guard
- Ⓓ someone who works at Ernie's

2. Cam goes to the music store
- Ⓕ to catch a thief.
- Ⓖ to take a picture with her mental camera.
- Ⓗ to buy the new Triceratops Pops CD.
- Ⓙ to hide from the Triceratops Pops.

3. What is true of magnetic strips?
- Ⓐ They can never be removed.
- Ⓑ They are useful to thieves.
- Ⓒ They were invented by Cam.
- Ⓓ They can set off an alarm.

4. Who is Jordan?
- Ⓕ Cam's friend
- Ⓖ a robber
- Ⓗ a security guard
- Ⓙ someone who works at Ernie's

5. Why doesn't Jordan's reason for the missing CDs make sense?
- Ⓐ He does not have a good memory.
- Ⓑ No one would buy six of the same CD.
- Ⓒ He did not check the computer.
- Ⓓ He is not a clear thinker.

6. What is the most likely reason for putting the woman in the raincoat in the story?
- Ⓕ It takes up extra space.
- Ⓖ She turns out to be the real thief.
- Ⓗ She solves the mystery.
- Ⓙ It shows there are many suspects.

7. How does the thief escape with CDs?
- Ⓐ by going out the back door
- Ⓑ by hiding the CDs in a video case
- Ⓒ by hiding the CDs in a watermelon
- Ⓓ by taking magnetic strips off CDs

8. How does going to the video store help Cam and Eric solve the crime?
- Ⓕ They find the thief there.
- Ⓖ The thief returns a video.
- Ⓗ They get the thief's address.
- Ⓙ The back door leads to the back door of the music store.

9. How do Barry's feelings about Cam and Eric change?
- Ⓐ from annoying them to helping them
- Ⓑ from disliking them to liking them
- Ⓒ from disliking them to hating them
- Ⓓ from ignoring them to valuing them

10. On a separate sheet of paper, write a short answer for this question:
What are three of the talents Cam and Eric use to solve this mystery?

© Harcourt

Julian's Glorious Summer

Reading Level

by Ann Cameron

► Theme Connection

In *Julian's Glorious Summer*, as in "The Stories Julian Tells," Ann Cameron spotlights the challenges and decisions that Julian faces as he grows up.

► Summary

When Gloria gets a new bike, Julian is upset because he does not know how to ride one. He works for his father for much of the summer as a way of avoiding Gloria, but his plans are foiled when his dad rewards him with a bicycle of his own.

► Building Background

Read the title of the story, and show students the cover. Talk about what the word *glorious* means, and have students give some ideas of what a glorious summer would be like. Then ask them what the opposite of a glorious summer would be like. Tell students that the purpose for reading this story is to be entertained. Ask volunteers to tell whether they expect this story to make them laugh, cry, feel frightened, think seriously about their lives, or react in another way.

Author Profile

Ann Cameron was born in Wisconsin, lived for some time in New York City, and now resides in Guatemala. Her books about Julian are based on a friend's tales of his own childhood. The Julian books focus on the trials and tribulations of growing up.

Additional Books by the Author
- *Julian, Secret Agent*
- *The Stories Huey Tells*
- *More Stories Julian Tells*

Vocabulary

Have students sort as many of the vocabulary words as possible into the categories shown below. See pages 296–299 for additional vocabulary activities. For definitions of the words, see the Glossary.

Words About Bikes	Words About Work and Money	Words for Feelings

Day 1
bicycle p. 6
glorious p. 10
handlebars p. 13
afraid p. 15
work p. 15

Day 2
mattress p. 19
furnace p. 22
steel p. 22

Day 3
happiness p. 37
suffering p. 40
spokes p. 42
pedals p. 42
fenders p. 42

Day 4
reward p. 45
balance p. 57

© Harcourt

	Response	Strategies	Skills
Day 1 **Chapters 1–2**	**Book Talk** • Synthesize • Identify with Characters • Draw Conclusions **Writing:** Personal Response	**READ AHEAD** **FOCUS STRATEGY** *Hidden Surprises*, p. T525	**SYNONYMS AND ANTONYMS** **FOCUS SKILL** *Hidden Surprises*, pp. T524–T525
Day 2 **Chapters 3–4**	**Book Talk** • Figurative Language • Author's Craft • Make Predictions **Writing:** Write Advice	Summarize *Journeys of Wonder*, p. T113	Sequence *Journeys of Wonder*, pp. T20–T21
Day 3 **Chapters 5–6**	**Book Talk** • Author's Craft • Speculate • Determine Characters' Traits **Writing:** Express Personal Opinion	Make and Confirm Predictions *Hidden Surprises*, p. T21	Characters' Feelings and Actions *Journeys of Wonder*, pp. T262–T263
Day 4 **Chapters 7–8**	**Book Talk** • Make Comparisons • Main Idea • Express Personal Opinions **Writing:** Personal Response	**READ AHEAD** **FOCUS STRATEGY** *Hidden Surprises*, p. T525	**SYNONYMS AND ANTONYMS** **FOCUS SKILL** *Hidden Surprises*, pp. T524–T525
Day 5 **Wrap-Up**	**Project** ✓ Make a Cast of Characters Poster • Inquiry Project **Writing** ✓ Friendly Letter *Journeys of Wonder*, pp. T652–T653 **Language Link** • Apostrophes **Assessment** ✓ Comprehension Test		

*Additional support is provided in *Collections*.
✓ Options for Assessment

Julian's Glorious Summer

BOOK TALK

After you read pages 5-18, meet with your group to discuss and answer the following questions:

❶ What are the two "stories" Julian tells?

❷ Why doesn't Julian want to see Gloria on a bike or talk about bikes with her?

❸ Whom do you think you are more like—Julian or Gloria? Explain why.

RESPONSE JOURNAL

Write about a time when you had a disagreement with a friend. How did you solve it?

Strategies Good Readers Use

FOCUS STRATEGY READ AHEAD

If you are not sure what is happening, a good strategy to use is to read ahead. Write one or two questions you expect will be answered when you read ahead.

SKILLS IN CONTEXT

FOCUS SKILL SYNONYMS AND ANTONYMS: PLAY A SYNONYM AND ANTONYM GAME A synonym is a word that means the same, or about the same, as another word. An antonym is a word that means the opposite, or about the opposite, of another word. Play a game with synonyms and antonyms.

What You Need

- **32 or more 3" x 5" cards**
- **writing tools**

What to Do

1. Work with a partner to find eight words from Chapters 1 and 2 that have synonyms and eight words that have antonyms. Write those words on cards.

2. On sixteen more cards, write one synonym or antonym for each word. Divide the cards into a synonym deck and an antonym deck. Exchange decks with another pair of students.

3. Pick a deck and shuffle the cards. Play Go Fish with the cards. Match each word with its antonym or synonym. Play again using the other deck.

Here are some pairs to get you started: *Synonyms:* glorious, wonderful; *antonyms:* shut, open

Think Ahead

Will anyone discover Julian's lies? If so, who?

© Harcourt

Julian's Glorious Summer

BOOK TALK

After you read pages 19–29, meet with your group to discuss and answer the following questions:

❶ Julian's dad asks him about his "story." Why does the author say "little red and blue flames were leaping" in Julian's dad's eyes?

❷ Why do you suppose the author decides to end Chapter 4 with Julian just lying on the grass?

❸ What do you think will happen to Julian?

> **Strategies Good Readers Use**
>
> **SUMMARIZE**
>
> Write one or more sentences that sum up what happens in Chapters 3 and 4.

RESPONSE JOURNAL

What advice would you like to give to Julian? Write it in your journal.

SKILLS IN CONTEXT

SEQUENCE: MAKE A SEQUENCE SIDEWALK Sequence is the order in which events happen in a story. When you list a sequence, you tell only the most important events. Create a "sidewalk" that shows important events in *Julian's Glorious Summer.*

What You Need

- **notebook paper**
- **squares of paper**
- **masking tape**
- **writing materials**

What to Do

1. Work with a small group to jot down the most important events in the story so far.

2. Neatly copy each event onto one square of paper.

3. In a space your teacher suggests, tape the squares to the floor in order to form a sidewalk.

4. Talk with your group about where your sidewalk might lead.

Here is the first event: Julian lies to Gloria about having to work for his dad all summer.

Think Ahead

Do you think Julian's dad will make him work all summer? Why or why not?

© Harcourt

Julian's Glorious Summer

BOOK TALK

After you read pages 30–44, meet with your group to discuss and answer the following questions:

❶ Why do you think the author keeps using the details about sharp rocks to show the relationship between Julian and Huey?

❷ What does Julian's mother really want to tell Julian?

❸ By the end of Chapter 6, you have learned a lot about Julian. How would you describe him?

RESPONSE JOURNAL

What feelings do you have about Julian? Do you feel sorry for him? Do you feel his problems are his own fault? Describe how you feel in your journal.

> **Strategies Good Readers Use**
>
> ### MAKE AND CONFIRM PREDICTIONS
>
> *W*rite down a prediction for the last two chapters. Remember to try to confirm it when you read Chapters 7–8.

SKILLS IN CONTEXT

CHARACTERS' FEELINGS AND ACTIONS: MAKE A WEB OF CONNECTIONS Sometimes the things that characters feel inside lead to actions they take. Julian is a realistic character whose actions are often based on his feelings. Make a web to show how Julian's actions reflect how he feels.

What You Need

- writing and drawing tools, including crayons or colored pencils
- drawing paper

What to Do

1. What is the one thing Julian feels that causes him to do almost everything he does in this book? Write the word for that feeling in a circle at the center of a large piece of paper.

2. Draw smaller circles near the center circle to show what Julian does as a result of this feeling. Draw lines to connect the smaller circles to the center circle. If you think of new feelings, add them too.

3. Color circles that show feelings with one color and circles that show actions with another color.

4. Display your web in the classroom.

Here are ideas for actions: *Julian tells Gloria a story.*

Think Ahead How will the book end?

© Harcourt

Julian's Glorious Summer

BOOK TALK

After you read pages 45–62, meet with your group to discuss and respond to the following questions or statements:

1 In *Julian's Glorious Summer*, real people do believable things. What else have you read in *Hidden Surprises* that shows real people and events?

2 How does Julian change in this book? What do you think the author wants to tell the reader by showing that change?

3 Name three things you liked about this book.

RESPONSE JOURNAL

Did you ever get a gift you did not want? What did you say and do? Write about it in your journal.

Strategies Good Readers Use

FOCUS STRATEGY READ AHEAD

Where did you need to read ahead to understand what was happening? Write down the page number. Tell what confused you or kept you reading.

SKILLS IN CONTEXT

FOCUS SKILL SYNONYMS AND ANTONYMS: SYNONYM AND ANTONYM HUNT A synonym is a word that means the same, or almost the same, as another word. An antonym is a word that means the opposite, or almost the opposite, of another word. Look for synonyms and antonyms in *Julian's Glorious Summer*.

What You Need

- **writing tools**
- **notebook paper**

What to Do

1. Synonyms for each of these words appear in the last two chapters of *Julian's Glorious Summer*: *terrible, pointed, think, snoozing, whole, chores, illustrations,* and *grinned*. Find them. Write each word and its synonym.

2. Antonyms for each of these words appear in the last two chapters of the book: *little, dead, away, easy, last, stand up, wonderful,* and *closed*. Find them. Write each word and its antonym.

3. Check your answers as a class.

Here is the first synonym: *terrible—bad*

Wrap-Up

▶ **Project** **MAKE A CAST OF CHARACTERS POSTER** Tell students their project is to make a poster showing the characters in *Julian's Glorious Summer*. Their finished poster should show the cast of characters and tell the most important information about each one.

• Ask students to begin planning by completing the copying master on page 139.
• Have students display their posters in the classsroom.
• Take time to discuss the posters students create.

▶ **Writing** **FRIENDLY LETTER** Have students respond to the following writing prompt: **Write a friendly letter that Julian might write at the end of the story. Imagine that he is telling a friend who lives far away about his summer.** Have students use the copying master on page 140 to plan their letters. Remind students to focus on letter-writing conventions. Use *Journeys of Wonder* pages T652–T653 for additional support. Rubrics for evaluating student writing can be found on pages 292–295.

▶ **Language Link** **APOSTROPHES** There are many uses of the apostrophe in this story. Some appear in contractions; others show possession. Ask students to make a list of at least ten words with apostrophes in the story. For each, have students tell what the apostrophe means. For example, for *don't*, students can write "do not." For *Julian's*, they can write "belonging to Julian."

Inquiry Project

What questions does *Julian's Glorious Summer* raise? What would students like to learn more about? Suggest they make a web of topics to explore possible ideas for an inquiry project. Then have students select a topic and use reference sources and the Internet to begin their project.

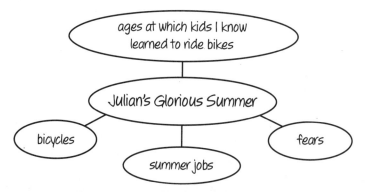

✔ **Comprehension Test** Test students' comprehension of *Julian's Glorious Summer* by having them complete the copying master on page 141.

© Harcourt

Name _____

Project Planner

Julian is the main character in *Julian's Glorious Summer*, but he is not the
only interesting or important character. Your job is to
identify all the characters that make the story interesting
and tell all about them on a poster.

What You Need
- poster board
- tape or paste
- scissors
- writing and drawing
  materials

☐ **Step 1.** List the five main characters.

_____

_____

_____

_____

☐ **Step 2.** Writing lightly in pencil, divide your poster board into five sections, one for
each character. You might want to make an extra-big section for Julian.

☐ **Step 3.** Use the web below to brainstorm the main ideas you want to tell about
Julian. Then make a web for each of the other characters on a separate
sheet of paper.

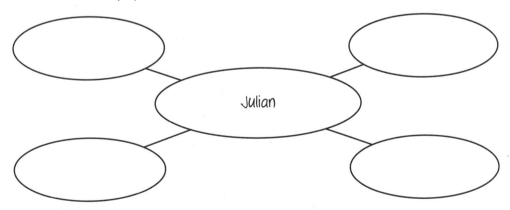

☐ **Step 4.** Design your poster. Draw or make construction paper cutouts of each
character. Be sure each character's name appears. List or draw details to
identify each one, such as "Julian's little brother."

☐ **Step 5.** Display your poster in the classroom.

Name _____

Friendly Letter

Write a letter that Julian might write at the end of the story. Imagine that he is telling a friend who lives far away about his summer. Complete the graphic organizer below to plan your letter. Then draft your letter.

Prewriting Graphic Organizer

Topic: _____

_____

Audience: _____

_____

Paragraph 1

Main Idea: _____

Details: _____

_____

Paragraph 2

Main Idea: _____

Details: _____

_____

Paragraph 3

Main Idea: _____

Details: _____

_____

© Harcourt

Name _____

Comprehension Test Test Prep

Read each question below. Then mark the letter for the answer you have chosen.

1. **What is the best way to describe the "stories" Julian tells?**
   - Ⓐ They have characters and a setting.
   - Ⓑ They have a plot.
   - Ⓒ They are lies.
   - Ⓓ They are facts.

2. **What does Julian truly want to do all summer?**
   - Ⓕ have fun
   - Ⓖ ride bikes
   - Ⓗ work to save money
   - Ⓙ help his dad

3. **What is Julian most afraid of?**
   - Ⓐ his dad getting angry at him
   - Ⓑ riding a bike
   - Ⓒ his little brother Huey
   - Ⓓ the sharp rocks under his mattress

4. **How does Julian's dad find out about Julian's work story?**
   - Ⓕ Gloria tells him.
   - Ⓖ Huey tells him.
   - Ⓗ Julian tells him.
   - Ⓙ Julian's mom tells him.

5. **When does Julian admit his feelings about bicycles?**
   - Ⓐ when Huey is finally kind to him
   - Ⓑ when Gloria asks him
   - Ⓒ when his mother talks to him alone
   - Ⓓ when he gets tired of weeding

6. **How long does Julian work before he gets his reward?**
   - Ⓕ all summer
   - Ⓗ one week
   - Ⓖ three weeks
   - Ⓙ three days

7. **What is Julian's "reward"?**
   - Ⓐ a new bicycle
   - Ⓑ enough money for a sports car
   - Ⓒ a week at summer camp
   - Ⓓ bike riding lessons

8. **Who teaches Julian to ride?**
   - Ⓕ Julian's dad
   - Ⓖ Julian's mom
   - Ⓗ Huey
   - Ⓙ Gloria

9. **What is the best way to describe Julian?**
   - Ⓐ a boy who is always afraid
   - Ⓑ a boy who is lazy
   - Ⓒ a boy who got over his fear
   - Ⓓ a boy who ruined his whole summer

10. **On a separate sheet of paper, write a short answer in response to the question below.**
    At first, summer is no fun for Julian. Then there is a turning point. (At a turning point, things change in a big way.) What is the turning point in this story? Explain what changes.

Coyote and the Laughing Butterflies

Reading Level

by Harriet Peck Taylor

Theme Connection
Like "Why Mosquitoes Buzz in People's Ears," *Coyote and the Laughing Butterflies* is a *pourquoi* tale, a type of folktale that answers the question "why" with respect to some aspect of nature. This folktale answers why butterflies never seem to fly straight.

Summary
Coyote's wife asks him to go to the big salty lake to get her some salt for cooking. When he stops to take a nap, a swarm of butterflies tricks him by lifting him and carrying him home again. When he awakes, he is puzzled, and his wife is annoyed that he has returned without the salt. On Coyote's second trip, the butterflies repeat the trick. Finally, as Coyote stops for a nap on his third trip, the butterflies take pity on him. This time they carry both him and his bag of salt home. To this day, the butterflies enjoy remembering the trick they played on Coyote. It is their laughter that makes them fly in a zigzag, fluttery way.

Building Background
Ask students if they ever wonder about why some things in nature are the way they are. Tell them that many people have tried to answer that question by telling stories. Explain that the stories were also meant to entertain people. *Coyote and the Laughing Butterflies* is an entertaining folktale. Have students read to be entertained and to find out the connection between Coyote and the laughing butterflies.

Author Profile
"My work reflects a playful approach to the world around me," says Harriet Peck Taylor. "My animals, perspectives, and colors are more naive and primitive, relying on my own personal vision and less on reality. They call out to the child who is in all of us." An established artist of batik paintings, Harriet Peck Taylor has also created several children's books, greeting cards, and other pieces illustrated with her colorful and fanciful batiks.

Additional Books by the Author
- *Coyote Places the Stars*
- *Ulaq and the Northern Lights*
- *When Bear Stole the Chinook*
- *Brother Wolf*

Vocabulary

Have students use the vocabulary words to complete a chart like the one below. See pages 296–299 for additional vocabulary activities. For definitions of the words, see the Glossary.

One Syllable	Two Syllables	Three Syllables	Four Syllables

Day 1
ancient p. 2
shoreline p. 2
lazily p. 2

Day 2
lounging p. 9
zigzagging p. 10
sighed p. 12

Day 3
willows p. 14
determined p. 17
thoughtful p. 17
frustration p. 19
nevertheless p. 19

Day 4
feast p. 20
twilight p. 20
flutter p. 22

	Response	Strategies	Skills
Day 1 Pages 2–7	**Book Talk** • Important Details • Express Personal Opinion • Generalize **Writing:** Write from a Character's Perspective	**USE TEXT STRUCTURE AND FORMAT** FOCUS STRATEGY *Journeys of Wonder,* p. T61	**SYLLABICATION** FOCUS SKILL *Journeys of Wonder,* pp. T60–T61
Day 2 Pages 8–13	**Book Talk** • Draw Conclusions • Speculate • Express Personal Opinion **Writing:** Write from a Character's Perspective	Create Mental Images *Hidden Surprises,* p. T567	Sequence *Journeys of Wonder,* pp. T20–T21
Day 3 Pages 14–19	**Book Talk** • Draw Conclusions • Determine Characters' Traits • Make Predictions **Writing:** Describe a Character's Feelings	Reread *Hidden Surprises,* p. T119	Draw Conclusions *Hidden Surprises,* pp. T322–T323
Day 4 Pages 20–22	**Book Talk** • Make Comparisons • Summarize • Fantasy and Reality **Writing:** Write an Invitation	**USE TEXT STRUCTURE AND FORMAT** FOCUS STRATEGY *Journeys of Wonder,* p. T61	**SYLLABICATION** FOCUS SKILL *Journeys of Wonder,* pp. T60–T61

Day 5
Wrap-Up

Project
✓ Design a Travel Poster
• Inquiry Project

Writing
✓ Paragraph That Contrasts
Journeys of Wonder, pp. T96–T97

Language Link
• How Insects Get Their Names

Assessment
✓ Comprehension Test

*Additional support is provided in *Collections.*
✓ Options for Assessment

Coyote and the Laughing Butterflies

BOOK TALK

After you read pages 2–7, meet with your group to discuss and answer the following questions:

❶ What is the setting of this story?

❷ Do you agree with Coyote's wife when she says that Coyote is lazy?

❸ What can you usually expect to find along the shore of a big lake?

RESPONSE JOURNAL

Imagine that you are one of the butterflies carrying Coyote. Describe how you feel as you are carrying him.

Strategies Good Readers Use

FOCUS STRATEGY **USE TEXT STRUCTURE AND FORMAT**

In many folktales, what happens to the main character repeats, or words and phrases repeat. You can use such patterns to predict what will happen next.

SKILLS IN CONTEXT

FOCUS SKILL **SYLLABICATION: WRITING AN IMAGE POEM** Divide a long word whose pronunciation you don't know into syllables. This will help you say or read the word. Then use context to understand what the word means. Use two-syllable words in an image poem. An image poem looks like whatever the poem is about. The words in the poem also tell about those things. For example, if you wrote an image poem about a skyscraper, you would use words that tell what a skyscraper is like, and the poem would look like a skyscraper. You can do the same for the setting of this story.

What You Need

- **scrap paper**
- **drawing paper**
- **pencil**

What to Do

1. Look through the part of the book you just read. On a piece of scrap paper, write down all the words that tell what the setting of the story is like.

2. Circle the words on your list that have two syllables.

3. Use the words you have circled to draw the scenery. You can repeat words as many times as you need to.

Here are some words to get you started: mountain, mesa, sagebrush

Think Ahead Do you think Coyote will get the salt on his next trip?

© Harcourt

Coyote and the Laughing Butterflies

BOOK TALK

After you read pages 8–13, meet with your group to discuss and answer the following questions:

1 How can you tell that Coyote wants to succeed this time?

2 Coyote's wife does not believe him. What might she know about Coyote that keeps her from trusting him?

3 If you could give Coyote advice on how to succeed, what would it be?

RESPONSE JOURNAL

Put yourself in Coyote's place. How do you feel about what has been happening?

Strategies Good Readers Use

CREATE MENTAL IMAGES

The words the author uses to describe this story's beautiful setting and the pictures she creates can help you see the setting in your mind.

SKILLS IN CONTEXT

SEQUENCE: BUTTERFLY MOBILE Coyote makes a plan that he tries to follow, but the butterflies outsmart him. You will notice that the sequence of events is almost the same each time. Being aware of the sequence of events can help you understand the story and characters better. Follow the directions below in sequence to make a beautiful butterfly.

What You Need

- **drawing paper and pencil**
- **scissors**
- **coloring materials**
- **tape**
- **string or yarn cut in different lengths**
- **wire coat hanger**

What to Do

1. Put your *right* foot on the left side of the paper. Have a friend trace your foot. It will be the butterfly's left wing.

2. Put your *left* foot to the right of the first wing, leaving space for the butterfly's body. Have your foot traced.

3. Add the butterfly's body, and color each wing. Remember to make the markings the same.

4. Tape string or yarn to the butterfly and attach to a coat hanger.

5. Add other butterflies to your mobile.

Here is an idea to get you started:
Butterflies often match the colors of the plants in the places where they live.

Think Ahead What is likely to happen the next time Coyote makes a trip to the salty lake?

© Harcourt

BOOK TALK

After you read pages 14–19, meet with your group to discuss and answer the following questions:

1 Why do you think Coyote took the shortcut rather than the trail this time?

2 Why does Coyote tell himself how thoughtful he is?

3 How might Coyote's experience change how he does things in the future?

RESPONSE JOURNAL

Describe how Coyote's wife feels when Coyote finally comes home with the salt?

Strategies Good Readers Use

REREAD

Coyote is probably going over in his mind what he has done. Readers can do the same thing. If you read something you do not understand, go back to reread it.

SKILLS IN CONTEXT

DRAW CONCLUSIONS: ANIMAL FLIPBOOK You can use story clues and your own experience to figure out something the author doesn't fully explain. This is called drawing a conclusion. Make an animal flipbook about one of the animals in the story. See if a classmate can use the clues you wrote and his or her knowledge of animals to figure out which animal you wrote about.

What You Need

- six pieces of drawing paper
- pencil and drawing tools
- stapler

What to Do

1. Staple five of the six pages together.

2. On each stapled page, write clues about your animal. Do not say the name of the animal you are describing.

3. On the sixth sheet of paper, draw a picture of your animal.

4. Trade books with a classmate, but do not give them your picture. See if they can figure out what animal you described. After your partner has drawn a conclusion, staple your picture to the front of your book.

Here's a clue to get you started:
I have a broad, flat tail. (beaver)

Think Ahead
What do you think Coyote's wife will do with the salt?

© Harcourt

Coyote and the Laughing Butterflies

BOOK TALK

After you read pages 20–22, meet with your group to discuss and answer the following questions:

❶ Which stories in *Journeys of Wonder* does this story remind you of?

❷ How does this story explain why butterflies fly as they do?

❸ What do you think might be the real reason butterflies move as they do?

RESPONSE JOURNAL

Write an invitation to your friends, inviting them to a feast to show thanks for something special.

> ### Strategies Good Readers Use
>
> **FOCUS STRATEGY** **USE TEXT STRUCTURE AND FORMAT**
>
> Think about the patterns that are repeated in this story. How do you think repeating a pattern might help someone retell the story?

SKILLS IN CONTEXT

FOCUS SKILL **SYLLABICATION: SYLLABLE SACK RACE** Tell about at least one word that you were able to pronounce because you knew about syllables. Work with a partner to create a syllable game.

What You Need

- **three large paper bags**
- **ten word cards**
- **felt-tip pen or dark crayon**
- **stopwatch or a clock that shows seconds**

What to Do

1. Write a different word from the story on each card. Write some words with one syllable, some with two syllables, and some with three syllables. Mix them up and put them in a deck.

2. Label the paper bags 1, 2, and 3. Line the bags up.

3. Trade cards with another partner team. Each team should sort the cards they receive as quickly as possible. Put the words with one syllable in bag 1, the words with two syllables in bag 2, and so on.

4. Each team should be timed to see who wins the race.

Here is an idea to get you started: Feast *would be in bag 1;* thoughtful *would be in bag 2.*

Wrap-Up

► **Project** DESIGN A TRAVEL POSTER Remind students that in *Coyote and the Laughing Butterflies,* the setting is not only beautiful but spectacular. Explain that many people visit New Mexico because they want to enjoy the scenery. They may have seen pictures of it on a travel poster, such as the kind travel agents, airlines, and others have in their windows or on the walls of their offices. Tell students they will be creating a travel poster using what they have learned about New Mexico.

• Organize students into groups, and discuss what kind of scenery they might show for New Mexico. Each scene should be somewhat different.
• Ask students to complete the copying master on page 149 to plan their posters.
• Have each group design an original travel poster.
• Have each group present its finished poster to the class.

► **Writing** PARAGRAPH THAT CONTRASTS Have students respond to the following prompt: **Write a paragraph that contrasts where Coyote lives with the setting of another story you have read.** Have students use the copying master on page 150 to plan their paragraph. Remind students to focus on word choice to bring out contrasts vividly. Use *Journeys of Wonder* pages T96–T97 for additional support. Rubrics for evaluating student writing are provided on pages 292–295.

► **Language Link** HOW INSECTS GET THEIR NAMES Explain to students that scientists have special names for insects like butterflies. Many people have also made up their own names for the different types of butterflies. Suggest that students look at a field guide or encyclopedia to find some of these names. Encourage them to speculate on how the different butterflies got their names. For example, ask students how they think the Tiger Swallowtail got its name.

Inquiry Project

Coyote and the Laughing Butterflies can be a springboard for inquiry into a variety of topics and ideas. Have students brainstorm topics they would like to know more about and organize their responses in a web. Students can use reference books and the Internet to begin their inquiry project.

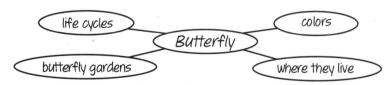

✔ **Comprehension Test** Test students' comprehension of *Coyote and the Laughing Butterflies* by having them complete the copying master on page 151.

Name _____

Project Planner

In *Coyote and the Laughing Butterflies*, the setting is an important part of the story. Travel posters about different places usually show exciting scenery and invite people to visit those places. Create a travel poster that shows the setting of this story.

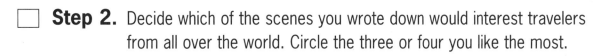

What You Need

- books with pictures of New Mexico
- scrap paper
- large pieces of drawing paper
- drawing and coloring tools

☐ **Step 1.** Discuss with your group the kinds of places you read about in this book. Write those places on the lines below.

_____ _____

_____ _____

_____ _____

☐ **Step 2.** Decide which of the scenes you wrote down would interest travelers from all over the world. Circle the three or four you like the most.

☐ **Step 3.** Plan your poster on scrap paper. Decide what words you will put on the poster to tell about the setting.

☐ **Step 4.** Draw your poster and add the words. Share your work with the class.

© Harcourt

Name _____

Paragraph That Contrasts

Write a paragraph that contrasts where Coyote lives with the setting of another story you have read. Use the graphic organizer below to help you plan your paragraph.

Prewriting Graphic Organizer

Topic: _____   **Audience:** _____

Main Idea: _____

Difference 1: _____
Details: _____
_____

Difference 2: _____
Details: _____
_____

Difference 3: _____
Details: _____
_____

Main Point Summarized: _____
_____

© Harcourt

Name _____

Comprehension Test

Read each question below. Then mark the letter for the answer you have chosen.

1. **Where is Coyote supposed to get salt for his wife?**

    Ⓐ the shore of a lake

    Ⓑ in the valley

    Ⓒ the top of a faraway hill

    Ⓓ in a salty lake

2. **Why do the butterflies decide to trick Coyote?**

    Ⓕ They are angry with him.

    Ⓖ Coyote's wife tells them to.

    Ⓗ Coyote looks so lazy.

    Ⓙ Everyone plays tricks on him.

3. **After the first trip, Coyote**

    Ⓐ lies about where he has been.

    Ⓑ tries to explain what happened.

    Ⓒ decides that he dreamed everything.

    Ⓓ promises to get the salt the next day.

4. **Which best describes how Coyote feels about this?**

    Ⓕ sad   Ⓗ puzzled

    Ⓖ angry   Ⓙ not worried

5. **Why is Coyote sure he has made the second trip?**

    Ⓐ He remembers filling the sack with salt.

    Ⓑ His back is tired.

    Ⓒ His legs are sore from running.

    Ⓓ He dreams about it all the way back.

6. **Why might the butterflies feel sorry for Coyote the third time?**

    Ⓕ This time he fills the sack with salt.

    Ⓖ He looks so tired and sore.

    Ⓗ Coyote's wife gives him just one more chance.

    Ⓙ Coyote's wife is making a feast.

7. **What is the cause of Coyote's frustration this time?**

    Ⓐ His wife is still angry at him.

    Ⓑ He still does not have the salt.

    Ⓒ He does not know how he got home.

    Ⓓ He is still sore from running.

8. **What does Coyote tell his wife about the salt?**

    Ⓕ He tells her how hard he had to work to get it.

    Ⓖ He tells her it was easy to get.

    Ⓗ He says nothing about it.

    Ⓙ He tells her why he is so puzzled.

9. **Why do the coyotes have the feast?**

    Ⓐ to give thanks for living on the mesa

    Ⓑ to use up all the salt they have

    Ⓒ to feed themselves

    Ⓓ to give thanks for the harvest

10. **On a separate sheet of paper, respond to the question below.**

    How would you describe Coyote?

© Harcourt

My Horse of the North

Reading Level

by Bruce McMillan

▶ Theme Connection
As students read *My Horse of the North*, they will learn about using horses for work. Margrét trains and rides her horse on a sheep roundup much as the cowboys and cowgirls in "Yippee-Yay!" train and ride their horses on cattle drives. Like the children in "If You Made a Million," who work to make money, Margrét and her horse work to help support the family sheep-farming business.

▶ Summary
Nine-year-old Margrét lives in Iceland. She works hard with her new horse, Perla, to get ready for *réttir*, the September roundup of sheep that is an annual Icelandic tradition. She and her friends practice rounding up cows, geese, and rams before joining the roundup at the end of the summer.

▶ Building Background
Tell students that *My Horse of the North* is nonfiction. Display the book cover, and show students some of the photographs inside. Show page 3, and have students find Iceland on a map. Talk about what Iceland is like. Explain to students that they will hear some Icelandic words. Have them read to be informed about Iceland.

Author Profile
Bruce McMillan is a photographer and writer whose previous book about Iceland, *Nights of the Pufflings*, was an ALA Notable Children's Book and a School Library Journal Best Book of the Year. In *My Horse of the North*, McMillan returns to Iceland—one of his favorite places in the world.

Additional Books by the Author
- *Summer Ice: Life Along the Antarctic Peninsula*
- *Going on a Whale Watch*

Vocabulary

Have students use the vocabulary words to complete a chart like the one below. See pages 296–299 for additional vocabulary activities. For definitions of the words, see the Glossary.

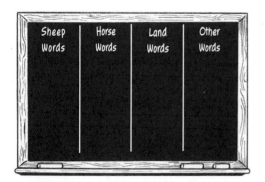

Sheep Words	Horse Words	Land Words	Other Words

Day 1	Day 2	Day 3	Day 4
wool p. 5	pasture p. 7	grooming p. 9	reins p. 14
	mane p. 7	herd p. 10	
	breed p. 7		
	ancestors p. 7		
	Vikings p. 7		

Day 5	Day 6	Day 7	Day 8
trot p. 19	roundup p. 23	ridge p. 24	stray p. 28
gallop p. 19		bleat p. 27	journey p. 28

© Harcourt

	Response	Strategies	Skills
Day 1 Pages 3–5	**Book Talk** • Important Details • Cause-Effect • Author's Purpose **Writing:** Personal Response	**USE CONTEXT TO CONFIRM MEANING** `FOCUS STRATEGY` *Journeys of Wonder, p. T407	**STUDY STRATEGIES** `FOCUS SKILL` *Journeys of Wonder, pp. T406–T407
Day 2 Pages 6–7	**Book Talk** • Author's Craft • Use Graphic Aids • Author's Viewpoint **Writing:** Express Personal Opinion	Use Prior Knowledge *Hidden Surprises, p. T71	Important Details *Journeys of Wonder, pp. T536–T537
Day 3 Pages 8–11	**Book Talk** • Determine Characters' Emotions • Draw Conclusions • Cause-Effect **Writing:** Personal Response	Reread *Hidden Surprises, p. T119	Compare and Contrast *Journeys of Wonder, pp. T304–T305
Day 4 Pages 12–15	**Book Talk** • Interpret Characters' Motivations • Use Graphic Aids • Make Judgments **Writing:** Identify with Characters	**USE CONTEXT TO CONFIRM MEANING** `FOCUS STRATEGY` *Journeys of Wonder, p. T407	**STUDY STRATEGIES** `FOCUS SKILL` *Journeys of Wonder, pp. T406–T407
Day 5 Pages 16–19	**Book Talk** • Generalize • Author's Viewpoint • Important Details **Writing:** Personal Response	**ADJUST READING RATE** `FOCUS STRATEGY` *Journeys of Wonder, p. T455	**PARAPHRASE** `FOCUS SKILL` *Journeys of Wonder, pp. T454–T455
Day 6 Pages 20–23	**Book Talk** • Cause-Effect • Main Idea • Important Details **Writing:** Determine Characters' Emotions	Read Ahead *Hidden Surprises, p. T525	Skim and Scan *Journeys of Wonder, pp. T196–T197
Day 7 Pages 24–27	**Book Talk** • Determine Characters' Emotion • Cause-Effect • Express Personal Opinion **Writing:** Express Personal Opinion	Create Mental Images *Hidden Surprises, p. T567	Locating Information *Hidden Surprises, pp. T566–T567
Day 8 Pages 28–31	**Book Talk** • Theme • Make Comparisons • Author's Craft **Writing:** Summarize/Personal Response	**ADJUST READING RATE** `FOCUS STRATEGY` *Journeys of Wonder, p. T455	**PARAPHRASE** `FOCUS SKILL` *Journeys of Wonder, pp. T454–T455
Days 9-10 **Wrap-Up**	**Project** ✓ Create a Travel Brochure • Inquiry Project	**Writing** ✓ Research Report *Journeys of Wonder, pp. T390–T391	**Language Link** • Illustrations **Assessment** ✓ Comprehension Test

*Additional support is provided in *Collections*.
✓ Options for Assessment

© Harcourt

My Horse of the North

BOOK TALK

After you read pages 3–5, meet with your group to discuss and answer the following questions:

1 What is the setting? Why is it important?

2 Why does Margrét look up to the hills?

3 Why doesn't the author tell you what *réttir* is? When do you think you will find out?

RESPONSE JOURNAL

Write about something you dream of doing. What can you do to get ready for it?

Strategies Good Readers Use

FOCUS STRATEGY USE TEXT TO CONFIRM MEANING

Explain how context helps you understand the words *roam* and *valley* on page 5.

SKILLS IN CONTEXT

FOCUS SKILL **STUDY STRATEGIES: *RÉTTIR* NOTEBOOK** Taking notes about new ideas is an important study strategy. As you read, take notes that will help you figure out what *réttir* is. The author does not define *réttir*, but he gives clues. As you read, record information about *réttir*.

What You Need

- **lined paper**
- **construction paper**
- **writing tools**

What to Do

1. Fold the construction paper in half, from short edge to short edge.

2. Staple two sheets of lined paper inside.

3. Write *What is réttir?* at the top of the first sheet of lined paper. Under this, write the heading *Clues* and the numbers 1–5. Leave space for more numbers.

4. Keep your notebook handy. When you find information about *réttir*, write the clues and record the page numbers.

5. Look over your clues once you finish the book. On the second page, write in your own words what *réttir* is.

Here is a clue to get you started: *happens at summer's end, page 5*

Think Ahead What do you think Margrét will do with her horse?

© Harcourt

My Horse of the North

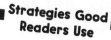

BOOK TALK

After you read pages 6–7, meet with your group to discuss and answer the following questions:

❶ What does the author do to help you read and understand the Icelandic words in this story?

❷ How do the pictures help you understand what Perla looks like?

❸ How do you know that the author admires Icelandic horses?

RESPONSE JOURNAL

What do you know about horses? Would you like to have one? Explain.

Strategies Good Readers Use

USE PRIOR KNOWLEDGE

What you already know can help you understand new information. List ideas in the story that you knew something about before you started reading.

SKILLS IN CONTEXT

IMPORTANT DETAILS: ICELANDIC HORSE WEB Identifying a main idea and its supporting details is an important part of understanding what you read. Make a web that shows main ideas and details about Perla.

What You Need

- drawing paper
- writing and drawing tools
- notebook paper

What to Do

1. Draw a picture of Perla in the center of your paper. Look at the book to get details for her color and shape.

2. Write *age*, *size*, *color*, and *breed* in each corner of your paper. Draw a circle around each main idea word. Draw a line from each circle to the picture of Perla.

3. Search page 7 for details about Perla's age, size, color, and breed. Write each detail underneath the main idea that it supports. Make lines to connect the main ideas and details to the picture of Perla.

Here is a detail to get you started: size: *small yet strong*

Think Ahead

Do you think Perla and Margrét will be a good team? Why?

© Harcourt

My Horse of the North

BOOK TALK

Read pages 8–11. Then meet with your group to discuss and answer the following questions:

❶ How does Margrét feel about Perla? How do you know?

❷ Why do Margrét and her friends need to practice for *réttir*?

❸ What is the problem with cows? How will the children solve this problem?

RESPONSE JOURNAL

What are the skills Margrét is practicing? What skills would you like to improve? How do you work on improving them?

SKILLS IN CONTEXT

COMPARE AND CONTRAST: COMPARISON FOLD-OVER Comparing two things can help you understand how things are alike. Contrasting two things can help you understand how they are different. Make a fold-over that compares and contrasts Margrét's life with yours.

What You Need

- **drawing paper**
- **scissors**
- **writing and drawing tools**

What to Do

1. Fold your paper in half, long side to long side. Crease the paper. Then fold the paper again, short side to short side. The fold lines should cross when you open your paper.

2. Cut from one long edge to the center line. Fold the cut pieces down over the whole side. On one cut piece, draw Margrét. On the other, draw a picture of yourself. Label each picture.

3. Under Margrét's picture, tell about Margrét's life. Under your picture, tell about your life.

4. Talk with a partner about how your life is like Margrét's life and how it is different.

Here is an idea to get you started:
We both have friends. Margrét practices herding skills, but I do not.

Think Ahead What animals do you think the children will try herding next?

© Harcourt

My Horse of the North

BOOK TALK

After you read pages 12–15, meet with your group to discuss and answer the following questions:

❶ Why do the children laugh at Margrét's idea?

❷ How do the pictures add to this part of the story?

❸ Do you think Margrét and Perla work well together? Explain why.

RESPONSE JOURNAL

Why do you think Margrét feels proud after herding the geese?

SKILLS IN CONTEXT

FOCUS SKILL **STUDY STRATEGY: GOOSE CAMEO POSTER** One important study strategy is using both text and pictures to understand an idea. Make a poster about geese that includes information from both the photographs and the text in *My Horse of the North.*

What You Need

- **drawing paper**
- **writing and drawing tools**
- **ruler**

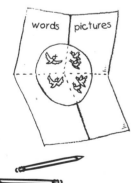

What to Do

1. Fold your paper in half, and in half again. Draw a large circle where the folds cross. Darken the fold lines above and below the circle.

2. Label the left side of the paper *Words* and the right side *Pictures*.

3. Write on the left side of the paper words and phrases from the book that describe the geese.

4. List on the right side details about the geese that you learn from the photographs.

5. Draw your own illustration of the geese in *My Horse of the North* inside the circle.

Here is a detail to get you started:
The geese honk and flap.

Think Ahead
Do you think Margrét and Perla will practice anymore? Why?

© Harcourt

My Horse of the North

BOOK TALK

After you read pages 16–19, meet with your group to discuss and answer the following questions:

1 In what ways are the sheep important to Margrét's family?

2 Why does the author call Margrét and Perla "a working team"?

3 The author says the children are skilled riders. What can they do?

RESPONSE JOURNAL

Think about something you do well. What skills does the task require? How did you learn the skills?

Strategies Good Readers Use

FOCUS STRATEGY ADJUST READING RATE

What parts of this story have you had to read more slowly? What parts have you read faster? Why?

SKILLS IN CONTEXT

FOCUS SKILL **PARAPHRASE: PARAPHRASE CARTOON** To paraphrase is to put ideas in your own words. You can leave out ideas, but what you write must have the same meaning as what you read. Paraphrase the sweater passage on page 16 to make a comic strip to show why and how Margrét will get a new sweater.

What You Need

- paper for drafting your paraphrase
- drawing paper
- writing and drawing tools

What to Do

1. Paraphrase the sweater passage on page 16. You can combine or rearrange ideas, but keep the author's meaning.

2. Decide how many pictures you will draw to illustrate your paraphrase. Use a ruler to divide the paper.

3. Draw your pictures in the boxes. Use your paraphrase to make captions.

Here is a paraphrased idea to get you started: Margrét's sweater is handmade.

Think Ahead What animals do you predict the children will try herding next?

© Harcourt

My Horse of the North

BOOK TALK

Read pages 20–23. Then meet with your group to discuss and answer the following questions:

1 How does Margrét know she and Perla are ready for *réttir*?

2 On page 23, what words tell you what *réttir* is? Did you guess earlier? How did you know?

3 Why is *réttir* important?

RESPONSE JOURNAL

How do you think Margrét feels as she leaves for *réttir*? Explain.

Strategies Good Readers Use

READ AHEAD

☆Often, readers can figure out the meaning of a new word or idea by reading ahead. Read ahead to figure out the meaning of *rams* (page 20).

SKILLS IN CONTEXT

SKIM AND SCAN: WINTER/SUMMER PAINTINGS: When you skim, you read quickly to find out what text is about. When you scan, you read quickly to find specific information. You do not read every word when you skim or scan. Skim and scan the book for details to help you create pictures of Iceland in summer and winter.

What You Need

- **note-taking paper**
- **drawing paper**
- **writing and drawing tools**

What to Do

1. Take notes about winter in Iceland from page 23. Include details about the weather and the sheep.
2. Draw a picture of Iceland in winter.
3. Scan the book to find information about summer in Iceland. Look at both text and pictures. Take notes.
4. Using your notes, draw a picture of Iceland in summer.
5. Give each picture a title and write your name on it. Display your pictures side by side.

Here is an idea to get you started: *"Lambs and their mothers roam freely in the mountains all summer." (page 5)*

Think Ahead
What do you think will happen during the roundup?

My Horse of the North

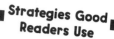

BOOK TALK

After you read pages 24–27, meet with your group to discuss and answer the following questions:

1 How does Margrét feel when she sees all the sheep? How do you know?

2 How has practice paid off for Margrét and Perla? What would be different if they had not practiced?

3 Would you like to ride in a *réttir*? Explain.

RESPONSE JOURNAL

What would you like about living in Iceland? Is there anything you would not enjoy?

Strategies Good Readers Use

CREATE MENTAL IMAGES

It is helpful to picture in your mind what an author describes. What do you "see" in your mind when you read about *réttir*?

SKILLS IN CONTEXT

LOCATING INFORMATION: ICELANDIC DICTIONARY Locating information is an important study skill. Often text clues, such as **bold type** and (parentheses), help readers locate information. *My Horse of the North* includes some Icelandic words. You can locate the Icelandic words by looking for their pronunciations and translations, which are given in (parentheses), CAPITAL LETTERS, and *italics*. Make a dictionary of Icelandic words.

What You Need

- **drawing paper, cut in half**
- **construction paper**
- **writing and drawing tools**
- **stapler**

What to Do

1. Find Icelandic words in *My Horse of the North*.
2. Write each word on a half-sheet of drawing paper. Add the pronunciation, translation, and a sentence that uses the word. Illustrate the word.
3. Put the pages in alphabetical order.
4. Make a folded construction paper cover.
5. Make a title page on the cover.

Here is an idea to get you started:
réttir (RRYET•ir) *roundup. Margrét rides Perla in the* réttir.

Think Ahead
What do you think will happen after *réttir*?

© Harcourt

My Horse of the North

BOOK TALK

Read pages 28–31. Then meet with your group to discuss and answer the following questions:

1 What stories have you read in *Journeys of Wonder* that seem similar to *My Horse of the North?*

2 What are some themes, or main ideas, in *My Horse of the North?*

3 What do you think the author had to do and learn about to create this book?

RESPONSE JOURNAL

How does Margrét help her family on the farm? What work does your family do? How do you help?

SKILLS IN CONTEXT

FOCUS SKILL **PARAPHRASE: PARAPHRASE BOOKLET** Remember that paraphrasing is saying things in your own words without changing the author's meaning. A main idea in this story is that Margrét practices for *réttir*. She practices on three kinds of animals before finally herding the ewes and lambs. Paraphrase and illustrate each step to make an accordion book.

What You Need

- **paper for planning**
- **writing paper**
- **drawing paper**
- **writing and drawing tools**
- **tape**

What to Do

1. Reread and paraphrase each part of the story: herding cows, herding geese, herding rams, and herding the ewes and lambs.

2. Write each paraphrase on writing paper, cut it out, and mount it on drawing paper. Illustrate each paraphrase.

3. Put the paraphrased pages in order, side by side.

4. Use tape on the back to join the pages. The pages can be folded like an accordion.

5. Share your accordion book with your classmates.

Here is a paraphrased idea to get you started: *First Margrét and Perla practice herding cows to the barn. This is too easy, because the cows go there by themselves, slowly. (page 10)*

Wrap-Up

▶ **Project** **CREATE A TRAVEL BROCHURE** Point out to students that they have learned a lot about Iceland by reading *My Horse of the North*. On the last page, the author suggests that readers contact the Icelandic Tourist Board for more information. Ask students what kinds of materials they might get from a tourist board. Show sample travel brochures. Talk about and list information that is usually included in a travel brochure. Tell students they will be creating a brochure about northern Iceland.

- Organize students into groups.
- Ask students to complete the copying master on page 163 to plan what will be in their brochures.
- Have each group design its own brochure using the information about Iceland presented in *My Horse of the North*. Students may wish to use a word processing program to publish their brochures.
- Have each group present its finished brochure to the class.

▶ **Writing** **RESEARCH REPORT** Have students respond to the following writing prompt: **Write a research report about one breed of horse.** Have students use the copying master on page 164 to plan their research reports. Remind students to focus on organization. Use *Journeys of Wonder* pages T390–T391 for additional support. Rubrics for evaluating student writing are provided on pages 292–295.

▶ **Language Link** **ILLUSTRATIONS** Explain to students that illustrations are very important in nonfiction texts. Illustrations include pictures, diagrams, and photographs. They show you what the text describes. Have students choose several illustrations that they like in *My Horse of the North*. Have them work with a partner to explain to each other what each picture shows.

Inquiry Project

My Horse of the North can be a springboard for inquiry into a variety of topics and ideas. Have students brainstorm topics they would like to know more about and organize their responses in a web. Students can use reference books and the Internet to begin their inquiry projects. They may also be able to use community resources.

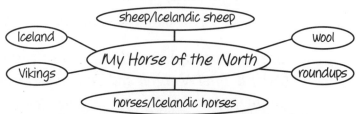

✔ **Comprehension Test** Test students' comprehension of *My Horse of the North* by having them complete the copying master on page 165.

Name _____

Project Planner

My Horse of the North tells you a lot about Iceland. Use ideas in *My Horse of the North* to create a travel brochure about northern Iceland for people who might visit there someday.

☐ **Step 1.** Discuss with your group the kinds of information useful in a travel brochure. Make a list of ideas you will include.

_____

_____

What You Need
- sketch paper
- drawing paper or oak tag
- writing and drawing tools
- reference sources

☐ **Step 2.** Brainstorm ideas and details from the story to use in your brochure. If you need more information, use reference sources. Use the web below to brainstorm information you will include in your brochure. You should discuss the following questions:

- What does the land look like?
- What can you do in Iceland?
- What is the climate like?
- What souvenirs can you buy there?

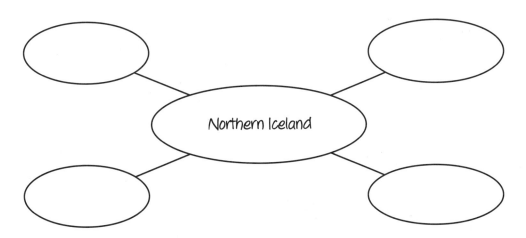

Northern Iceland

☐ **Step 3.** Create the brochure with your group. Fold a piece of paper into a brochure. Write and illustrate the information in your web to make a brochure that will make people want to visit northern Iceland.

☐ **Step 4.** As a group, present your brochure to the class.

Research Report

Write a research report about a breed of horse. Use the graphic organizer to help you plan your research report. Then write your report.

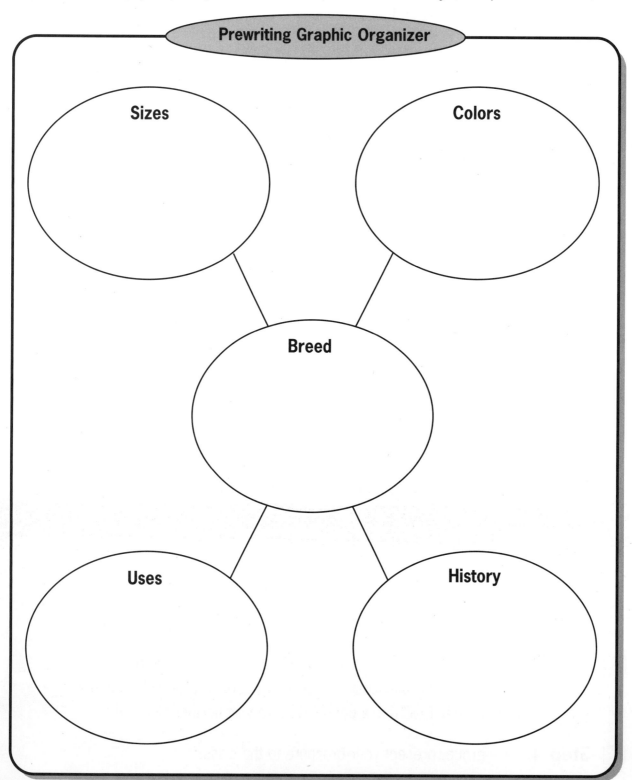

Prewriting Graphic Organizer

Sizes

Colors

Breed

Uses

History

Name _____

Comprehension Test Test Prep

Read each question below. Then mark the letter for the answer you have chosen.

1. **When does Iceland's sheep roundup take place?**
   Ⓐ spring
   Ⓑ beginning of summer
   Ⓒ September
   Ⓓ winter

2. **Why are the sheep in the mountains?**
   Ⓕ They ran away.
   Ⓖ They are roaming free to eat grass and grow wool.
   Ⓗ Margrét let them loose by accident.
   Ⓙ Other animals chased them away from the farm.

3. **What kind of animal is Perla?**
   Ⓐ ram
   Ⓑ lamb
   Ⓒ Icelandic horse
   Ⓓ Icelandic pony

4. **What is Margrét's dream?**
   Ⓕ to have a new sweater
   Ⓖ to get a horse
   Ⓗ to make new friends
   Ⓙ to ride in a roundup

5. **What will Margrét's mother do after *réttir*?**
   Ⓐ knit Margrét a sweater
   Ⓑ buy sheep
   Ⓒ get Margrét a new horse
   Ⓓ sell the farm

6. **Which animals are the easiest to herd?**
   Ⓕ ewes and lambs
   Ⓖ cows
   Ⓗ geese
   Ⓙ rams

7. **What is the Icelandic word for *roundup*?**
   Ⓐ *f'fa*   Ⓒ *hestur*
   Ⓑ *gæser*   Ⓓ *réttir*

8. **Why do Margrét and her friends ride so much?**
   Ⓕ Their parents make them.
   Ⓖ If they learn to ride, they can have horses of their own.
   Ⓗ They want to be ready for *réttir*.
   Ⓙ They have nothing else to do.

9. **Which is a main idea in *My Horse of the North*?**
   Ⓐ Children can help with family work.
   Ⓑ Roundups are too dangerous for children.
   Ⓒ Iceland is a hard place to live.
   Ⓓ Practice is a waste of time.

10. **On a separate sheet of paper, write a short answer in response to the question below.**
    In your own words, describe Iceland's *réttir*.

Mama Provi and the Pot of Rice

Reading Level

by Sylvia Rosa-Casanova

Theme Connection

In "Alejandro's Gift," Alejandro solves the problem of his loneliness by building a water hole for desert animals, adapting his plan to achieve success. In *Mama Provi and the Pot of Rice*, Mama Provi also solves a problem, how to cheer up her sick granddaughter. As Alejandro shares what he has with the animals who live nearby, so Mama Provi shares with her neighbors. Food is her gift, as Alejandro's gift is the water hole.

Author Profile

Sylvia Rosa-Casanova grew up in New York City, the setting for *Mama Provi and the Pot of Rice*, which is her first book for children. Mama Provi is based on Rosa-Casanova's grandmother, who also liked to cook.

Summary

Mama Provi's granddaughter, Lucy, is ill and cannot visit. Mama Provi makes Lucy a delicious *arroz con pollo* to cheer her up. As she walks up the seven flights to Lucy's apartment, Mama Provi meets many neighbors, who trade something they themselves have cooked or baked for some of her chicken and rice. By the time she reaches Lucy's door, Mama Provi is carrying a multicultural feast.

Building Background

Tell students that *Mama Provi and the Pot of Rice* is realistic fiction. The story is set in a city apartment building. Invite students to share what they know about apartment buildings. Look at the covers and some illustrations together. Identify Mama Provi, the main character. Have children read to be entertained and to find out where Mama Provi is going and what is in her big shopping bag.

Vocabulary

sk students to work with a partner to pair vocabulary words and create sentences for them. See pages 296–299 for additional vocabulary activities. For definitions of the words, see the Glossary.

Word Pairs	Sentences
delicious, aroma	The delicious ginger-bread had a spicy aroma.

Day 1	Day 2	Day 3	Day 4
apartment building p. 2	elevator p. 11	immediately p. 20	enchanting p. 27
granddaughter p. 2	aroma p. 11	bumped p. 25	tremendous p. 30
tales p. 4	briskly p. 11		
chicken pox p. 8	generous p. 18		
delicious p. 8			

© Harcourt

	Response	Strategies	Skills
Day 1 Pages 2–9	**Book Talk** • Make Judgments • Cause-Effect • Interpret Characters' Motivations **Writing:** Personal Response	**READ AHEAD** `FOCUS STRATEGY` *Journeys of Wonder,* p. T581	**PROBLEM SOLVING** `FOCUS SKILL` *Journeys of Wonder,* pp. T580–T581
Day 2 Pages 10–19	**Book Talk** • Important Details • Summarize • Determine Characters' Traits **Writing:** Author's Craft	Use Context to Confirm Meaning *Hidden Surprises,* p. T613	Important Details *Journeys of Wonder,* pp. T536–T537
Day 3 Pages 20–25	**Book Talk** • Cause-Effect • Make Comparisons • Generalize **Writing:** Express Personal Opinion	Self-Question *Journeys of Wonder,* p. T21	Sequence *Journeys of Wonder,* pp. T20–T21
Day 4 Pages 26–30	**Book Talk** • Make Comparisons • Theme • Author's Craft **Writing:** Make Connections	**READ AHEAD** `FOCUS STRATEGY` *Journeys of Wonder,* p. T581	**PROBLEM SOLVING** `FOCUS SKILL` *Journeys of Wonder,* pp. T580–T581
Day 5 Wrap-Up	**Project** ✓ Make a Story Bag • Inquiry Project **Writing** ✓ Persuasive Dialogue *Journeys of Wonder*, pp. T608–T609 **Language Link** • Vivid Words **Assessment** ✓ Comprehension Test		

*Additional support is provided in *Collections.*
✓ Options for Assessment

Mama Provi and the Pot of Rice • 167

Mama Provi and the Pot of Rice

BOOK TALK

After you read pages 2–9, meet with your group to discuss and answer the following questions:

1 What is special about Lucy's relationship with Mama Provi?

2 Why does Mama Provi always make a lot of food?

3 Why is Mama Provi making *arroz con pollo*?

RESPONSE JOURNAL

Lucy does special things with her grandmother. Write about someone you like to do special things with.

Strategies Good Readers Use

FOCUS STRATEGY READ AHEAD

Give an example to show where reading ahead helped you understand something in the story.

SKILLS IN CONTEXT

FOCUS SKILL PROBLEM SOLVING: PROBLEM-PLAN FLAP PICTURE Understanding how story characters solve problems can help readers solve their own problems. Make a flap picture that shows a problem and a plan from the story.

What You Need

- **drawing paper**
- **ruler**
- **writing and drawing tools**
- **clear tape**

What to Do

1. Draw a picture of the outside of the apartment building. Make it eight stories tall. Place it over a sheet of paper.
2. Cut out the building, cutting through both papers.
3. Cut off the bottom floor of the building. Line up the bottom of it with the bottom of the plain paper, and tape across the top edge to form a flap.
4. Cut off the top floor and line it up with the top of the plain paper. Tape it to the top edge to form a flap.
5. Now tape the middle of the building in place.
6. Lift the flap and write *problem* on the inside. Draw a picture that shows the problem with Lucy.
7. Write *plan* inside the bottom flap. Draw a picture of Mama Provi working on her plan.

Here is an idea to get you started:
One Saturday, Lucy was sick and could not visit.

Think Ahead
What will Mama Provi do after she makes the *arroz con pollo*?

© Harcourt

Mama Provi and the Pot of Rice

BOOK TALK

After you read pages 10–19, meet with your group to discuss and answer the following questions:

1 Where is Mama Provi going?

2 What happens as Mama Provi goes up the stairs?

3 What sort of person is Mama Provi? How do you know?

RESPONSE JOURNAL

How does the author make this story interesting?

SKILLS IN CONTEXT

IMPORTANT DETAILS: CHARACTER ENCOUNTER CARTOON Details answer questions such as *who*, *what*, *when*, *where*, *why*, and *how*. Details help readers understand what is happening in a story. Create a cartoon or comic strip that shows the details of a meeting between Mama Provi and one of her neighbors.

What You Need

- **paper for planning**
- **drawing paper**
- **writing and drawing tools**

What to Do

1. Plan a cartoon or comic strip about the meeting between Mama Provi and one of her neighbors. Include details that show who is involved, where they are, what happens, and what they are doing.

2. You may use speech balloons or captions for some information.

3. Fold the drawing paper to form the number of boxes you will need.

4. Draw your cartoon or comic strip in the boxes.

Here is an idea to get you started:

You could show Mama Provi resting on the second floor landing smelling something delicious.

Think Ahead
What do you predict will happen next?

© Harcourt

Mama Provi and the Pot of Rice

The market

BOOK TALK

After you read pages 20–25, meet with your group to discuss and answer the following questions:

1 Why is Mrs. Bazzini waiting for Mama Provi?

2 What is different about Mama Provi's meeting with Mrs. Woo?

3 What can you say about Mama Provi's neighbors?

RESPONSE JOURNAL

What makes someone a good neighbor?

Strategies Good Readers Use

SELF-QUESTION

Good readers ask themselves questions to be sure they understand what they are reading. What questions can you ask yourself to make sure you understand this story?

SKILLS IN CONTEXT

SEQUENCE: SEQUENCING GAME CARDS Sequence is the order of events or ideas. Understanding sequence is an important part of understanding what you read. Draw details from the story on cards. Play a game with a classmate to sequence the events.

What You Need

- index cards or paper cut into squares
- writing and drawing tools

What to Do

1. Look again at pages 2–25. Find six important events. Write each event on a separate index card.

2. Trade cards with a classmate. Put the events your classmate chose in the correct order.

3. Ask your classmate if you put his or her cards in the right order. If you disagree about the order, check the book.

Here is an event to get you started:

Mama Provi makes arroz con pollo.

Think Ahead
Where will Mama Provi go next?

Mama Provi and the Pot of Rice

BOOK TALK

After you read pages 26–30, meet with your group to discuss and answer the following questions:

❶ What stories have you read in *Journeys of Wonder* that seem similar to *Mama Provi and the Pot of Rice?*

❷ What are some themes in *Mama Provi and the Pot of Rice?*

❸ How do you think the author got the idea for this story?

> **Strategies Good Readers Use**
>
> **FOCUS STRATEGY** **READ AHEAD**
>
> How did reading ahead help you understand this story? What were some things you learned by reading ahead?

RESPONSE JOURNAL

What can you learn from Mama Provi about solving problems?

SKILLS IN CONTEXT

FOCUS SKILL **PROBLEM SOLVING: PROBLEM-SOLVING CHART** Remember that understanding how characters solve problems can help readers think of ways to solve problems themselves. The steps in problem solving are understanding the problem, making a plan, carrying out the plan, and examining the solution. Use a problem-solving chart to understand how Mama Provi solved her problem.

What You Need

- **drawing paper**
- **writing and drawing tools**

What to Do

1. Fold the paper in half and in half again. You should have four sections when you unfold the paper.
2. Write *Problem, Plan, Actions,* and *Examine the Solution* as the titles of the sections.
3. Fill in each section with details from the story.
4. Share your chart with a partner. Discuss how the plan changes as Mama Provi goes up the stairs and whether the plan works. Can you think of a better solution?

Here is the problem to get you started: *Lucy has the chicken pox and cannot visit Mama Provi.*

© Harcourt

Wrap-Up

▶ **Project** **MAKE A STORY BAG** Remind students that Mama Provi tells stories to Lucy. Have students make a story bag and use it to retell this tale. Ask them to complete the copying master on page 173 to plan their scenes. Have each group retell the story for the class.

▶ **Writing** **PERSUASIVE DIALOGUE** Have students respond to the following writing prompt: **Write a dialogue to persuade a neighbor to help you organize a neighborhood feast.** Have students use the copying master on page 174 to brainstorm reasons and details. Remind students to focus on word choice. Use *Journeys of Wonder*, pages T608–T609 for additional support. Rubrics for evaluating student writing are provided on pages 292–295.

▶ **Language Link** **VIVID WORDS** Explain to students that the author uses many words to describe smells. Have students find and list the words and their descriptions. Talk about the effects of different words. Then have students write a sentence describing the smell of a favorite food.

Inquiry Project

Mama Provi and the Pot of Rice can be a springboard for inquiry into a variety of topics and ideas. Have students brainstorm topics they would like to know more about and organize their responses in a web. Students can use reference books and the Internet to begin their inquiry projects. They may also be able to use community resources.

✔ **Comprehension Test** Test students' comprehension of *Mama Provi and the Pot of Rice* by having them complete the copying master on page 175.

Name _____

Project Planner

One of the special activities Mama Provi and Lucy share is Mama Provi's telling stories to Lucy. Make a story bag and use it to retell this tale.

☐ **Step 1.** Discuss with your group how you want to retell the story. Make a list of the important events that you want to include.

What You Need
- paper bag
- drawing paper
- scissors
- writing and drawing tools
- ribbon or twine
- stapler

☐ **Step 2.** Work with your group to assign all of the tasks that need to be completed for you to retell *Mama Provi and the Pot of Rice*. Use the chart below to record what each member of the group will be responsible for. You should consider the following questions:
- Who will make Mama Provi's bag?
- Who will draw and cut out a picture of each food?
- How will you retell the story? Will you have a narrator? Will the characters speak?

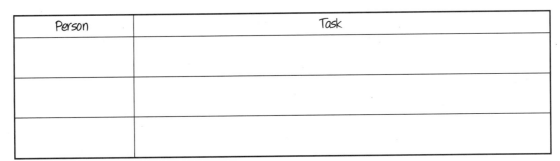

Person	Task

☐ **Step 3.** Fill the bag with the cutout foods and organize your retelling around them. Work together to write the retelling.

☐ **Step 4.** Rehearse the story, using the bag and foods as props.

☐ **Step 5.** As a group, use your bag to retell the story for the class.

Persuasive Dialogue

Write a dialogue to persuade a neighbor to help you organize a neighborhood feast. Use the graphic organizer below to plan your dialogue.

Prewriting Graphic Organizer

Topic: _____   Audience: _____

Characters: _____

Opinion/action requested: _____

_____

Reason 1 (details): _____

_____

Reason 2 (details): _____

_____

Reason 3 (details): _____

_____

Conclusion/action agreed to: _____

_____

© Harcourt

Name _____

Comprehension Test

Read each question below. Then mark the letter for the answer you have chosen.

1. **Where does Lucy live?**
   - Ⓐ next door to Mama Provi
   - Ⓑ in the next town
   - Ⓒ on the eighth floor of Mama Provi's building
   - Ⓓ in Mama Provi's apartment

2. **Why can't Lucy visit Mama Provi?**
   - Ⓕ Mama Provi lives too far away.
   - Ⓖ Lucy has chicken pox.
   - Ⓗ Mama Provi is sick.
   - Ⓙ Lucy has too much homework.

3. **What is Mama Provi's special dish?**
   - Ⓐ *frijoles*
   - Ⓑ *arroz con pollo*
   - Ⓒ chicken soup
   - Ⓓ apple pie

4. **Why does Mama Provi make her special dish?**
   - Ⓕ She wants to cheer up Lucy.
   - Ⓖ She wants to share with her neighbors.
   - Ⓗ She is going to a birthday party.
   - Ⓙ She is having company for dinner.

5. **What happens as Mama Provi is climbing the stairs?**
   - Ⓐ She drops her special dish.
   - Ⓑ She meets Lucy coming down.
   - Ⓒ She forgets where she is going.
   - Ⓓ She trades food with her neighbors.

6. **Why does Mama Provi knock on her neighbors' doors?**
   - Ⓕ She is lonely and hungry.
   - Ⓖ She needs help to carry her bag.
   - Ⓗ She wants to see who is sick.
   - Ⓙ She smells good things cooking.

7. **What is in Mama Provi's bag at the top of the stairs?**
   - Ⓐ a full pot of her special dish
   - Ⓑ a feast of lots of special foods
   - Ⓒ games and toys for Lucy
   - Ⓓ nothing

8. **How does Lucy feel when she sees Mama Provi?**
   - Ⓕ angry
   - Ⓖ lonely
   - Ⓗ healthy
   - Ⓙ happy

9. **Which is a theme in *Mama Provi and the Pot of Rice*?**
   - Ⓐ Anyone can cook well.
   - Ⓑ Neighbors can be unkind.
   - Ⓒ Chicken pox is uncomfortable.
   - Ⓓ When people share their talents, everyone benefits.

10. **Write a short answer in response to the question below.**
    Mama Provi wanted to cheer up her granddaughter. Do you think she did? Support your answer with details from the story.

What Do Authors Do?

Reading Level

by Eileen Christelow

▶ **Theme Connection** In *What Do Authors Do?* authors find ideas from their own experiences and turn them into something special: books. In "Arthur Writes a Story" and "Marta's Magnets," characters also use their own experiences to create or do something special.

▶ **Summary** In comic-strip form with added captions, the author follows the experiences of two author-neighbors. The two neighbors go through the publishing process step-by-step, from the moment a writer gets a story idea through the writing, editing, designing, printing, binding, and selling of the book.

▶ **Building Background** Tell students that this is an informational story about two authors. Readers learn from start to finish what the authors do to write books. You might ask students to tell what they know about the process of making books once the story and illustrations are done. Have students set a purpose for reading *What Do Authors Do?* by writing one or more questions about the publishing process that they hope the book will answer.

Author Profile

Eileen Christelow is an author and illustrator based in Dummerston, Vermont. Her most popular books are for very young children and include *Five Little Monkeys Jumping on the Bed.* She says that when she visited schools, children often asked her if she had to draw the pictures and type the words for every copy of her books and if she liked her job. These questions inspired her to write this book.

Additional Books by the Author
• *What Do Illustrators Do?*
• *Don't Wake Up Mama!*
• *The Five-Dog Night*

Vocabulary

Have students use the vocabulary words to complete a chart like the one below. See pages 296–299 for additional vocabulary activities. For definitions of the words, see the Glossary.

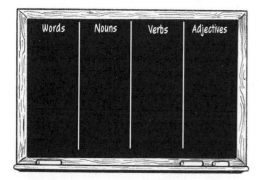

Words	Nouns	Verbs	Adjectives

Day 1
authors p. 2
ideas p. 2

Day 2
lists p. 6
illustrators p. 6
sketches p. 6
information p. 7

Day 3
suggestions p. 12

Day 4
publishers p. 16
rejection p. 17

Day 5
editors p. 19
changes p. 21

Day 6
design p. 22
dedication p. 25

Day 7
corrections p. 26
printers p. 27
warehouses p. 28

Day 8
reviews p. 30
autograph p. 31

© Harcourt

	Response	Strategies	Skills
Day 1 Pages 2–5	**Book Talk** • Note Details • Important Details • Cause-Effect **Writing:** Personal Response	**MAKE AND CONFIRM PREDICTIONS** `FOCUS STRATEGY` *Hidden Surprises,* p. T21	**PREFIXES AND SUFFIXES** `FOCUS SKILL` *Hidden Surprises,* pp. T20–T21
Day 2 Pages 6–9	**Book Talk** • Important Details • Sequence • Classify **Writing:** Relate to Characters	Use Text Structure and Format *Hidden Surprises,* p. T371	Compare and Contrast *Journeys of Wonder,* pp. T304–T305
Day 3 Pages 10–13	**Book Talk** • Summarize • Speculate • Draw Conclusions **Writing:** Personal Response	Self-Question *Hidden Surprises,* p. T453	Draw Conclusions *Hidden Surprises,* pp. T322–T323
Day 4 Pages 14–17	**Book Talk** • Classify • Text Structure • Main Idea **Writing:** Paraphrase	**MAKE AND CONFIRM PREDICTIONS** `FOCUS STRATEGY` *Hidden Surprises,* p. T21	**PREFIXES AND SUFFIXES** `FOCUS SKILL` *Hidden Surprises,* pp. T20–T21
Day 5 Pages 18–21	**Book Talk** • Cause-Effect • Classify • Author's Purpose **Writing:** Personal Response	**USE PRIOR KNOWLEDGE** `FOCUS STRATEGY` *Hidden Surprises,* p. T71	**WORD IDENTIFICATION STRATEGIES** `FOCUS SKILL` *Hidden Surprises,* pp. T70–T71
Day 6 Pages 22–25	**Book Talk** • Sequence • Generalize • Speculate **Writing:** Personal Opinion	Read Ahead *Hidden Surprises,* p. T525	Author's Purpose *Hidden Surprises,* pp. T702–T703
Day 7 Pages 26–29	**Book Talk** • Note Details • Use Context • Draw Conclusions **Writing:** Personal Response	Summarize *Hidden Surprises,* p. T161	Sequence *Journeys of Wonder,* pp. T20–T21
Day 8 Pages 30–34	**Book Talk** • Make Comparisons • Author's Purpose • Express Personal Opinion **Writing:** Personal Response	**USE PRIOR KNOWLEDGE** `FOCUS STRATEGY` *Hidden Surprises,* p. T71	**WORD IDENTIFICATION STRATEGIES** `FOCUS SKILL` *Hidden Surprises,* pp. T70–T71

| **Days**
9–10
Wrap-Up | **Project**
✓ Make a Flowchart
• Inquiry Project | **Writing**
✓ Personal Narrative
Hidden Surprises,
pp. T54–T55 | **Language Link**
• Humor

Assessment
✓ Comprehension Test |

*Additional support is provided in *Collections.*
✓ Options for Assessment

© Harcourt

What Do Authors Do?

BOOK TALK

After you read pages 2–5, meet with your group to discuss and answer the following questions:

1 This story is about two authors. What kind of book does each author plan to write?

2 Who are Rufus and Max?

3 Where do the authors get the idea for their books?

RESPONSE JOURNAL

Think about the "strangest moment" when the authors get their ideas. What is strange about it?

Strategies Good Readers Use

FOCUS STRATEGY **MAKE AND CONFIRM PREDICTIONS**

*N*ow that you have read the first five pages, list three things you think will happen in this book. Try to confirm them as you read.

SKILLS IN CONTEXT

FOCUS SKILL **PREFIXES AND SUFFIXES: PLAY A SUFFIX GAME** A *prefix* is a beginning word part that changes the meaning of the base word. A suffix is an ending word part that changes the meaning of a base word. The first line of the story says, "Authors get ideas for books at the *strangest* moments!" *Strangest* is made from the word *strange* plus the suffix *-est*. (There is also a spelling change.)

What You Need

- **fourteen 3" x 5" cards**
- **writing materials**

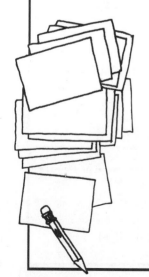

What to Do

1. Work with a partner. Write each of these words on a separate card: *cute, sweet, fast, weird, small, large, smart, crazy, silly, wet, strange, long, big, loud.*

2. Shuffle the cards, and take turns drawing a card.

3. Write a new word that ends with *-est* for each word you draw. Remember that the spelling of some words will change.

4. Use each new word in a sentence about Max, Rufus, or this book.

Here is a sentence to get you started: *Max's owner thinks Max is the smartest cat in the world.*

Think Ahead What will each author do next?

© Harcourt

What Do Authors Do?

BOOK TALK

After you read pages 6–9, meet with your group to discuss and answer the following questions:

❶ What prewriting do the authors do?

❷ What happens after the authors prewrite?

❸ There are really four main characters. You could classify, or group, these characters two different ways. What ways are these?

RESPONSE JOURNAL

Which author is more like you? Why?

Strategies Good Readers Use

USE TEXT STRUCTURE AND FORMAT

There are two parts to most pages of this story, or two places on the page where there are words. Write what they are.

SKILLS IN CONTEXT

COMPARE AND CONTRAST: MAKE A VENN DIAGRAM When you compare, you look for how things are alike. When you contrast, you look for how they are different. How are the authors in this story the same? How are they different?

What You Need

- **something to make or trace circles with**
- **paper, card-board, or poster board**
- **writing tools**

What to Do

1. Make two overlapping circles.
2. Label one circle *Author 1*. Label the other circle *Author 2*. Label the overlapping part *Both*.
3. Write as many ideas as you can about how each author is different and how both are alike.
4. Compare your diagram with a classmate's diagram. Did your classmate's diagram have any similarities or differences you could add to your diagram?

Here is an idea to get you started:
Both authors find outside sources.

Author 2

Author 1   Both

man   find outside sources   woman

Think Ahead
What do authors do after they gather information?

© Harcourt

What Do Authors Do?

BOOK TALK

After you read pages 10–13, meet with your group to discuss and answer the following questions:

1 What steps in the writing process have you read about so far? Which step do you think is the most important?

2 Why do authors throw some writing out?

3 What do people do in a writers' group? How might being a part of a writer's group be helpful to an author?

RESPONSE JOURNAL

Do you like to share your writing with others to get their opinions? Why or why not?

SKILLS IN CONTEXT

DRAW CONCLUSIONS: "DRAWING" CONCLUSIONS When you read, you should use story clues and what you know to draw conclusions. You can draw conclusions about the characters, events, and the overall message of a story.

What You Need

- **drawing paper**
- **writing tools**

What to Do

1. Draw three things the authors use to help them write their stories. Look at the pictures in the book to help you.

2. Inside each item, write a conclusion you can draw about what authors do.

3. Discuss your conclusions with a group of classmates. Then hang your drawings in the classroom.

Here is one thing you could draw:
a computer

Writers look up information.

Think Ahead
What will the author tell about next?

© Harcourt

What Do Authors Do?

BOOK TALK

After you read pages 14–17, meet with your group to discuss and answer the following questions:

❶ What problems do writers face? How do they go about solving these problems?

❷ What do the cartoons show about rejection letters that the words do not tell?

❸ What is one main idea you have learned so far about writers?

RESPONSE JOURNAL

The authors in this book get "stuck" while writing their stories. Describe how you get "unstuck" when you are writing.

Strategies Good Readers Use

FOCUS STRATEGY MAKE AND CONFIRM PREDICTIONS

Go back and check the predictions you made after you read page 5. Add to or change the predictions now that you have read more.

SKILLS IN CONTEXT

FOCUS SKILL **PREFIXES AND SUFFIXES: UN- FUN** The prefix *un-* means "not." It can be added to the beginning of some words to make new words.

What You Need

- twenty index cards
- writing tools

What to Do

1. Find the word with *un-* in the reading for today.
2. Write on the cards 20 words that might or might not be combined with *un-*. For example, *done* and *happy* can be combined with *un-* to make real words. Words such as *look*, and *start* cannot be combined with *un-* to make real words.
3. Shuffle your cards and exchange your deck with another pair or group.
4. Take turns picking cards. Try combining each word with the prefix *un-*. Tell whether it forms a real word and what it means. If necessary, look the word up in a dictionary.
5. Make a list of real words with *un-*.

Here are some more words you could write: *paid, do, pack, fold*

Think Ahead
What will the author tell about next?

What Do Authors Do?

BOOK TALK

After you read pages 18–21, meet with your group to discuss and answer the following questions:

1 Why doesn't writing end when a publisher likes a book?

2 What kinds of changes might authors have to make? Do you think these changes make their books better? Explain.

3 What has the author of this book told you so far about the writing process?

RESPONSE JOURNAL

How would you feel if a publisher asked you to change your book? Explain.

Strategies Good Readers Use

FOCUS STRATEGY USE PRIOR KNOWLEDGE

Using prior knowledge can help you understand what you read. How does what you know about writing help you understand the process the authors go through?

SKILLS IN CONTEXT

FOCUS SKILL WORD IDENTIFICATION STRATEGIES: PARTS TO WHOLES You can use many different word identification strategies to figure out words you do not know. These strategies include finding smaller parts of a large word, such as prefixes and suffixes, or finding words that form parts of larger words.

What You Need

- writing tools
- paper

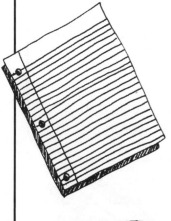

What to Do

1. Find words in this book that contain smaller words, and write them on a sheet of paper. Then list the smaller words that can be found in the larger words. For example, if you find the word *editor*, you would write *edit* on your list.

2. Trade your list of smaller words with a partner. Find and write all the larger words. For example, for *edit* you would write *editor*.

3. Use your list of larger words to check your partner's work.

Here are some larger words to get you started: *sometimes, interview*

Think Ahead What still has to happen before the book is finished?

© Harcourt

What Do Authors Do?

BOOK TALK

After you read pages 22–25, meet with your group to discuss and answer the following questions:

1 What happens right after the book writing is done?

2 How much say do authors have in how their books are illustrated?

3 Why do you think it takes so long to do the illustrations?

RESPONSE JOURNAL

Would you like to be a book designer? Why or why not?

Strategies Good Readers Use

READ AHEAD

When you do not understand something, read ahead to see if you can find more information about what you don't understand.

SKILLS IN CONTEXT

AUTHOR'S PURPOSE: A POSTER OF PURPOSES An author has a reason for writing a book. The words, pictures, and details an author includes help to get that reason across.

What You Need

- **poster board**
- **markers**

What to Do

1. Identify three choices the author makes, such as what to include, what to tell in a caption, and what to show in a cartoon.

2. List the choices on your poster.

3. Write a reason why the author made each choice.

4. Discuss with a group what the author's purpose is. Do her choices help her get her purpose across?

Here is an idea to get you started:

On page 22, the designer thinks about kinds of type. What is the purpose of showing the kinds of type as they would appear on the page? Why not just name them?

1. What to Include

2. What to Tell in a Caption

Think Ahead

What still has to happen before the book is in bookstores?

What Do Authors Do?

BOOK TALK

After you read pages 26–29, meet with your group to discuss and answer the following questions:

1 How are books printed?

2 The authors do not see their books until they are printed and bound. What does *bound* mean?

3 From start to finish, how long do you think it takes to write and make a book?

RESPONSE JOURNAL

What did you learn that you did not already know about how a book is made?

SKILLS IN CONTEXT

SEQUENCE: PRINT BY NUMBER Sequence is the order in which things happen. Understanding sequence can help you better understand what you read.

What You Need

- **self-stick notes**
- **writing materials**

What to Do

1. Number a set of self-stick notes from 1 to 7.

2. Read page 27 and carefully study the diagram. Label the steps in the printing process by placing the self-stick note with the number *1* on it next to what happens first, and so on.

3. Compare your work with a partner. Discuss the way you labeled each step. Make changes if needed.

Here is how to start: *Place the self-stick note with the number 1 on it next to the words "Big sheets of paper go in here."*

Think Ahead What comes after the celebration?

© Harcourt

What Do Authors Do?

BOOK TALK

After you read pages 30–34, meet with your group to discuss and respond to the following questions or statements:

❶ What selections in *Hidden Surprises* also teach you about a process?

❷ Write one or two sentences that tell why the author wrote the book and what her main idea is.

❸ Do you think this book does a good job of giving information? Tell why or why not.

RESPONSE JOURNAL

Do you like the way this book ends? Explain.

Strategies Good Readers Use

FOCUS STRATEGY USE PRIOR KNOWLEDGE

You can use things you already know to help you understand what you are reading. What are some things you already knew about authors before you read this book?

SKILLS IN CONTEXT

FOCUS SKILL **WORD IDENTIFICATION STRATEGIES: A BLIZZARD OF CLUES** You can use more than one word identification strategy to figure out a word. For example, you might sound out the word, look for spelling patterns, find other words that give clues, and see how the word is used in a sentence.

What You Need

- **large sheet of paper**
- **writing tools**

What to Do

1. Write *blizzard* in large letters across a sheet of paper.

2. Underline letters or letter pairs that make sounds you know. Say the sounds as you underline them.

3. Break the word into syllables by drawing a line between its two parts.

4. Look at page 32. Find the word *blizzard*. Around *blizzard* on your paper, write words from that page that help you figure out what the word means.

5. Show your paper to a classmate. Say the word *blizzard* and tell what it means.

Here is one way to start: *Underline the letters* bl *and say their sound.*

Wrap-Up

▶ **Project** **MAKE A FLOWCHART** *What Do Authors Do?* tells the steps in the process of making a book. Tell students they will be making flowcharts to show these steps in order.

- Have students form small groups and complete the Project Planner on page 187.
- Ask them to use construction paper or poster board to make a large flowchart that clearly shows these steps and their order.
- Remind students that they should write each step as clearly and briefly as possible.
- Provide time for groups to present and compare their ideas.

▶ **Writing** **PERSONAL NARRATIVE** Have students respond to the following writing prompt: **Write a personal narrative about something that took you a long time to make or do.** Have students use the copying master on page 188 to plan the narrative. Remind students to focus on word choice. Use *Hidden Surprises* pages T54–T55 for additional support. Rubrics for evaluating student writing can be found on pages 292–295.

▶ **Language Link** **HUMOR** The mistakes, or *typos*, the writers find in their books are funny. Have students write down two examples of funny mistakes and tell how the writer of *What Do Authors Do?* uses them to make the reader laugh.

═══════════ **Inquiry Project** ═══════════

What questions do students still have about how books are made? Students might enjoy learning more about printing presses and the careers of editors and others in publishing. Suggest students use a K-W-L chart to get started. They can use print and nonprint sources to find information to complete their chart.

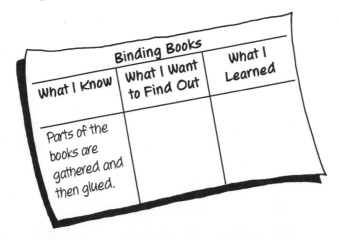

✔ **Comprehension Test** Test students' comprehension of *What Do Authors Do?* by having them complete the copying master on page 189.

Name _____

Project Planner

You have read about the many steps it takes to turn an idea into a book. Your job is to show them in a clear, orderly way.

☐ **Step 1.** List as many steps as you can in the process of making a book. Do not worry about the order right now.

_____

_____

_____

_____

_____

What You Need
- poster board
- writing materials

☐ **Step 2.** Use the organizer below to put your steps in order. If you need to, add more ovals on the back of your paper.

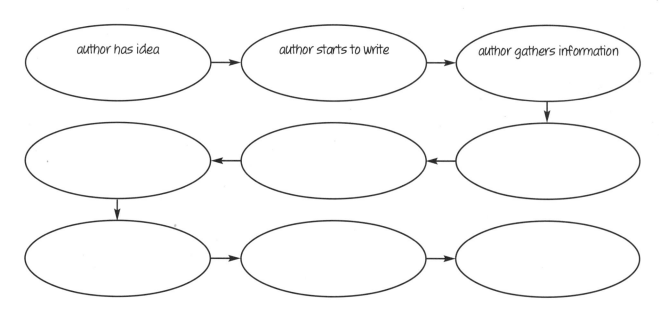

author has idea → author starts to write → author gathers information

☐ **Step 3.** Make a plan for copying your flowchart organizer onto the poster board. Work with your group to decide the clearest, shortest way to write each step. Give your work a title.

☐ **Step 4.** Explain your flowchart to the class.

© Harcourt

Personal Narrative

Write a personal narrative about something that took you a long time to make or do. How did you begin? What happened next? What did you do after that? How did it all end up? Plan your writing by listing the steps in order.

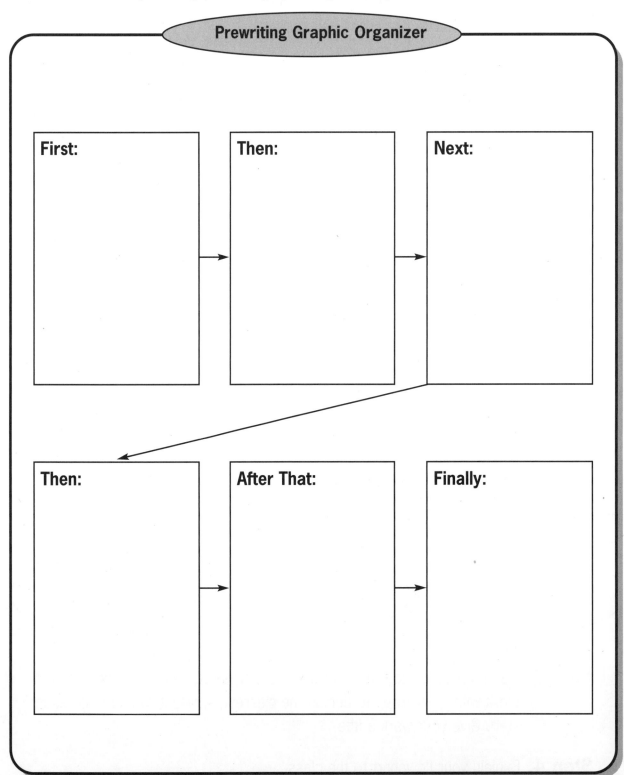

Prewriting Graphic Organizer

First:

Then:

Next:

Then:

After That:

Finally:

Name _____

Comprehension Test

Read each question below. Then mark the letter for the answer you have chosen.

1. **At the beginning of the book, what are the authors going to write about?**
   - Ⓐ their home
   - Ⓒ their pets
   - Ⓑ their friendship
   - Ⓓ the weather

2. **Which prewriting method does one of the authors use?**
   - Ⓕ freewriting
   - Ⓖ clustering
   - Ⓗ lists and outlines
   - Ⓙ a sequence chart

3. **In this book, how do authors get unstuck?**
   - Ⓐ by doing something else
   - Ⓑ by working with a writers' group
   - Ⓒ by interviewing other people
   - Ⓓ by not putting the writing down

4. **In the world of books, what is a dummy?**
   - Ⓕ a book that does not make sense
   - Ⓖ an illustration
   - Ⓗ a rough draft of the story
   - Ⓙ pictures and words on pages

5. **What does a rejection letter say?**
   - Ⓐ A contract needs to be signed.
   - Ⓑ A publisher does not want a book.
   - Ⓒ A publisher does want a book.
   - Ⓓ A publisher wants the author to make changes.

6. **What do authors usually do right after their book is accepted by a publisher?**
   - Ⓕ meet with the editor
   - Ⓖ start the next book
   - Ⓗ begin changing the book
   - Ⓙ read their reviews

7. **When is the book stitched together?**
   - Ⓐ right before the book is printed
   - Ⓑ before signatures are made
   - Ⓒ before it is glued into the cover
   - Ⓓ after type size and paper are chosen

8. **What do the authors in this book do after their books are published?**
   - Ⓕ make some changes
   - Ⓖ join a writers' group
   - Ⓗ write a dedication
   - Ⓙ meet their readers

9. **At the end of the book, what do the authors decide to write about?**
   - Ⓐ their home
   - Ⓒ their pets
   - Ⓑ their friendship
   - Ⓓ the weather

10. **On a separate sheet of paper, write a short answer in response to the question below.**
    What would you like and what would you dislike about being an author?

© Harcourt

Earth: Our Planet in Space

Reading Level

by Seymour Simon

▶ Theme Connection

"The Armadillo from Amarillo" offers a fictional look at Earth from space. "Visitors from Space" is a nonfiction account of comets. As students read *Earth: Our Planet in Space*, they will get a "real" look at Earth from space.

▶ Summary

The author reveals many of the features that make Earth unique among planets by showing photographs of Earth that were taken from space. He explores the effects of Earth's rotation, revolution, atmosphere, and magnetic field. He also looks at its geographical features and the ways in which human habitation has affected the planet.

▶ Building Background

Tell students that *Earth: Our Planet in Space* is a nonfiction book. Ask what students already know about Earth. Look at the book cover and some of the illustrations and talk about them. Explain that one purpose for reading is to be informed. Suggest that students read to find out new facts about Earth.

Author Profile

More than half of Seymour Simon's 150 science books have been named Outstanding Trade Books for Children by the National Science Teachers Association. His books on the human body and the planets in our Solar System are particularly admired. He is also the author of the Einstein Anderson series of scientific mysteries.

Additional Books by the Author

- *Animal Fact/Animal Fable*
- *Earthquakes*
- *Comets, Meteors, and Asteroids*

Vocabulary

Have students work in groups and use their prior knowledge to answer the questions below. See pages 296–299 for additional vocabulary activities. For definitions of the words, see the Glossary.

1. Who can travel past the <u>layer</u> of air that surrounds Earth?
2. How can humans make <u>photographs</u> of the <u>Solar System</u>?
3. How do scientists <u>measure distance</u>?
4. How do scientists measure <u>temperature</u>?
5. Does a <u>top</u> spin better when it is <u>tilted</u> or not?
6. What shape is an <u>orbit</u>, and why?
7. What are the dangers of <u>radiation</u> in our <u>atmosphere</u>?
8. How do the two sides of a <u>magnet</u> work differently?
9. What does an <u>aurora</u> look like?
10. What causes a mountain to <u>erode</u> so that a <u>valley</u> is formed?
11. What would an <u>astronaut</u> be trained to <u>explore</u>?

Day 1	Day 2	Day 3	Day 4
layer p. 2	Solar System p. 6	measure p. 8	orbit p. 12
	photograph p. 6	top p. 11	distance p. 12
			temperature p. 12

Day 5	Day 6	Day 7	Day 8
tilted p. 14	atmosphere p. 17	valley p. 21	astronaut p. 25
	magnet p. 18	eroded p. 22	explore p. 26
	radiation p. 18		
	aurora p. 18		

	Response	Strategies	Skills
Day 1 Pages 1–3	**Book Talk** • Generalize • Important Details • Retell **Writing:** Personal Response	**USE CONTEXT TO CONFIRM MEANING** `FOCUS STRATEGY` *Journeys of Wonder, p. T669	**REFERENTS** `FOCUS SKILL` *Journeys of Wonder, pp. T668–T669
Day 2 Pages 4–7	**Book Talk** • Important Details • Make Comparisons • Draw Conclusions **Writing:** Write a Description	Adjust Reading Rate *Journeys of Wonder, p. T455	Locating Information *Hidden Surprises, pp. T566–T567
Day 3 Pages 8–11	**Book Talk** • Make Inferences • Figurative Language • Summarize **Writing:** Personal Response	Reread *Hidden Surprises, p. T119	Paraphrase *Journeys of Wonder, pp. T454–T455
Day 4 Pages 12–13	**Book Talk** • Draw Conclusions • Important Details • Speculate **Writing:** Express Personal Opinion	**USE CONTEXT TO CONFIRM MEANING** `FOCUS STRATEGY` *Journeys of Wonder, p. T669	**REFERENTS** `FOCUS SKILL` *Journeys of Wonder, pp. T668–T669
Day 5 Pages 14–15	**Book Talk** • Summarize • Draw Conclusions • Synthesize **Writing:** Write a Description	**USE TEXT STRUCTURE AND FORMAT** `FOCUS STRATEGY` *Journeys of Wonder, p. T719	**NOTE TAKING** `FOCUS SKILL` *Journeys of Wonder, pp. T718–T719
Day 6 Pages 16–18	**Book Talk** • Make Judgments • Understand Figurative Language • Cause-Effect **Writing:** Write a Description	Create Mental Images *Hidden Surprises, p. T567	Important Details *Journeys of Wonder, pp. T536–T537
Day 7 Pages 19–23	**Book Talk** • Important Details • Summarize • Draw Conclusions/ Author's Purpose **Writing:** Cause and Effect	Use Graphic Aids *Hidden Surprises, p. T409	Cause and Effect *Journeys of Wonder, pp. T624–T625
Day 8 Pages 24–26	**Book Talk** • Make Comparisons • Theme • Express Personal Opinion **Writing:** Personal Response	**USE TEXT STRUCTURE AND FORMAT** `FOCUS STRATEGY` *Journeys of Wonder, p. T719	**NOTE TAKING** `FOCUS SKILL` *Journeys of Wonder, pp. T718–T719
Days 9–10 **Wrap-Up**	**Project** ✓ Make a Model of Earth in Space • Inquiry Project	**Writing** ✓ Rhymed Poem *Journeys of Wonder, pp. T702–T703	**Language Link** • Science Fiction **Assessment** ✓ Comprehension Test

*Additional support is provided in *Collections*.

✓ Options for Assessment

© Harcourt

Earth: Our Planet in Space

BOOK TALK

After you read pages 1-3, meet with your group to discuss and answer the following questions:

1 How is it true that all people live in the same place?

2 Earth is in space, but something separates Earth from space. What is it?

3 What do each of the colors in the photograph on page 3 represent?

RESPONSE JOURNAL

What do you think of the photograph on page 3? What are your thoughts and feelings as you look at it?

Strategies Good Readers Use

FOCUS STRATEGY **USE CONTEXT TO CONFIRM MEANING**

Readers use context to understand the meaning of a word or idea. How can you use context to find the meaning of a word in this book?

SKILLS IN CONTEXT

FOCUS SKILL **REFERENTS: REPRODUCE EARTH AS SEEN FROM SPACE** Writers use pronouns such as *it* and *them* to avoid repeating the words that they refer to. The word a pronoun refers to is called its *referent*. The directions for this project use pronouns and referents. The pronouns are underlined. Write on a sheet of paper the referent of each underlined word. Then follow the directions to create a model of Earth as seen from space.

What You Need

- notebook paper
- 17" x 22" drawing paper
- large bowl or lid
- writing and drawing tools
- cotton ball

What to Do

1. Find the picture on page 3. You are going to make a copy of <u>this</u>.
2. Draw Earth by placing a bowl on your drawing paper and drawing around <u>it</u>.
3. The gray places in the picture are land. Outline <u>them</u> on your paper.
4. The dark places are seas. Color <u>them</u> blue.
5. Pull a cotton ball until <u>it</u> is thin. Glue <u>it</u> over parts of your drawing. Make <u>it</u> look like the clouds that surround Earth.

Here is a hint to get you started:
In number 2, bowl *is the referent for* it.

Think Ahead What else will the book tell you about Earth?

© Harcourt

Earth: Our Planet in Space

BOOK TALK

After you read pages 4–7, meet with your group to discuss and answer the following questions:

1 How does the author define *planet*?

2 How is the sun different from Earth?

3 What planets are missing from the picture on pages 6 and 7? Why?

TELESCOPE

RESPONSE JOURNAL

Imagine that you are standing on the moon and looking out into space. Describe what you see.

> ### Strategies Good Readers Use
>
> ### ADJUST READING RATE
>
> Good readers change their reading speed while they read. What happened to your reading speed when you read page 6? Why?

SKILLS IN CONTEXT

LOCATING INFORMATION: USE REFERENCES TO LABEL A PICTURE Sometimes an author does not provide all the information you need to understand what you are reading. When this happens, good readers go to reference sources for help. Reference sources include dictionaries, encyclopedias, and other resources. Use the text on page 6 and reference sources to reproduce and label the photograph on pages 6 and 7.

What You Need

- **drawing paper**
- **writing and drawing tools**
- **reference sources (encyclopedia, book about the planets)**
- **clear tape**

What to Do

1. Draw the picture on pages 6 and 7.

2. Label the parts that are clearly identified in the text on page 6.

3. Use reference sources to identify and label the other planets.

4. Draw and label the planets that are missing on pages 6 and 7 on a separate piece of paper. Tape this paper to the bottom edge of your drawing.

Here is a sentence to get you started: *Earth is shown rising over the surface of the moon.*

Think Ahead

Do you expect to read more about Earth or more about the other planets?

© Harcourt

Earth: Our Planet in Space

BOOK TALK

After you read pages 8–11, meet with your group to discuss and answer the following questions:

1 Why would people long ago have thought Earth was flat?

2 How is Earth like a ball? How is it like a top?

3 Why does Earth have night and day?

RESPONSE JOURNAL

How do you feel when you look at the sky at night? What do you wonder or think about?

> **Strategies Good Readers Use**
>
> **REREAD**
>
> *R*ereading helps readers find or check information. When have you used the strategy of rereading in this book?

SKILLS IN CONTEXT

PARAPHRASE: PICTURES AND PARAPHRASES Paraphrasing is putting ideas in your own words. This can help you understand what you have read. Make your own drawings. Write paraphrases that explain what your pictures show.

What You Need

- drawing paper
- writing and drawing tools

What to Do

1. Fold a sheet of drawing paper in half, short side to short side. Open it up again.

2. Draw Earth's shadow traveling across the moon on the left side of your paper. Under your drawing, write a title and paraphrase of the first paragraph on page 8 to explain the illustration.

3. Draw day and night on Earth on the right side of your paper. Then write a title and paraphrase a paragraph from pages 8–11 to explain why we have day and night on Earth.

Here is the beginning of a paraphrase to get you started: *This picture shows Earth's shadow moving across the moon. The curve of the shadow shows . . .*

Think Ahead
The Earth spins around the sun. How far is Earth from the sun?

© Harcourt

Earth: Our Planet in Space

BOOK TALK

After you read pages 12 and 13, meet with your group to discuss and answer the following questions:

1 How many times have you traveled around the sun? How do you know?

2 How close are Earth and the sun? Why is this important?

3 What would happen if Earth's orbit changed?

RESPONSE JOURNAL

Do you think there could be life on other planets?

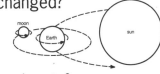

Strategies Good Readers Use

FOCUS STRATEGY USE CONTEXT TO CONFIRM MEANING

Give examples to show how you have used context to confirm meaning as you read this book.

SKILLS IN CONTEXT

FOCUS SKILL **REFERENTS: REFERENT RECORD** Writers use pronouns to avoid repeating words. The word a pronoun takes the place of is its referent. Revisit *Earth: Our Planet in Space* to find examples of pronouns and referents.

What You Need

- **drawing paper**
- **writing tools**

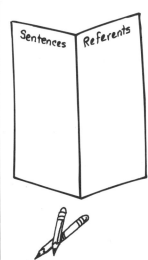

What to Do

1. Fold your paper in half, long side to long side. Now open it up.

2. Write *Sentences* at the top of the left side and *Referents* at the top of the right side.

3. Search pages 1–12 for sentences that use pronouns. Choose five of these sentences. Copy them onto your paper under *Sentences*.

4. Number each sentence. Circle the pronouns.

5. Look at the sentence or go back to the book to find the referent of each pronoun. Write the referent for each pronoun under *Referents*.

Here's a sentence to get you started: *While Earth is spinning, it also travels around the sun in a path called an orbit.*

Think Ahead What happens during a year on Earth? What might the author explain next?

© Harcourt

Earth: Our Planet in Space

BOOK TALK

After you read pages 14 and 15, meet with your group to discuss and answer the following questions:

1 What important information is given on pages 14 and 15?

2 Where do you think the seasons change least? Why?

3 What happens to the length of days and nights as the seasons change? Why?

RESPONSE JOURNAL

Describe what the seasons are like where you live. Which is your favorite? Why?

Strategies Good Readers Use

FOCUS STRATEGY USE TEXT STRUCTURE AND FORMAT

Captions and labels give important information. How do the labels help you understand the illustrations on pages 14 and 15?

SKILLS IN CONTEXT

FOCUS SKILL **NOTE TAKING: EARTH NOTES PUZZLE** Taking notes helps readers understand and remember what they have read. The best way to take notes is to write the important information in your own words. Make a puzzle using notes that you take from the book.

What You Need

- writing paper
- drawing paper
- writing and drawing tools
- scissors
- glue

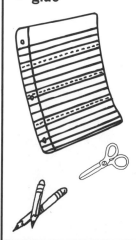

What to Do

1. Reread pages 14–15. Take notes about the Earth's seasons. Write one note on every other line.
2. Glue your note-taking paper to a sheet of drawing paper. Make a picture on the back of the drawing paper.
3. Cut your notes into strips. Cut between your notes so you have one idea on each strip.
4. Mix up the strips. Try to put your notes back together in order.
5. Turn over the strips. If you are right, you will see your picture as you drew it. If not, try again.

Here is a note to get you started:
When the northern half of Earth is tilted toward the sun, the northern half of Earth has summer.

Think Ahead
What keeps the Earth from getting too hot during summer?

© Harcourt

BOOK TALK

After you read pages 16–18, meet with your group to discuss and answer the following questions:

❶ How important is Earth's atmosphere? Why?

❷ Why does the author say that Earth's magnetic field is like a shield?

❸ What is an aurora? What causes it?

RESPONSE JOURNAL

How would you explain an aurora to someone who has never seen one?

SKILLS IN CONTEXT

IMPORTANT DETAILS: DIAGRAM OF EARTH'S ATMOSPHERE AND MAGNETIC FIELD

Details help readers understand main ideas. Details answer the questions *who, where, when, why, what,* and *how.* Draw a diagram that shows Earth, its atmosphere, and its magnetic field as you picture them.

What You Need

- **paper for taking notes**
- **drawing paper**
- **writing and drawing tools**

What to Do

1. Draw a circle on your paper to represent Earth. Leave space around it to draw the atmosphere and the magnetic field.

2. Find details in the book that help you understand the atmosphere. Draw and label the atmosphere on your diagram. Under the label, list details that tell *what, where,* and *why* about the atmosphere.

3. Find details in the book that help you understand the magnetic field. Draw and label the magnetic field on your diagram. Under the label, list details that tell *what, where,* and *why* about the magnetic field.

Here is a sentence to get you started:
Earth has a blanket of air around it that keeps it from getting too hot or too cold.

Think Ahead
The author is zooming in closer to Earth. What will he look at next?

Earth: Our Planet in Space

BOOK TALK

After you read pages 19–23, meet with your group to discuss and answer the following questions:

1 How much of Earth is covered by oceans? Why is this fact important for people to know?

2 How do natural forces change Earth's surface? How fast do they work?

3 How do you think the photos on pages 22–24 were taken? Why would the author use these photos instead of photos taken on the land?

RESPONSE JOURNAL

Describe a place where you have seen water at work. How is it changing the land?

Strategies Good Readers Use

USE GRAPHIC AIDS

Graphic aids, such as maps, diagrams, and pictures, help readers understand what they read. Graphic aids can also add information. Explain what you see in the pictures on pages 20, 22, and 23.

SKILLS IN CONTEXT

CAUSE AND EFFECT: EROSION CAUSE-AND-EFFECT FLAP CHART An event (what happens) usually has a cause (a reason why the event happens). Understanding cause-and-effect relationships helps you understand what you read. Use *Earth: Our Planet in Space* to find causes and effects of natural forces that change land. Make a flap chart to show these relationships.

What You Need

- **17" x 22" drawing paper**
- **writing and drawing tools**
- **scissors**

What to Do

1. Fold a piece of drawing paper in half the long way. Fold it into quarters, then eighths. Open the paper.

2. Cut each line from the left edge to the center. You will end up with four flaps that fold over the uncut half of your paper.

3. With the paper folded, draw and write on each flap a cause that involves a river, a waterfall, ice, or snow.

4. Under each flap, tell or show how the natural force changes land.

Here are details to get you started: *"The dark line is a deep river valley"* (effect). *"Over many years the river has scraped deep into the land"* (cause).

Think Ahead Do any other forces change land?

© Harcourt

BOOK TALK

After you read pages 24–26, meet with your group to discuss and answer the following questions:

1 What stories in *Journeys of Wonder* have you read that seem similar to *Earth: Our Planet in Space*? Explain.

2 What are some themes in *Earth: Our Planet in Space*?

3 Do you think space exploration should continue? Why?

RESPONSE JOURNAL

What topic in this book is most interesting to you? Why? What reference sources can you use to learn more about this topic?

Strategies Good Readers Use

FOCUS STRATEGY USE TEXT STRUCTURE AND FORMAT

Illustrations and captions help readers understand ideas. Give examples of how text structure and format helped you understand this book.

SKILLS IN CONTEXT

FOCUS SKILL **NOTE TAKING: "WHAT PEOPLE DO" CHART** Taking notes helps readers understand and remember what they have read. The best way to take notes is to write the important information in your own words. Take notes on the human activities described on pages 24–26. Record the information in a chart.

What You Need

- writing paper
- writing tools
- ruler

What to Do

1. Title your paper *What People Do*.
2. Make a two-column chart. Make the first column about an inch wide. Make the second column at least five inches wide.
3. Label the first column *Page Number* and the second column *Important Information*.
4. Reread pages 24–26. Take notes about what people do. Write the notes and page numbers on your chart. Use your own words when you can.
5. Write the book title and the author's name above or below your chart.

Here is an example to get you started: *page 24: People change the land by farming and digging for rocks.*

Wrap-Up

▶ **Project** MAKE A MODEL OF EARTH IN SPACE Talk with students about the title of the book. Tell students that they will be using information from the book to help them make a model of Earth in space.

- Organize students into groups and have them discuss the information they will need to make the model.
- Ask students to complete the copying master on page 201 to plan their models.
- Have each group present its model to the class.

▶ **Writing** RHYMED POEM Have students respond to the following writing prompt: **Write a rhymed poem about Earth.** Have students use the copying master on page 202 to brainstorm ideas and details. Remind students to focus on word choice. Use *Journeys of Wonder* pages T702–T703 for additional support. Rubrics for evaluating student writing are provided on pages 292–295.

▶ **Language Link** SCIENCE FICTION Explain to students that science fiction writing combines science and imagination. Invite students to think of science fiction stories and movies set in space. Have them talk about the stories' characters, settings, and plots. Ask them to explain what parts of the story are science-based and what parts are imaginary.

Inquiry Project

Earth: Our Planet in Space can be a springboard for inquiry into a variety of topics and ideas. Have students brainstorm topics they would like to know more about and organize their responses in a web. Students can use reference books and the Internet to begin their inquiry projects. They may also be able to use community resources.

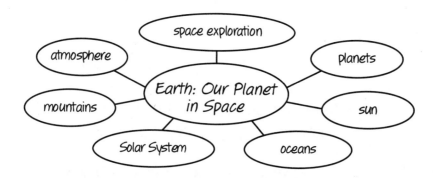

✔ **Comprehension Test** Test students' comprehension of *Earth: Our Planet in Space* by having them complete the copying master on page 203.

Name _____

Project Planner

In *Earth: Our Planet in Space*, you learned about how Earth looks from
space. Use information from this book to help you create a model of Earth in space.

☐ **Step 1.** Plan with your group what a model of Earth
as seen in space might show. Make a list
of all the things you want to include.

_____

_____

_____

_____

_____

What You Need
- black paper
- drawing paper
- writing and drawing tools
- scissors
- glue

☐ **Step 2.** Discuss what you learned about Earth and the Solar System from *Earth: Our Planet in Space*. Use the web below to brainstorm information to include in your model.

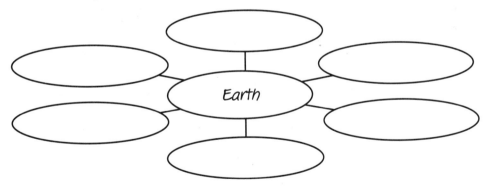

Earth

☐ **Step 3.** Make a sketch to plan your model. Draw, color, and cut out the pieces for your model. Arrange them on the black paper and glue them down.

☐ **Step 4.** Write a label that identifies and gives details about each piece of the model and attach it to the paper.

☐ **Step 5.** Present your model to the class.

Name _____

Rhymed Poem

Write a rhymed poem about Earth. Use information you have learned about Earth in your poem. Use the graphic organizer below to plan your poem.

Prewriting Graphic Organizer

Topic: _____

Audience: _____

Rhyme Pattern: _____

Beat Pattern: _____

Image 1: _____

Comparison/colorful words: _____

_____

Image 2: _____

Comparison/colorful words: _____

_____

Image 3: _____

Comparison/colorful words: _____

_____

© Harcourt

Name _____

Comprehension Test (Test Prep)

Read each question below. Then mark the letter for the answer you have chosen.

1. **What can you see when you look at Earth from space?**
   - Ⓐ your house
   - Ⓑ New York City
   - Ⓒ seas and land
   - Ⓓ people

2. **What is the sun?**
   - Ⓕ a planet
   - Ⓖ a star
   - Ⓗ a moon
   - Ⓙ a shadow

3. **How big is the sun?**
   - Ⓐ a million times bigger than Earth
   - Ⓑ the same size as Earth
   - Ⓒ the same size as the moon
   - Ⓓ less than half the size of Earth

4. **How many planets orbit our sun?**
   - Ⓕ none
   - Ⓖ four
   - Ⓗ six
   - Ⓙ nine

5. **Why do we have day and night on Earth?**
   - Ⓐ because Earth spins like a top
   - Ⓑ because Earth is slightly pear-shaped
   - Ⓒ because the sun rises and sets
   - Ⓓ because Earth orbits the sun

6. **How long does it take Earth to orbit the sun?**
   - Ⓕ twenty-four hours
   - Ⓖ one year
   - Ⓗ ninety-three years
   - Ⓙ ninety-three million years

7. **Which is *not* in Earth's atmosphere?**
   - Ⓐ dust
   - Ⓒ water
   - Ⓑ gases
   - Ⓓ minerals

8. **What would happen if Earth's magnetic field were destroyed?**
   - Ⓕ Radiation from the sun would destroy life.
   - Ⓖ Space travel would be easier.
   - Ⓗ The surface of Earth would change quickly.
   - Ⓙ It would always be daytime.

9. **Which is a main idea in *Earth: Our Planet in Space*?**
   - Ⓐ Earth is a unique planet.
   - Ⓑ People make Earth a special place.
   - Ⓒ Space travel will soon be common.
   - Ⓓ People should take care of Earth.

10. **On a separate sheet of paper, write a short answer in response to the question below.**
    Why can Earth support life? Think about Earth's atmosphere, its magnetic field, and its distance from the sun.

The Chickenhouse House

Reading Level

by Ellen Howard

▶ Theme Connection

As students read *The Chickenhouse House*, they will learn about a girl whose family moves into a chickenhouse. As in "Cloudy with a Chance of Meatballs" and "The Crowded House," change helps story characters appreciate the meaning of "home."

▶ Summary

Alena and her family move by horse-drawn wagon from Grandfather's house to a new farm on the prairie. For the first winter, they live in the chickenhouse, the only building that Alena's father has built. In the spring, once the crops are planted, her parents and their friends and relatives work together to build a big, new house. Although Alena had disliked the chickenhouse when she first arrived, she has come to love its coziness, and finds the new house too big. With her father's help, she comes to cope with change.

▶ Building Background

Tell students that *The Chickenhouse House* is historical fiction about a girl whose family lives for a while in a chickenhouse. Explain that the story is set in the past. Have students discuss what life was like for early settlers in America, based on their reading and what they know. Then have students read to be entertained and to find out why Alena and her family live in a chickenhouse and what the chickenhouse looks like.

Author Profile

Award-winning author Ellen Howard once remarked that the joy of writing a book "goes on and on, as we watch our book go out into the world in the same way we watch our children grow up." Howard often sets her books in earlier times, basing plot events on stories told to her by her grandmother.

Additional Books by the Author
- *Circle of Giving*
- *When Daylight Comes*
- *Gillyflower*

Vocabulary

Have students examine the vocabulary words and think of ways to group them. Then have them create a chart like the one below. Ask them to create headings for groups of words that are related by subject, structure, or meaning. See pages 296–299 for additional vocabulary activities. For definitions of the words, see the Glossary.

Words about Feelings	Words about Weather	Words w/ Prefixes or Suffixes	Words w/ More Than One Meaning

Day 1	Day 2	Day 3	Day 4
wagon p. 1	quilts p. 10	cleared p. 15	blizzard p. 21
prairie p. 2	fetch p. 11	helper p. 17	favorite p. 21
building p. 4	unpack p. 14		stocking p. 22
bare p. 7			
homey p. 8			

Day 5	Day 6	Day 7	Day 8
spells p. 25	cellar p. 31	settled p. 39	silence p. 46
plow p. 26	frame p. 35	lonely p. 41	cozy p. 49
unbroken p. 27	carpenter p. 36	icy p. 42	

© Harcourt

	Response	Strategies	Skills
Day 1 **Chapter 1**	**Book Talk** • Important Details • Main Idea • Summarize **Writing:** Draw Conclusions	**MAKE AND CONFIRM PREDICTIONS** `FOCUS STRATEGY` *Journeys of Wonder*, p. T153	**FIGURATIVE LANGUAGE** `FOCUS SKILL` *Journeys of Wonder*, pp. T152–T153
Day 2 **Chapter 2**	**Book Talk** • Cause-Effect • Sequence • Author's Craft **Writing:** Personal Response	Use Prior Knowledge *Hidden Surprises*, p. T71	Reality and Fantasy *Hidden Surprises*, pp. T452–T453
Day 3 **Chapter 3**	**Book Talk** • Compare and Contrast • Determine Characters' Emotions • Draw Conclusions **Writing:** Make Comparisons	Self-Question *Hidden Surprises*, p. T453	Fact and Opinion *Journeys of Wonder*, pp. T112–T113
Day 4 **Chapter 4**	**Book Talk** • Author's Craft • Make Comparisons • Author's Viewpoint **Writing:** Author's Purpose	**MAKE AND CONFIRM PREDICTIONS** `FOCUS STRATEGY` *Journeys of Wonder*, p. T153	**FIGURATIVE LANGUAGE** `FOCUS SKILL` *Journeys of Wonder*, pp. T152–T153
Day 5 **Chapter 5**	**Book Talk** • Draw Conclusions • Sequence • Speculate **Writing:** Personal Response	**CREATE MENTAL IMAGES** `FOCUS STRATEGY` *Journeys of Wonder*, p. T197	**SKIM AND SCAN** `FOCUS SKILL` *Journeys of Wonder*, pp. T196–T197
Day 6 **Chapter 6**	**Book Talk** • Synthesize • Summarize • Determine Characters' Emotions **Writing:** Summarize	Reread *Hidden Surprises*, p. T119	Sequence *Journeys of Wonder*, pp. T20–T21
Day 7 **Chapter 7**	**Book Talk** • Author's Craft • Figurative Language • Determine Characters' Emotions **Writing:** Identify with Characters	Summarize *Hidden Surprises*, p. T161	Story Elements *Hidden Surprises*, pp. T274–T275
Day 8 **Chapter 8**	**Book Talk** • Make Comparisons • Determine Theme • Identify with Characters **Writing:** Synthesize	**CREATE MENTAL IMAGES** `FOCUS STRATEGY` *Journeys of Wonder*, p. T197	**SKIM AND SCAN** `FOCUS SKILL` *Journeys of Wonder*, pp. T196–T197
Days 9–10 **Wrap-Up**	**Project** ✓ Create a Prairie Diorama • Inquiry Project	**Writing** ✓ Comparison and Contrast Essay *Journeys of Wonder*, pp. T44–T45, T96–T97	**Language Link** • Sensory Words **Assessment** ✓ Comprehension Test

*Additional support is provided in *Collections*.
✓ Options for Assessment

The Chickenhouse House

BOOK TALK

After you read Chapter 1, meet with your group
to discuss and answer the following questions:

1 What time of year is it when the story begins? Give three
details that help you picture the story setting.

2 Why do Alena and her family have to live in the chickenhouse?

3 What are Alena's first impressions
of the chickenhouse?

Strategies Good Readers Use

FOCUS STRATEGY MAKE AND CONFIRM PREDICTIONS
*P*redict whether Alena will like living in a chicken-house. Check your prediction as you read.

RESPONSE JOURNAL

Are Alena's experiences what you expected for the children of settlers? Explain.

SKILLS IN CONTEXT

FOCUS SKILL **FIGURATIVE LANGUAGE: DEAR DIARY** When writers use figurative language, they say one thing but mean another. Write a diary entry that
Alena might have written as she sat on the blanket beside Fritz. Use figurative
language to tell about the events described in Chapter 1.

What You Need

- notebook paper
- construction paper
- hole punch
- yarn
- pen or pencil
- drawing tools

What to Do

1. Look for details in Chapter 1 that tell what Alena sees
and feels. List them on a sheet of notebook paper.

2. Circle the details you will include in your diary. Think
about how to describe them with figurative language.

3. Write your diary entry on a clean sheet of paper.

4. Use construction paper to make an illustrated cover.
Punch holes in your diary entry, extra sheets of paper,
and your cover. Use yarn to bind the cover and pages.

5. Add to your diary as you finish reading the remaining
chapters.

Alena's Diary

Here is an example to get you started:
*Alena looked at the prairie grass: "I looked
out over a golden sea of prairie grass."*

Think Ahead
What will Alena's family have to do as they settle into their new home?

© Harcourt

BOOK TALK

After you read Chapter 2, meet with your group to discuss and answer the following questions:

1 Why does Alena have trouble going to sleep her first night in the chickenhouse?

2 What happens the morning after the family moves into the chickenhouse?

3 What does the line "Her eyes stung and she cried, perhaps because of the smoke" suggest about Alena's feelings? How else does the author show what Alena is feeling?

RESPONSE JOURNAL

What would you say to cheer up Alena?

Strategies Good Readers Use

USE PRIOR KNOWLEDGE

Write three things you know about the early settlers that helped you understand the characters and events in the story.

SKILLS IN CONTEXT

REALITY AND FANTASY: TOPSY'S WORLD COMIC STRIP Realistic stories tell about people, places, and events that could really exist. Stories that are fantasies tell about things that are make-believe. *The Chickenhouse House* is a realistic story. When Alena talks to Topsy, Topsy does not answer because cows do not talk. Create a comic strip called "Topsy's World" in which Topsy talks to Alena.

What You Need

- notebook paper
- oaktag strip
- ruler
- writing and drawing tools

What to Do

1. Revisit Chapter 1 to recall Alena's feelings about the chickenhouse. Reread Alena's conversation with Topsy in Chapter 2. Jot down details on notebook paper.

2. Decide what Topsy might say to Alena.

3. Use a ruler to divide an oaktag strip into four frames.

4. Use your notes to create your comic strip. Put Topsy's words and Alena's words in speech balloons.

5. Present your comic strip to your classmates.

Here is a question to get you started: *What might Topsy say when Alena asks, "Don't you miss your big barn, Topsy?"*

Think Ahead How will Alena feel the next time she visits her grandparents' house?

© Harcourt

The Chickenhouse House

BOOK TALK

After you read Chapter 3, meet with your group to discuss and answer the following questions:

1 How have Alena's feelings about the chickenhouse changed since the beginning of the story?

2 How do you think Alena feels when her grandmother hugs Emily and tells Emily that she is a good helper?

3 Why is Alena glad when it is time to leave her grandparents' house on Thanksgiving Day?

RESPONSE JOURNAL

How was Thanksgiving dinner at Grandmother's like other family celebrations you have read about or experienced yourself?

> **Strategies Good Readers Use**
>
> ### SELF-QUESTION
>
> Write two questions you asked yourself about characters and events as you read. How did asking questions help you understand the characters' feelings?

SKILLS IN CONTEXT

FACT AND OPINION: IS THAT A FACT? A fact is a statement that can be checked or proven. An opinion tells what someone feels or believes, and cannot be proven. Create a game called "Is That a Fact?"

What You Need

- **notebook paper**
- **ten index cards**
- **writing tools**

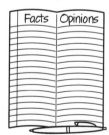

What to Do

1. Find five facts and five opinions in Chapter 3. List them in two columns on a sheet of notebook paper. Then write each fact and opinion on a separate index card.

2. Read a card aloud to a partner. If your partner correctly identifies the statement as a fact or an opinion, your partner gets the card. If not, explain why it is a fact or an opinion and keep the card.

3. Take turns until you have both read all of your cards. The person with the most cards wins.

Here are sentences from the story to get you started: *"Baby Fritz napped in his crib." (fact)*
"It was rather nice, listening to the rain on the roof of the chickenhouse house." (opinion)

Think Ahead — What will the winter holidays be like?

© Harcourt

The Chickenhouse House

BOOK TALK

After you read Chapter 4, meet with your group to discuss and answer the following questions:

1. What details help you picture what winter is like on the prairie?

2. Compare how William reacts to his stocking to how Alena reacts. What do Alena's reactions tell you about her?

3. How do you think the author feels about families and holidays? What clues do you get from the story?

RESPONSE JOURNAL

What do you think the author wants you to feel about the chickenhouse house?

Strategies Good Readers Use

FOCUS STRATEGY MAKE AND CONFIRM PREDICTIONS

Write down predictions about what the family will do when spring comes. Confirm or revise your predictions when you read Chapter 5.

SKILLS IN CONTEXT

FOCUS SKILL **FIGURATIVE LANGUAGE: TELL ME A RIDDLE!** Figurative language often includes words or phrases that have more than one meaning. To understand figurative language, think about what meaning makes the most sense. Alena's family has to stay inside during the blizzard. Imagine that they tell each other riddles. Using figurative language from the story, create a book of riddles.

What You Need

- notebook paper
- construction paper
- writing and drawing materials

The Chickenhouse House Riddles

What to Do

1. Revisit Chapters 1–4. List words with more than one meaning that you can use in riddles. Circle the words that you will use to write two riddles.

2. Write each riddle at the top of a sheet of paper. Write the answer in smaller letters upside down at the bottom.

3. Work with your classmates to assemble the riddles in a book. Add an illustrated construction paper cover.

4. Read riddles from your book aloud.

Here is an example from the story to get you started: *"Alena could hear the wind howl."* A riddle might be: What howls at night and begins with w but isn't a wolf? (wind)

Think Ahead
How will the prairie change when winter ends?

© Harcourt

The Chickenhouse House

BOOK TALK

After you read Chapter 5, meet with your group to discuss and answer the following questions:

1 What story clues help you know that churning butter is hard work?

2 What does Father have to do on the farm before he can build the house?

3 What does Alena probably know about birds and their nests that makes her put on her mittens?

RESPONSE JOURNAL

Is Alena sad simply because the bird left its nest? Explain.

SKILLS IN CONTEXT

FOCUS SKILL **SKIM AND SCAN: SKIM AND SCAN BOOKMARK** When you skim a story, you read very quickly to find out how it is organized and what it is about. When you scan a story, you read very quickly to find specific information. You do not read every word when you skim or scan. Imagine that you are looking at *The Chickenhouse House* for the first time. Create a bookmark that has skimming and scanning rules.

What You Need

- **7" x 2½" piece of stiff white paper**
- **writing and drawing tools**

What to Do

1. Think about how to skim Chapter 5 to find out what it is about and how to scan it for specific information.

2. Write rules for skimming and scanning on one side of the bookmark.

3. Using the rules you wrote, skim and scan Chapter 5. Write the main idea of Chapter 5 and two details on the back of the bookmark.

Here is an idea to help you get started:
Scan to find signs of spring on the prairie.

Rules for Skimming and Scanning

Think Ahead
Do you think Father will build the new house all by himself?

© Harcourt

BOOK TALK

After you read Chapter 6, meet with your group to discuss and answer the following questions:

❶ Why is it important to keep the cellar cool in summer?

❷ What happens on house-raising day?

❸ How do you think Alena feels when she finds out that it will be a while before the family can move into the new house?

RESPONSE JOURNAL

How do family and neighbors help Alena's family? Why do you think they are so willing to help?

Strategies Good Readers Use

REREAD

*W*rite about a time when rereading an earlier passage in the story helped you understand a character's feelings or actions later in the story.

SKILLS IN CONTEXT

SEQUENCE: HOUSE-BUILDING CHECKLIST   When you tell the sequence of events in a story, you tell the order in which they happened. Alena and her family are getting closer to moving into their new house. Create a checklist to keep track of each step in the house-building process as described in Chapter 6.

What You Need

- notebook paper
- writing tools

What to Do

1. Revisit Chapter 6 to review the sequence describing how Alena's house was built. Write all the steps on a sheet of paper. Include steps still to be completed. Number them in the order that they happen.

2. Copy the steps on a clean sheet of paper. Draw small check boxes next to each step.

3. Check each step that has been completed by the end of Chapter 6. Check off the remaining items as you read.

Here is an idea from the story to help you get started: *The first thing Father did to prepare to build the new house was burn off prairie grass on the rise.*

☐ 1. Burn off prairie grass on rise of ground.
☐ 2. Dig the cellar with the help of family and friends.
☐ 3. Line cellar walls with stone slabs.

Think Ahead
Will Alena feel at home in the big, new house?

The Chickenhouse House

BOOK TALK

After you read Chapter 7, meet with your group to discuss and answer the following questions:

1 How does the author show you that Alena has grown since she moved from her grandfather's house?

2 What does the author mean when she says that "Alena had a funny feeling at the bottom of her stomach"?

3 How do you know that Alena does not feel at home in the big, new house? What does she do?

RESPONSE JOURNAL

Would you have been happy or unhappy to move into the new house if you were Alena? Why?

Strategies Good Readers Use

SUMMARIZE

Write a brief summary of what happens in Chapter 7. Use your own words and tell only the most important parts.

SKILLS IN CONTEXT

STORY ELEMENTS: WHAT IF? Thinking about the way the setting, characters, and plot work together can help you understand and enjoy a story. Create a story-elements game in which you change what happens in the story.

What You Need

- notebook paper
- paper plate
- cardboard
- bracket to attach spinner
- writing tools

What to Do

1. Review Chapter 7. Jot down ideas for a new character, setting detail, story event, and ending for the chapter.

2. Work with a small group. Divide a paper plate into four sections. Write one of these words in each section: *setting, character, event, ending*. Draw an arrow on the cardboard. Write *What if?* on the arrow. Cut it out and attach it to the center of the plate with a bracket.

3. Spin the arrow. Wherever the arrow lands, tell your idea for a change. Begin with *What if . . . ?* Take turns spinning the arrow and telling your ideas.

Here's an idea to help you get started: *What if it was raining when Alena went out to the chickenhouse?*

Think Ahead
What will happen to the chickenhouse? How will Alena feel?

© Harcourt

The Chickenhouse House

BOOK TALK

After you read Chapter 8, meet with your group to discuss and answer the following questions:

1 What stories in *Journeys of Wonder* show characters who have odd or strange homes?

2 What message about home do you think the author wants readers to understand?

3 How does Alena's story help you understand what life was like for children of settlers on the prairie?

RESPONSE JOURNAL

How did living in the chickenhouse house change Alena?

> **Strategies Good Readers Use**
>
> **FOCUS STRATEGY** **CREATE MENTAL IMAGES**
>
> *W*rite one or two sentences to explain how creating mental pictures helped you understand and enjoy what you read in Chapter 8.

SKILLS IN CONTEXT

FOCUS SKILL **SKIM AND SCAN: BOOK JACKET** You skim to find the main idea of a story. You scan to find specific information. Imagine that *The Chickenhouse House* was published one chapter at a time in small booklets. Design and create a book jacket for *Chapter 8: The Chickenhouse House*, using what you know about skimming and scanning to get information to include on your book jacket.

What You Need

- **notebook paper**
- **construction paper**
- **ruler and scissors**
- **writing and drawing tools**
- **paste**

What to Do

1. Skim Chapter 8 to find its main idea. Scan to find three details. Jot down the main idea and details.

2. Make two columns on a clean sheet of paper. In one column, write a short paragraph telling what Chapter 8 is mainly about. In the other, write specific details. Use your notes to help you write. Cut the columns apart.

3. Fold a piece of construction paper in half to make a cover. Write the title and decorate your cover with illustrations that tell about the chapter.

4. Open the paper. Paste the main idea along the left edge and the details along the right edge.

5. Present your book jacket to your classmates.

Here is a detail to get you started: *Father puts nesting boxes in the chickenhouse to prepare for the arrival of two dozen chicks.*

© Harcourt

Wrap-Up

▶ **Project** **CREATE A PRAIRIE DIORAMA** Remind students that this story is about settlers who began a new life on the open prairie. Tell them that they will research the American prairie in the days of the early settlers and then create a diorama to help them better understand Alena's experiences.
- Organize students into small discussion groups.
- Have them share both what they have learned about the prairie and early settlers from reading and what else they might like to learn.
- Ask them to complete the copying master on page 215 to plan what they will include in their dioramas.
- Then have each group work together to design and build their dioramas.

▶ **Writing** **COMPARISON AND CONTRAST ESSAY** Have students respond to the following writing prompt: **Write a short essay that compares and contrasts the chickenhouse to the new house.** Remind students to focus on organization. Have students use the copying master on page 216 to plan their essays. Use *Journeys of Wonder* pages T44–T45 and T96–T97 for additional support. Rubrics for evaluating student writing are provided on pages 292–295.

▶ **Language Link** **SENSORY WORDS** Point out to students that sensory words describe how things look, sound, smell, feel, and taste. Writers use sensory words to help readers feel as if they are part of the story. Ask students to create a sensory word web, with circles for each of the five senses: *Sight, Hearing, Taste, Smell,* and *Touch.* Then have them record sensory words and phrases from *The Chickenhouse House* that help them feel as if they are experiencing events along with Alena.

Inquiry Project

The Chickenhouse House can be a springboard for inquiry into many different topics and ideas. Ask students to brainstorm prairie environment topics that they would like to know more about and organize their responses in a web. Encourage students to plan and do their research using reference books and the Internet. You may choose to tie in several of the students' inquiry projects with their wrap-up project.

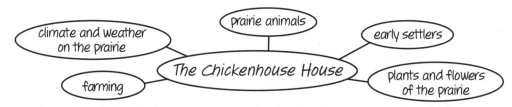

✔ **Comprehension Test** Test students' comprehension of *The Chickenhouse House* by having them complete the copying master on page 217.

Name _____

Project Planner

Use what you learned from reading this story and from additional research to create a diorama that shows a prairie setting in the days of the settlers.

☐ **Step 1.** Discuss with your group what kinds of details your diorama will include. Jot down your ideas.

_____

_____

_____

What You Need

- empty shoe box
- drawing materials
- construction paper
- scissors
- paste
- reference sources

☐ **Step 2.** Discuss with your group what you learned about the prairie from reading *The Chickenhouse House*. Use the graphic organizer below to brainstorm additional facts and details to use in your diorama.

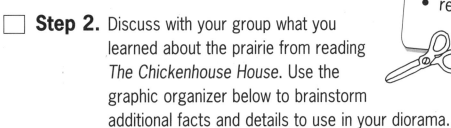

THE PRAIRIE ENVIRONMENT		
WEATHER AND LANDSCAPE	PLANTS	ANIMALS

☐ **Step 3.** Decide how to display the information in a diorama. You can show one season or divide your diorama into four sections to show all four seasons.

☐ **Step 4.** Build your diorama. Create a background landscape. Arrange cutout figures of plants and animals. Include a figure of Alena's chickenhouse house.

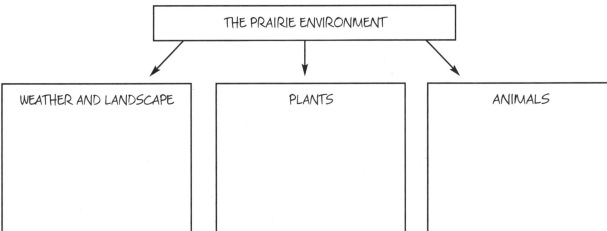

☐ **Step 5.** Present the diorama to the class.

Name _____

Comparison and Contrast Essay

Write a short essay that compares and contrasts the chickenhouse to Alena's new house. Before you begin, complete the Venn diagram below to brainstorm what is the same and what is different about the two houses. When you write your essay, write one paragraph about how the houses are alike and another paragraph about how they are different. In your last paragraph, write a conclusion that tells something about both houses.

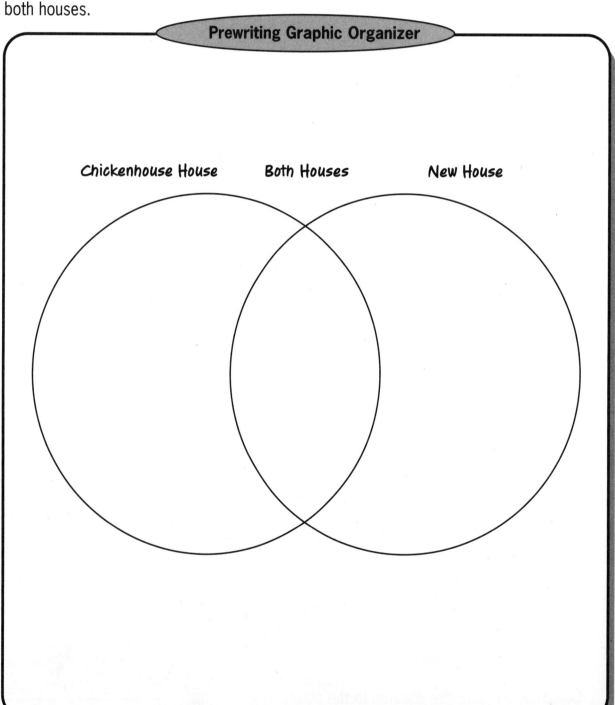

Prewriting Graphic Organizer

Chickenhouse House   Both Houses   New House

Name _____

Comprehension Test

Read each question below. Then mark the letter for the answer you have chosen.

1. **The chickenhouse has windows because—**
   - Ⓐ chickens need lots of sunlight.
   - Ⓑ Alena's family will live in it.
   - Ⓒ it used to be Grandfather's home.
   - Ⓓ all chickenhouses have windows.

2. **How many actual rooms are there in the chickenhouse?**
   - Ⓕ one
   - Ⓖ two
   - Ⓗ four
   - Ⓙ six

3. **How might Alena describe Grandfather's house on Thanksgiving?**
   - Ⓐ quiet but fun
   - Ⓑ dim and bare
   - Ⓒ warm and cozy
   - Ⓓ crowded and noisy

4. **On Christmas, Alena worries that—**
   - Ⓕ William will lick the window.
   - Ⓖ dinner will be canceled.
   - Ⓗ Saint Nicholas will not find her.
   - Ⓙ wind will blow down the chicken-house.

5. **Which of these would you probably *not* see on the prairie?**
   - Ⓐ little-boys'-breeches and Johnny-jump-ups
   - Ⓑ tall grass and cottonwood trees
   - Ⓒ robins and thrushes
   - Ⓓ palm trees and seagulls

6. **How long does it take to frame, roof, and side the new house?**
   - Ⓕ about one year
   - Ⓖ about two days
   - Ⓗ about one month
   - Ⓙ all summer

7. **What does the family do just before moving out of the chickenhouse?**
   - Ⓐ move furniture into the new house
   - Ⓑ hang wallpaper
   - Ⓒ whitewash the cellar
   - Ⓓ build a winding staircase

8. **How does Alena feel as she looks out the window of her new room?**
   - Ⓕ She misses the oak tree.
   - Ⓖ She misses her grandparents.
   - Ⓗ She wants to decorate her room.
   - Ⓙ She misses the chickenhouse.

9. **What is a nesting box?**
   - Ⓐ a box that holds a nest that falls from a tree
   - Ⓑ a box to keep chicks warm and dry
   - Ⓒ a box that sits inside another box
   - Ⓓ another name for a robin's nest

10. **On a separate sheet of paper, write a short answer to this question:**
    What does Alena mean when she says, "It may take a little while for the chicks to get used to their chickenhouse house"?

© Harcourt

Aldo Ice Cream

by Johanna Hurwitz

Reading Level

▶ Theme Connection
As students read *Aldo Ice Cream*, they will learn about family relationships and community connections. Like the family in "The Three Little Javelinas," Aldo's family is close. In addition, the characters in both stories are able to solve problems.

▶ Summary
It is summer vacation, and nine-year-old Aldo Sossi has several goals. By the end of the summer, he wants to learn to swim, teach his friend DeDe's dog some new tricks, earn enough money to buy his sister an ice-cream freezer for her birthday, and eat every flavor of ice cream sold in a local store. The summer fills up with other accomplishments as well, as Aldo reaches out in friendship to some elderly housebound neighbors and wins the Grubby Sneakers Contest.

▶ Building Background
Tell students that *Aldo Ice Cream* is realistic fiction. Aldo's parents and two sisters are supporting characters. Ask students if they always get along with their siblings. Have they ever done something special for a sibling? Explain that Aldo and his mom deliver Meals-on-Wheels to elderly people. Ask students to share what they know about volunteer services in their community. Invite students to read to be entertained.

Author Profile
At the age of ten, award-winning author Johanna Hurwitz had already decided that she would be a writer and a librarian. Like *Aldo Ice Cream*, many of Hurwitz's books star fourth-grader Aldo Sossi and his older sisters. "I write for children because I am especially interested in that period of life," she has said. "There is an intensity and seriousness about childhood which fascinates me."

Additional Books by the Author
- *The Adventures of Ali Baba Bernstein*
- *Aldo Applesauce*
- *Baseball Fever*

Vocabulary

Have groups work together to write the words on one set of index cards and the definitions on another set of index cards. Then have the groups place the cards face down to play a memory game in which they take turns trying to pick matching words and definitions. See pages 296–299 for additional vocabulary activities. For definitions of the words, see the Glossary.

Day 1	Day 2	Day 3	Day 4
vegetarian p. 25	equivalent p. 52	gloomy p. 80	disqualified p. 110
somber p. 29	ichthyology p. 53	acquire p. 82	reduced p. 113
extravagant p. 31	appetizing p. 54	fund p. 88	mortified p. 116
	proclaimed p. 65		mournfully p. 117
	hurricane p. 65		

	Response	Strategies	Skills
▶ Day 1 **Chapters 1–2**	**Book Talk** • Determine Characters' Traits • Summarize • Determine Characters' Emotions **Writing:** Personal Response	**USE PRIOR KNOWLEDGE** `FOCUS STRATEGY` *Journeys of Wonder,* p. T305	**COMPARE AND CONTRAST** `FOCUS SKILL` *Journeys of Wonder,* pp. T304–T305
▶ Day 2 **Chapters 3–5**	**Book Talk** • Express Personal Opinion • Cause/Effect • Make Judgments **Writing:** Make Comparisons	Read Ahead *Hidden Surprises,* p. T525	Sequence *Journeys of Wonder,* pp. T20–T21
▶ Day 3 **Chapters 6–7**	**Book Talk** • Cause/Effect • Important Details • Draw Conclusions **Writing:** Respond to Story	Reread *Hidden Surprises,* p. T119	Story Elements *Hidden Surprises,* pp. T274–T275
▶ Day 4 **Chapters 8–9**	**Book Talk** • Make Comparisons • Determine Theme • Make Judgments **Writing:** Personal Response	**USE PRIOR KNOWLEDGE** `FOCUS STRATEGY` *Journeys of Wonder,* p. T305	**COMPARE AND CONTRAST** `FOCUS SKILL` *Journeys of Wonder,* pp. T304–T305

▶ Day 5
Wrap-Up

Project
✓ Make a Board Game
• Inquiry Project

Writing
✓ Research Report
Journeys of Wonder, pp. T330–T331

Language Link
• Dialogue

Assessment
✓ Comprehension Test

*Additional support is provided in *Collections.*
✓ Options for Assessment

Aldo Ice Cream

BOOK TALK

Read Chapters 1 and 2. Then meet with your group to discuss and answer the following questions:

1 What are Aldo's character traits? Give examples from the story to support your ideas.

2 What are Aldo's goals? How is he working toward them?

3 How do you know that Aldo likes helping his mother deliver meals-on-wheels?

RESPONSE JOURNAL

Write about some goals you have.

Strategies Good Readers Use

FOCUS STRATEGY USE PRIOR KNOWLEDGE

What parts of this story do you have experience with? Write two examples to show how what you already know helps you understand the story.

SKILLS IN CONTEXT

FOCUS SKILL COMPARE AND CONTRAST: COMPARE AND CONTRAST DIAGRAM Comparing characters can help you learn more about them. Aldo and DeDe are best friends. Make a Venn diagram to compare and contrast their traits, feelings, and actions.

What You Need

- drawing paper
- round or oval object, such as a small bowl or a large lid
- writing and drawing tools

What to Do

1. Put the round or oval object on your paper, but not in the center, and trace around it.
2. Move the object over to trace your second circle. Make sure that your second circle overlaps the first.
3. Above the middle section, write *Both*. Above one circle, write *Aldo*. Above the other circle, write *DeDe*.
4. In the middle section, write how Aldo and DeDe are alike. In the outer sections, write how each character is different.

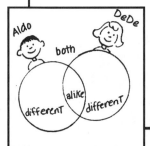

Here is an idea to get you started:
Aldo: *loves to try new things*
DeDe: *sticks with what she likes.*

Think Ahead
Do you think Aldo's and Karen's wishes will come true? Explain.

© Harcourt

Aldo Ice Cream

BOOK TALK

Read Chapters 3–5. Then meet with your group to discuss and answer the following questions:

❶ What do you think of the quarter-a-day plan?

❷ How does Mr. Puccini change, and why?

❸ What do you think of Aldo's "cats-on-wheels" plan? How well does the plan work?

RESPONSE JOURNAL

Compare Aldo's sisters. Which of them do you like better, and why?

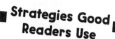

Strategies Good Readers Use

READ AHEAD

☆Often, readers figure out the meaning of a word by reading ahead. Try this strategy with *ichthyology* (page 53) and *restricted* (page 55).

SKILLS IN CONTEXT

SEQUENCE: COMIC STRIP SEQUENCE Sequence is the order of events or ideas. Comic strips show events in sequence. Make a comic strip to show the sequence of events in Aldo's cats-on-wheels plan to cheer up Mrs. Nardo. Look at the illustration on page 58. What events happen before the event in the picture? What events happen after? List the main events in sequence. Mark the events you want to include in your comic strip.

What You Need

- **drawing paper**
- **writing and drawing tools**
- **ruler**

What to Do

1. Using your ruler, divide your paper into quarters.
2. Draw the events in order. Put one drawing in each box. Use a new sheet of paper to show more events.
3. Label each event.
4. Color your drawings.
5. Leave your comic strip as is, or cut the pictures apart and use them in a sequencing game.

Here is an idea to get you started:

Aldo picked the cat up and put him into the carton.

Think Ahead
What do you think will happen next in the story? List some predictions.

Aldo Ice Cream

BOOK TALK

Read Chapters 6 and 7. Then meet with your group to discuss and answer the following questions:

❶ What happens because Aldo reads the *Pennysaver*?

❷ What is the deal Aldo makes with his mother?

❸ Why is Aldo worried about Trevor?

RESPONSE JOURNAL

Imagine that you want to make some money. Which of Aldo's methods would you try? Why? What other methods might you try?

Strategies Good Readers Use

REREAD

*R*ereading helps readers check information and notice details. Reread the part of the story that helps you answer one of the questions you just discussed.

SKILLS IN CONTEXT

STORY ELEMENTS: STORY ELEMENTS WIND SOCK Story elements include characters, setting, plot, and theme. Make a wind sock that shows the story elements in *Aldo Ice Cream*.

What You Need

- **construction paper, light colors**
- **writing tools**
- **scissors**
- **stapler or tape**
- **ribbon or yarn**

What to Do

1. Cut two pieces of construction paper in thirds, for a total of six pieces.
2. Write *Characters* at the top of one strip and list all the characters. Write a few words to describe each one. Illustrate the main character.
3. Label three other strips *Setting*, *Plot*, and *Themes*. Describe and illustrate the setting(s), list the plot events, and write the theme(s).
4. Write the title and author on the last two strips. Staple or tape the ends to form a ring. Attach a piece of ribbon to it to make a handle.
5. Staple or tape each paper strip around the ring.

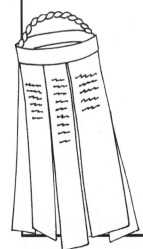

Here is an idea to get you started:
Use the pictures and chapter titles to help you decide what to include in each section of your wind sock.

Think Ahead
What do you think will happen in the contest?

© Harcourt

Aldo Ice Cream

BOOK TALK

Read Chapters 8 and 9. Then meet with your group to discuss and answer the following questions:

1 What stories have you read that seem similar to *Aldo Ice Cream*? Explain.

2 What are some themes, or main ideas, in *Aldo Ice Cream*?

3 Did you like the way the story turned out? Why?

RESPONSE JOURNAL

What do you like about this story? Is it the characters, setting, plot, or theme? Is it something else? Explain.

> **Strategies Good Readers Use**
>
> **FOCUS STRATEGY USE PRIOR KNOWLEDGE**
>
> You can use your experiences and knowledge to connect with story characters. Have you ever been in a contest like Aldo?

SKILLS IN CONTEXT

FOCUS SKILL **COMPARE AND CONTRAST: SOLUTION COMPARISON CHART** Often, the main character in a story has a problem to solve. He or she may try several ways to solve it before finding a solution that works. Aldo tries three methods for raising the funds to buy Karen's gift. Make a chart that summarizes each method and evaluates the results. The chart will help you compare Aldo's methods.

What You Need

- **17" x 22" drawing paper**
- **writing tools**

What to Do

1. Fold your paper in thirds.

2. In each section, copy the form at the left.

3. Fill out a form for each method Aldo tried. Give the method a number and a title, such as *1. Get a job*. For *Summary*, tell how Aldo tried to get money. For *Evaluation*, tell what happened. Write *yes* or *no* to answer the last question.

Here is an idea to get you started: *"Suddenly his eye stopped at an ad that sounded perfect for himself."* (page 34) HINT: Method 2 is in Chapter 3, and Method 3 starts in Chapter 6.

Wrap-Up

▶ Project   MAKE A BOARD GAME

Tell students they are going to make a board game based on *Aldo Ice Cream*. Invite them to name some simple, familiar board games and compare how they are played. For example, how is the board designed? What else is needed to play? Note some ideas for making games based on *Aldo Ice Cream*. For example, details from the story could become spaces on a board or questions on cards in a draw pile.

- Organize students into groups and have them decide what tasks will be involved in making a game.
- Have them complete the copying master on page 225 to plan what they will do and who will do each part.
- Schedule a game day where everyone can play the finished games.

▶ Writing   RESEARCH REPORT

Have students respond to the following writing prompt: **Write a research report about hurricanes**. Review the prewriting strategies and note-taking strategies, and have students take notes on hurricanes. Have students use the copying master on page 226 to help them create an outline for their report. Remind them that using an outline helps them to organize their ideas. Use *Journeys of Wonder*, pages T330–T331 for additional support. Rubrics for evaluating student writing can be found on pages 292–295.

▶ Language Link   DIALOGUE

Explain to students that a character's words can show what the character is like. For example, on page 30 Karen says about the ice-cream machine, "Actually, everyone in the family would get pleasure out of it." Her words show thoughtfulness and generosity. Have students find conversations in the story, read them aloud with one or more partners, and decide what traits or feelings the dialogue shows. Students can then use dialogue to compare and contrast characters.

Inquiry Project

Aldo Ice Cream can be a springboard for inquiry into a variety of topics and ideas. Have students brainstorm topics they would like to know more about and organize their responses in a web. Students can use reference books and the Internet to begin their inquiry projects. For some projects, they may be able to explore community resources.

✔ Comprehension Test

Test students' comprehension of *Aldo Ice Cream* by having them complete the copying master on page 227.

Name _____

Project Planner

In *Aldo Ice Cream* the main character rolls through his summer by setting goals, planning strategies, taking chances, and changing course when necessary. Use ideas in the story to create a board game based on *Aldo Ice Cream*.

☐ **Step 1.** Discuss with your group some familiar board games. Use the chart below to compare the board, other parts, and the point of each game. Decide these elements for your own game.

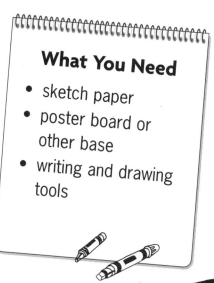

What You Need
- sketch paper
- poster board or other base
- writing and drawing tools

Name of Game	Description of Board	Other Parts	Point of the Game
Game 1:			
Game 2:			
Game 3:			
Our Game:			

☐ **Step 2.** Together, brainstorm a list of ideas and details from the story to use in your game. Consider characters, setting, plot, and key ideas. How will you use these elements? What other information will you use or need to find? On a separate sheet of paper, make a web of your ideas.

☐ **Step 3.** As a group, talk about what you need to do to create your game. Make a list of tasks and who will do each one.

☐ **Step 4.** Work together to create the game board, other materials, and list of rules. Each person in the group should do a piece of the project.

☐ **Step 5.** As a group, share your game with the class. Let other groups play your game, while you play theirs.

© Harcourt

Research Report

Write a research report about hurricanes. Take notes from various
resources on hurricanes. Then organize your notes and group ideas that seem to go
together. Use the graphic organizer below to write an outline for your report. Then use
the outline to write your report.

Prewriting Graphic Organizer

Title: _____

Introduction: _____

   A. _____

   B. _____

Middle: _____

   A. _____

      1. _____

      2. _____

   B. _____

      1. _____

      2. _____

Conclusion: _____

© Harcourt

Name _____

Comprehension Test

 Test Prep

Read each question below. Then mark the letter for the answer you have chosen.

1. **What is the setting of *Aldo Ice Cream*?**
   - Ⓐ winter
   - Ⓑ spring
   - Ⓒ summer
   - Ⓓ autumn

2. **Which is *not* one of Aldo's goals?**
   - Ⓕ teaching DeDe's dog tricks
   - Ⓖ learning to swim
   - Ⓗ trying every flavor of ice cream
   - Ⓙ learning to ride a bicycle

3. **How does Aldo meet Mr. Puccini?**
   - Ⓐ by helping his mom deliver Meals-on-Wheels
   - Ⓑ by visiting DeDe at her grandparents' house
   - Ⓒ by entering the Grubby-Sneaker Contest
   - Ⓓ by asking questions at the pet store

4. **Who wants an ice-cream maker?**
   - Ⓕ Aldo's mother
   - Ⓖ Aldo's friend DeDe
   - Ⓗ Aldo's sister Karen
   - Ⓙ Aldo's sister Elaine

5. **How does Aldo make friends with Mrs. Nardo?**
   - Ⓐ He brings his cat to visit her.
   - Ⓑ He invites her over for lunch.
   - Ⓒ He takes an interest in her pet fish.
   - Ⓓ He delivers her newspaper.

6. **What will happen if Aldo wins the Grubby-Sneaker Contest?**
   - Ⓕ His family will get new shoes.
   - Ⓖ His mom will give him his sneaker money to buy the ice-cream maker.
   - Ⓗ Aldo will get a trophy.
   - Ⓙ He will win a vacation for his family.

7. **Why is Aldo worried about Trevor?**
   - Ⓐ He is mean to Aldo.
   - Ⓑ He wants Aldo's sneakers.
   - Ⓒ He has the dirtiest sneakers.
   - Ⓓ DeDe likes Trevor better than Aldo.

8. **DeDe helps Aldo win by**
   - Ⓕ helping Aldo get his sneakers dirty.
   - Ⓖ helping him find his sneakers.
   - Ⓗ telling the judge Trevor is visiting.
   - Ⓙ telling his mother about the contest.

9. **Which is a main idea in *Aldo Ice Cream*?**
   - Ⓐ Families need ice-cream makers.
   - Ⓑ Family and friends make life happier.
   - Ⓒ Some friends are better than others.
   - Ⓓ People should not enter unfair contests.

10. **On a separate sheet of paper, answer the question below.**
    Imagine that you are Mr. Puccini or Mrs. Nardo. Explain how you met Aldo. Tell what you think of Aldo and why.

The Wave

Reading Level

by Margaret Hodges

Author Profile

Margaret Hodges is best known for her retellings of classical legends and myths. Her main characters include Saint Francis of Assisi, Joan of Arc, Gulliver, King Arthur, Saint George, Saint Patrick, Johnny Appleseed, Psyche, and Baldur from Norse mythology.

Additional Books by the Author
- *Hidden in the Sand*
- *Silent Night: The Song and Its Story*
- *The True Tale of Johnny Appleseed*

Theme Connection In *The Wave*, students will encounter a wise old man who understands nature. As in "Turtle Bay," students will see this wise old man using his knowledge to help others.

Summary After a mild earthquake, the villagers gather on the shore to watch the sea roll back. Watching from his mountaintop home, Ojiisan recognizes the meaning of the receding sea. To call the villagers away from certain death, he sets fire to his rice fields. The villagers run up the mountain, planning to help fight the fire. As a result, all are saved from the tidal wave that destroys the village.

Building Background Display the book cover, read the title, and show some of the illustrations. Ask students to tell what they know about earthquakes and tidal waves. Then have students set a purpose for reading *The Wave* by sharing a prediction with a partner about what kind of wave this is and what it will do.

Vocabulary

Have students complete a chart like the one below for the vocabulary words. Have them supply the kind of word that works best: a synonym, an antonym, or a related word. See pages 296–299 for additional vocabulary activities. For definitions of the words, see the Glossary.

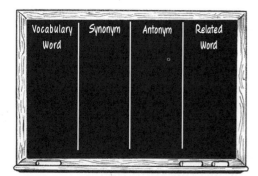

Vocabulary Word	Synonym	Antonym	Related Word

Day 1	Day 2	Day 3	Day 4
calm p. 1	torch p. 15	horizon p. 22	ebbed p. 34
waves p. 1	flames p. 16	muttered p. 26	typhoon p. 34
storm p. 1	blaze p. 20	tidal wave p. 29	debt p. 38
celebrate p. 7			
festival p. 9			
earthquake p. 9			

© Harcourt

	Response	Strategies	Skills
Day 1 Pages 1–11	**Book Talk** • Note Details • Compare and Contrast • Make Predictions **Writing:** Respond to a Character	**USE CONTEXT TO CONFIRM MEANING** FOCUS STRATEGY *Hidden Surprises,* p. T323	**DRAW CONCLUSIONS** FOCUS SKILL *Hidden Surprises,* pp. T322–T323
Day 2 Pages 12–21	**Book Talk** • Compare and Contrast • Retell • Determine Characters' Emotions **Writing:** Journal Entry from Character's Viewpoint	Create Mental Images *Hidden Surprises,* p. T567	Figurative Language *Journeys of Wonder,* pp. T152–T153
Day 3 Pages 22–33	**Book Talk** • Note Details • Make Judgments • Sequence **Writing:** Personal Opinion	Self-Question *Hidden Surprises,* p. T453	Homophones *Hidden Surprises,* pp. T656–T657
Day 4 Pages 34–38	**Book Talk** • Make Comparisons • Determine Theme • Express Personal Opinion **Writing:** Continue the Story	**USE CONTEXT TO CONFIRM MEANING** FOCUS STRATEGY *Hidden Surprises,* p. T323	**DRAW CONCLUSIONS** FOCUS SKILL *Hidden Surprises,* pp. T322–T323
Day 5 Wrap-Up	**Project** ✓ Write a TV Ad • Inquiry Project **Writing** ✓ Description *Hidden Surprises,* pp. T102–T103 **Language Link** • Vocabulary Power **Assessment** ✓ Comprehension Test		

*Additional support is provided in *Collections.*
✓ Options for Assessment

The Wave

BOOK TALK

After you read pages 1–11, meet with your group to discuss and answer the following questions:

1 What is "all the wealth of the people" in this story?

2 What makes Ojiisan different from the other villagers?

3 What do you think is going to happen?

RESPONSE JOURNAL

What do you think of Ojiisan so far? In your journal, tell why you would or would not like to meet him.

> **Strategies Good Readers Use**
>
> **FOCUS STRATEGY USE CONTEXT TO CONFIRM MEANING**
>
> *L*ist the context clues you could use to find the meaning of the word *harvest* on page 3.

SKILLS IN CONTEXT

FOCUS SKILL **DRAW CONCLUSIONS: MAKE A DIAGRAM** Sometimes an author does not state an idea directly. You can figure it out for yourself by drawing a conclusion. When you draw conclusions, you put words and ideas from the story together with your own knowledge.

What You Need

- **cardboard, paper, or poster board**
- **writing tools and a straight edge**

What to Do

1. Decide on one conclusion you can draw from this section of the story.

2. Illustrate how you drew the conclusion. First, draw one box, label it *Story Clue*, and write the clue. Second, draw another box, label it *My Knowledge*, and write what you know already. Third, draw a box, label it *Conclusion*, and write your conclusion.

3. Connect the boxes with symbols such as arrows.

4. Display your diagram.

Here is an idea to get you started:

Story Clue: *The villagers' houses are all right next to the bay.*

Think Ahead
What could happen when there is an earthquake?

© Harcourt

The Wave

BOOK TALK

After you read pages 12–21, meet with your group to discuss and answer the following questions:

❶ Why does Ojiisan understand what is happening when the other villagers do not?

❷ How does Ojiisan draw the villagers out of danger?

❸ How do you think Ojiisan feels about what he must do?

RESPONSE JOURNAL

Imagine you are Tada. Tell what you are thinking as Grandfather burns the fields.

Strategies Good Readers Use

CREATE MENTAL IMAGES

Picture in your mind what the shore looks like when the sea "runs away from the land." Make a sketch showing how unusual this looks.

SKILLS IN CONTEXT

FIGURATIVE LANGUAGE: ILLUSTRATE STORY IMAGES Figurative language creates a picture in your mind. Often, it makes comparisons that help you understand the events or feelings in a story.

What You Need

- crayons, paints, pastels, torn paper and glue, or other materials for making pictures
- paper

What to Do

1. Find the description on page 20 of the people hurrying up from the village. Or find another example of figurative language.
2. Show what the author helps you "see." You can draw, paint, or use bits of torn paper and glue.
3. Label your drawing with the words from the story that describe it.
4. Hang your illustration in the classroom.

Here is another idea from the story: *"Flames raced through Ojiisan's fields."*

Think Ahead What will Ojiisan do now?

The Wave

BOOK TALK

After you read pages 22–33, meet with your group to discuss and answer the following questions:

1 Who goes to Ojiisan's fields?

2 Do you think that Ojiisan was wise to burn his fields? Explain.

3 After everyone reaches Ojiisan's rice field, what happens next?

RESPONSE JOURNAL

What is your opinion of Ojiisan? What is your opinion of the villagers? Record your feelings in your journal.

> **Strategies Good Readers Use**
>
> ### SELF-QUESTION
>
> Write a question about something in the book you are not sure you understand. How could you find the answer to this question?

SKILLS IN CONTEXT

HOMOPHONES: PLAY A HOMOPHONE MATCHING GAME Homophones are words that sound alike but are spelled differently. For example, *see* and *sea* are homophones. On pages 22–33, there are at least 14 words that have homophones. How many can you find?

What You Need

- writing tools
- at least 30 index cards

What to Do

1. Write on index cards each of the words from the reading that have homophones. Write one homophone for each on separate cards.
2. Shuffle the cards, and lay them out face down.
3. With a partner, take turns turning over two cards at a time. If you make a match, keep the cards. If not, return the cards face down to the playing surface.

Here are some words from pages 22–33 and their homophones:
wait, weight; seen, scene; whole, hole

Think Ahead
What will be destroyed? Who or what will be saved?

© Harcourt

BOOK TALK

After you read pages 34–38, meet with your group to discuss and answer the following questions:

1. In *The Wave*, one person uses wisdom and courage to save a whole village. What other selections in *Hidden Surprises* show smart thinking and good actions that help others?

2. What do you think is the most important idea in this story?

3. What did you think was exciting or boring about this story?

RESPONSE JOURNAL

What do you think life was like for the people after the tidal wave? Tell about it in your journal.

Strategies Good Readers Use

FOCUS STRATEGY **USE CONTEXT TO CONFIRM MEANING**

Write a word from the story that you did not know. Then write the words that come before or after it that help you understand its meaning. Finally, write a meaning for the word.

SKILLS IN CONTEXT

FOCUS SKILL **DRAW CONCLUSIONS: GIVE A HOW-TO SPEECH** When you draw conclusions, you do so step-by-step. You use what the story says and you put it together with your own knowledge.

What You Need

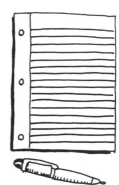

- writing materials

What to Do

1. Identify two or three conclusions you drew while reading. Write them down. Then write down the story clues and the knowledge you combined to draw the conclusions.

2. Prepare a short how-to speech on how to draw a conclusion. Describe the process you used while reading *The Wave*.

3. Present your speech to the class.

Here are some ideas to get you started: *You might have drawn conclusions about tidal waves, the relationship between Tada and Ojiisan, or life in Japan long ago.*

Wrap-Up

▶ Project
WRITE A TV AD Have students imagine that *The Wave* is being made into a major motion picture. Their job is to plan an ad for it that will appear on television.
- Organize students into groups to think about the words, sounds, and images that will appear in this ad.
- Have them complete the copying master on page 235.
- Provide an opportunity to present their ad ideas to the class.

▶ Writing
DESCRIPTION Have students respond to the following writing prompt: **Write a description of the tidal wave that hits the village.** Have students use the copying master on page 236 to plan their descriptions. Encourage students to make effective word choices. Use *Hidden Surprises* pages T102–T103 for additional support. Rubrics for evaluating student writing are provided on pages 292–295.

▶ Language Link
VOCABULARY POWER Many words in this story relate to fire and burning. Have students make a chart listing words from the story that name each of the following: things that burn, colors of burning things, results of burning, tools to burn with, action words that tell about burning, and other words related to burning.

Inquiry Project

The Wave can be a springboard for inquiry into a variety of topics that students would like to learn more about. Have students brainstorm topics such as Japan long ago, Japanese festivals, growing rice, or tidal waves. Remind students that a good way to find answers to their questions is by doing research and taking notes.

> Rice
> -important grain in Asia
> -like wheat in the United States
> -grown in wet areas called paddies

✔ **Comprehension Test** Test students' comprehension of *The Wave* by having them complete the copying master on page 237.

Name _____

Project Planner

Imagine that *The Wave* is being made into a movie. Write the words for the movie ad. Next to the words, write some ideas for pictures, or draw some sketches to show on the screen. Also, note some sounds or music that viewers should hear.

☐ **Step 1.** What should a viewer learn about *The Wave* in order to want to see it? You want to make it sound exciting but you don't want to give it away completely. List below some ideas for what viewers might see, hear, and learn in your ad.

What You Need

• writing and drawing materials

_____

_____

_____

_____

☐ **Step 2.** Plan your TV ad. Use the flowchart below to list some of the words, pictures, and sounds that might go together.

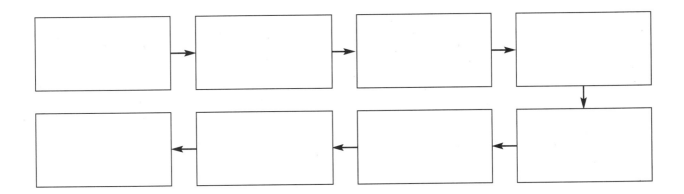

☐ **Step 3.** Work with your group to write your ad. Be sure to include words, sounds, and pictures that will go together to create interest.

☐ **Step 4.** Exchange your ideas with other groups. Tell which ideas you like best.

Description

Write a description of the tidal wave that hits the village. You can add details not given in the story. Use this organizer to plan your writing.

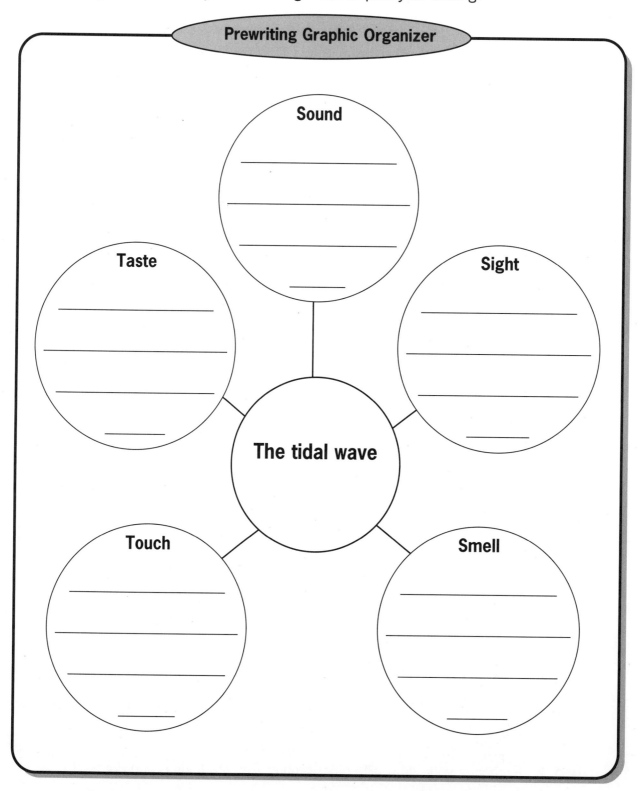

Prewriting Graphic Organizer

Sound

Taste

Sight

The tidal wave

Touch

Smell

Name _____

Comprehension Test

Read each question below. Then mark the letter for the answer you have chosen.

1. **When and where does this story take place?**
   - Ⓐ not long ago in Japan
   - Ⓑ long ago in Japan
   - Ⓒ not long ago in Hawaii
   - Ⓓ long ago on an island far away

2. **Why are the rice fields so important?**
   - Ⓕ They are beautiful.
   - Ⓖ They are next to the temple.
   - Ⓗ They are the reason for the festival.
   - Ⓙ They are the wealth of the people.

3. **Who is Tada?**
   - Ⓐ a villager who lives by the sea
   - Ⓑ the son of Ojiisan
   - Ⓒ the grandson of Ojiisan
   - Ⓓ the person who tells the story

4. **Why doesn't the idea of an earthquake frighten Tada?**
   - Ⓕ Japan has many earthquakes.
   - Ⓖ Earthquakes do not do much damage.
   - Ⓗ Ojiisan protects Tada from earthquakes.
   - Ⓙ Earthquakes are good for the land.

5. **What does Ojiisan alone realize?**
   - Ⓐ that the sea is rising
   - Ⓑ that a tidal wave is coming
   - Ⓒ that the earthquake will never stop
   - Ⓓ that the village has been destroyed

6. **Why is Ojiisan able to use his own fields as a warning?**
   - Ⓕ They are next to the sea.
   - Ⓖ They are in the center of the village.
   - Ⓗ They are high up the mountain.
   - Ⓙ They are the largest in the village.

7. **Why does Ojiisan choose fire as a method of warning?**
   - Ⓐ It is the fastest, best method.
   - Ⓑ People will come to watch it.
   - Ⓒ It will burn the whole village.
   - Ⓓ It is what his grandfather taught him to do.

8. **Why do the villagers come running when they see the fire?**
   - Ⓕ They know a tidal wave is coming.
   - Ⓖ They know there must be danger.
   - Ⓗ They know that an earthquake is coming.
   - Ⓙ They come to help put the fire out.

9. **Which words best describe Ojiisan?**
   - Ⓐ wise, old, selfish
   - Ⓑ wise, quick-thinking, kind
   - Ⓒ friendly, chatty, rich
   - Ⓓ kind, thoughtful, slow

10. **On a separate sheet of paper, write a short answer in response to the question below.**
    What did you learn about tidal waves in this book?

© Harcourt

Ramona Quimby, Age 8

Reading Level

by Beverly Cleary

Theme Connection
Like "Centerfield Ballhawk," *Ramona Quimby, Age 8* spotlights growing up and family relationships.

Summary
Ramona is having a hard time adjusting to third grade. She worries about her teacher disliking her, the boy she calls Yard Ape making fun of her, and her parents needing more money. With the help of a mysterious stranger, Ramona learns that although every family has its ups and downs, sticking together is vital.

Building Background
Tell students that *Ramona Quimby, Age 8* is a realistic story about a third-grade girl. Ask students to name some of the experiences that eight-year-olds have. Also ask them to talk about what it is like to start third grade and start a new school. Explain that this story is written to entertain. Have students write a prediction about what will happen to Ramona.

Author Profile
Beverly Cleary worked as a librarian before she published her first book for children in 1950. Since that time, Cleary has written dozens of books for middle-school and younger readers. Several of them star Ramona, one of her most popular characters.

Additional Books by the Author
- *Beezus and Ramona*
- *Henry Huggins*
- *Emily's Runaway Imagination*

Vocabulary

Have students write sentences using as many vocabulary words as they can. For example, "She finished her *homework* and met her friends at the *playground*." "The *principal* was *anxious* to see what the *excitement* on the *playground* was all about." See pages 296–299 for additional vocabulary activities. For definitions of the words, see the Glossary.

> She finished her *homework* and met her friends at the *playground*.

Day 1	Day 2	Day 3	Day 4
excitement p. 11	fad p. 56	mechanic p. 112	sobs p. 167
cafeteria p. 25	giggles p. 61	patient p. 127	stranger p. 178
anxious p. 26	principal p. 64	commercials p. 132	
playground p. 29	nuisance p. 68		
homework p. 52			

	Response	Strategies	Skills
Day 1 Chapters 1–2	**Book Talk** • Determine Characters' Traits • Synthesize • Author's Craft **Writing:** Express Personal Opinion	**USE REFERENCE SOURCES** `FOCUS STRATEGY` *Hidden Surprises,* p. T657	**HOMOGRAPHS AND HOMOPHONES** `FOCUS SKILL` *Hidden Surprises,* pp. T656–T657
Day 2 Chapters 3–5	**Book Talk** • Classify • Determine Characters' Traits • Note Details **Writing:** Relate to Character	Use Graphic Aids *Hidden Surprises,* p. T409	Characters' Feelings and Actions *Journeys of Wonder,* pp. T262–T263
Day 3 Chapters 6–7	**Book Talk** • Retell • Interpret Characters' Emotions • Make Predictions **Writing:** Write a Personal Narrative	Summarize *Hidden Surprises,* p. T161	Prefixes and Suffixes *Hidden Surprises,* pp. T20–T21
Day 4 Chapters 8–9	**Book Talk** • Make Comparisons • Theme/Author's Perspective • Express Personal Opinion **Writing:** Write Advice for a Character	**USE REFERENCE SOURCES** `FOCUS STRATEGY` *Hidden Surprises,* p. T657	**HOMOGRAPHS AND HOMOPHONES** `FOCUS SKILL` *Hidden Surprises,* pp. T656–T657

Day 5
Wrap-Up

Project
✓ Make a Book Cover
• Inquiry Project

Writing
✓ Persuasive Review
Hidden Surprises, pp. T596–T597

Language Link
• Common and Proper Nouns

Assessment
✓ Comprehension Test

© Harcourt

*Additional support is provided in *Collections.*
✓ Options for Assessment

Ramona Quimby, Age 8

BOOK TALK

After you read pages 11–54, meet with your group to discuss and answer the following questions:

1 What is Ramona like?

2 Ramona feels as if a lot depends on her. Why?

3 How does the author make Ramona's day seem like a real first day at school?

RESPONSE JOURNAL

Would you like to go to third grade at Ramona's school, ride on her bus, and be in her class? Why or why not?

Strategies Good Readers Use

FOCUS STRATEGY **USE REFERENCE SOURCES**

Tell what reference source you could use to find the meaning of the word *quivery* on page 11. Then write its meaning.

SKILLS IN CONTEXT

FOCUS SKILL **HOMOGRAPHS AND HOMOPHONES: PLAY A MATCHING GAME** *Homographs* are words that have the same spellings but different pronunciations and meanings. *Homophones* are words that sound alike but have different spellings and meanings. Use homophones in *Ramona Quimby, Age 8* to play a matching game.

What You Need

- **twenty-four index cards**
- **writing tools**

What to Do

1. Work in a group of four. Write these words on separate cards: *too, write, weak, wear, due, new, hear, bee, hi, won,* and *weave.* On pages 11–22, find homophones for these words and write them on cards.

2. Shuffle the cards and deal out all of them.

3. Take any pairs of homophones you have out of your hand. Tell the meaning of each word.

4. Call out "Pass." Everyone should then pass one unwanted card to the right, face down. Then repeat Step 3.

5. Repeat Step 4 until someone has no cards and wins.

Here is one homophone you will find: *we've*

Think Ahead What problems do you think Ramona will face?

BOOK TALK

After you read pages 55–108, meet with your group to discuss and answer the following questions:

1 What kinds of problems does Ramona have in school?

2 What does the strange meat that Mrs. Quimby serves for dinner one night show about the Quimby family?

3 What is funny about the meal that Ramona and her sister make?

> **Strategies Good Readers Use**
>
> ### USE GRAPHIC AIDS
>
> With a partner, talk about what the picture on page 68 shows and how it helps you understand the story.

RESPONSE JOURNAL

Write about a time when you felt the same way as Ramona did when she cracked the egg on her head or heard her teacher talk about her.

SKILLS IN CONTEXT

CHARACTERS' FEELINGS AND ACTIONS: MAKE A CHARACTER WEB Readers get to know story characters from their feelings and their actions. Create a character web poster to show what you have learned about Ramona.

What You Need

- writing paper
- large paper or poster board
- writing and art materials

What to Do

1. In the middle of a sheet of writing paper, draw a circle. Write *Ramona* inside.

2. Use lines to connect four more large circles to the *Ramona* circle. Write *Looks, Thinks, Does,* and *Says* inside.

3. In the first three circles, list some details about what Ramona looks like and wears, the things she thinks and worries about, and what she does. In the final circle, list the things Ramona says that tell the most about her.

4. Neatly copy your character web onto poster board or paper. Label it *All About Ramona.*

5. Display your web in the classroom.

Here is one idea: *Under* Looks, *you might list "wears squeaky sandals."*

Think Ahead Could other disasters be waiting to happen? Explain.

Ramona Quimby, Age 8

BOOK TALK

After you read pages 109–144, meet with your group to discuss and answer the following questions:

❶ What disaster happens to Ramona in school?

❷ Why does Ramona cry when her mother comes to get her at school?

❸ What do you think will happen when Ramona tries to "sell" her book?

Strategies Good Readers Use

SUMMARIZE

Write two or three sentences that tell the most important things that have happened in the book so far.

RESPONSE JOURNAL

What embarrassing things have happened to you at school? Write about one of them.

SKILLS IN CONTEXT

PREFIXES AND SUFFIXES: PLAY A SUFFIX GAME The author says that Ramona's parents are usually cheerful. *Cheerful* is made from the word *cheer* plus the suffix *-ful*. The author also says that Ramona's father pushes the car slowly down the driveway. *Slowly* is made from the word *slow* plus the suffix *-ly*. You can add suffixes to words to create new words. Play a suffix game to make new words and use them in sentences about Ramona or *Ramona Quimby, Age 8*.

What You Need

- fifteen index cards
- writing materials

What to Do

1. Work in a group of three. Write one of these words on each of the cards: *equal, final, wonder, quick, spoon, dread, special, total, real, care, friend, thank, play, usual, sad.*

2. Mix up the cards. With two classmates, take turns drawing a card.

3. For each word you draw, write a new word that ends with *-ful* or *-ly*.

4. Using the new word, say a sentence about Ramona or this book.

Here is a sentence to get you started: *Ramona felt dreadful after she threw up at school.*

Think Ahead
How will Ramona "sell" her book?

© Harcourt

Ramona Quimby, Age 8

BOOK TALK

After you read pages 145–190, meet with your group to discuss and respond to the following questions or statements:

1 *Ramona Quimby, Age 8* is about an everyday kid who has some funny and worrisome things happen to her. What characters in *Hidden Surprises* does she remind you of? Why?

2 What do you think the author of this book thinks is very important in life?

3 Name one thing you liked about this book and one thing you did not like.

RESPONSE JOURNAL

Write some advice you would give to Ramona.

Strategies Good Readers Use

FOCUS STRATEGY USE REFERENCE SOURCES

Imagine you want to learn more about television commercials. Where would you look? Write one or more places where you might find information.

SKILLS IN CONTEXT

FOCUS SKILL **HOMOGRAPHS AND HOMOPHONES: PLAY A HOMOPHONE MATCHING GAME**
Homophones are words that sound alike but are spelled differently and have different meanings. For example, the words *flew* and *flu* are homophones. Use homophones in the book to play a matching game.

What You Need

- writing tools
- thirty index cards

What to Do

1. Work in a group of three. Write these words on separate cards: *waste, your, four, who's, write, seam, sew, reed, sea, sum, fourth, eight, weigh, tows, through.* Find homophones for them on pages 145–152. Write the homophones on separate cards, too.

2. Shuffle the cards and hand them out face down.

3. Take turns turning over two cards. If you make a pair, say the meaning of each word and keep the cards. If not, return the cards face down to the playing surface. Let another player take a turn.

Here is one set of homophones to get you started: reed *and* read

Wrap-Up

▶ **Project** **MAKE A BOOK COVER** Show students a book cover, or remind them of book covers they have made to protect their school books. Tell them that they will make a book cover for *Ramona Quimby, Age 8* that will show what the book is about.

• Organize students into groups.
• Ask groups to complete the copying master on page 245.
• Provide an opportunity to discuss the covers that students create.

▶ **Writing** **PERSUASIVE REVIEW** Have students respond to the following writing prompt: **Write a review of *Ramona Quimby, Age 8* to persuade other students to read the book.** Have students use the copying master on page 246 to plan a persuasive review. Remind them to use special care when choosing words. Use *Hidden Surprises* pages T596–T597 for additional support. Rubrics for evaluating student writing are provided on pages 292–295.

▶ **Language Link** **COMMON AND PROPER NOUNS** Common nouns are easy to find in this book. Have students make a list of five nouns. Proper nouns are a little more difficult to find. Ask students to make a list of ten of them, including at least four proper nouns that do *not* name people.

Inquiry Project

Reading *Ramona Quimby, Age 8* may spark interest and inquiry into other topics. To help students find ideas for exploring, suggest they make a web like this one:

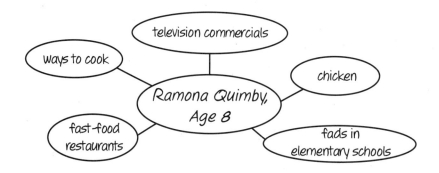

✔ **Comprehension Test** Test students' comprehension of *Ramona Quimby, Age 8* by having them complete the copying master on page 247.

Name _____

Project Planner

Ramona is full of little worries. What can an illustrator show about her story? Your job is to make a book cover with at least five drawings that show something important in the book.

☐ **Step 1.** With your group, discuss ideas for pictures of things that tell about Ramona (people may be too hard to draw) and things that happen to her. List your ideas below.

_____

_____

_____

_____

What You Need

- construction paper, a large brown paper bag, or other paper
- tape or glue stick
- scissors
- writing and drawing materials

☐ **Step 2.** Choose 5 or more of the best ideas to illustrate. Use the space below to plan where you will place each image. Remember that the cover needs the title and author both on the front and on the spine. Don't forget the back of your book jacket!

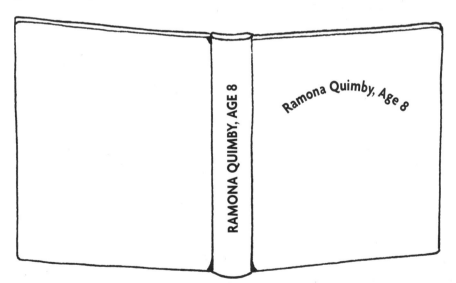

☐ **Step 3.** Make your cover. Fold it to fit a book you have. Tape or glue the flaps to another part of the cover and not to the book.

☐ **Step 4.** Display your cover in the classroom.

© Harcourt

Persuasive Review

Write a review of *Ramona Quimby, Age 8* to persuade other students to read the book. Use the graphic organizer below to plan your review.

Prewriting Graphic Organizer

Topic: _____

Audience: _____

Opinion: _____

_____

Reason 1: _____

Details: _____

Reason 2: _____

Details: _____

Reason 3: _____

Details: _____

Opinion Restated/Action Requested: _____

_____

© Harcourt

Comprehension Test

Test Prep

Read each question below. Then mark the letter for the answer you have chosen.

1. **What is the biggest problem in the Quimby house?**
   - Ⓐ Ramona is starting third grade.
   - Ⓑ Ramona and Beezus do not get along.
   - Ⓒ Ramona's parents are short on money.
   - Ⓓ Ramona's parents are out of work.

2. **Who is Willa Jean?**
   - Ⓕ Mrs. Whaley
   - Ⓖ Mrs. Larson's daughter
   - Ⓗ a young child
   - Ⓙ a teenager

3. **Which best describes Yard Ape?**
   - Ⓐ Beezus's best friend
   - Ⓑ the class bully
   - Ⓒ someone who likes Ramona
   - Ⓓ someone who hates Ramona

4. **What is true about Mr. Quimby?**
   - Ⓕ He has taught art for years.
   - Ⓖ He is going back to college so he can be a teacher.
   - Ⓗ He wants to work in the supermarket forever.
   - Ⓙ He doesn't like to eat out.

5. **What is true about Mrs. Quimby?**
   - Ⓐ She is always impatient.
   - Ⓑ She stays at home all day.
   - Ⓒ She loves her daughters.
   - Ⓓ She lets her children do anything.

6. **Which best describes the dinner that Ramona and Beezus make?**
   - Ⓕ creative
   - Ⓖ impossible to eat
   - Ⓗ delicious
   - Ⓙ a complete disaster

7. **What is true about Mrs. Whaley?**
   - Ⓐ She thinks Ramona is a nuisance.
   - Ⓑ She thinks Ramona played the egg joke on purpose.
   - Ⓒ She thinks Ramona likes to show off.
   - Ⓓ She thinks Ramona is perfect.

8. **Which best describes the ad Ramona uses to "sell" her book?**
   - Ⓕ dull
   - Ⓖ fun and creative
   - Ⓗ like everyone else's ad
   - Ⓙ a disaster

9. **Why does the stranger pay the dinner bill?**
   - Ⓐ He thinks the Quimbys are nice.
   - Ⓑ He owns the restaurant.
   - Ⓒ He knows Mr. Quimby teaches art.
   - Ⓓ He knows the Quimbys need the money.

10. **On a separate sheet of paper, write a short answer to these questions:** How are Beezus and Ramona alike? How are they different?

© Harcourt

Bonesy and Isabel

Reading Level

by Michael J. Rosen

Theme Connection

As students read *Bonesy and Isabel*, they will learn more about human-animal relationships. Isabel, the main human character, has a special relationship with a dog, as Leah in "Leah's Pony" has a special relationship with her pony.

Summary

Vera and Ivan adopt Isabel, a girl from El Salvador. Although Isabel speaks little English, she discovers that all the animals on the farm and the people in her new family communicate in gentle ways that mean "We care for you." Her special friend is an old dog named Bonesy. When he dies of old age, Isabel and her family are united in a sadness that needs no translation.

Author Profile

Michael J. Rosen has had a diverse and distinguished literary career. In addition to writing and designing books for children, he has compiled literary anthologies, including poetry collections, with themes related to social issues.

Additional Books by the Author
- *Elijah's Angel: A Story for Chanukah and Christmas*
- *All Eyes on the Pond*
- *A School for Pompey Walker*

Building Background

Tell students that *Bonesy and Isabel* is a realistic fiction story. Isabel, the girl in the story, comes from El Salvador to live on a farm in the United States. Have students find El Salvador on a map. Explain that the official language of El Salvador is Spanish. Invite students to think and share what it might be like for Isabel to join a new family in a new country. What would be hard? What could make her new life easier? Tell students that a dog named Bonesy helps Isabel bond with and become part of her adoptive family. Have them read to learn more about the relationship between Bonesy and Isabel.

Vocabulary

Have students preview the vocabulary words and group the words they think are related. A sample web is given. See pages 296–299 for additional vocabulary activities. For definitions of the words, see the Glossary.

Day 1	Day 2	Day 3	Day 4
creatures p. 2	resident p. 11	linens p. 17	brimming p. 23
Labrador retriever p. 2	companion p. 13	nudged p. 19	translation p. 23
abandoned p. 6	pronounced p. 13	rouse p. 20	vanished p. 25
language p. 6	arthritis p. 13	drafts p. 20	

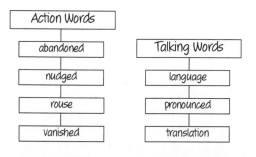

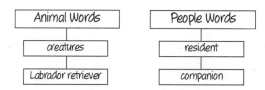

© Harcourt

	Response	Strategies	Skills
Day 1 **Pages 2–9**	**Book Talk** • Story Elements • Main Idea • Author's Purpose **Writing:** Make Inferences	**REREAD** FOCUS STRATEGY *Journeys of Wonder,* p. T263	**CHARACTERS'** FOCUS SKILL **FEELINGS AND** **ACTIONS** *Journeys of Wonder,* pp. T262–T263
Day 2 **Pages 10–15**	**Book Talk** • Determine Characters' Traits • Make Comparisons • Determine Characters' Emotions **Writing:** Write a Description/ Personal Response	Create Mental Images *Hidden Surprises,* p. T567	Main Idea *Hidden Surprises,* pp. T612–T613
Day 3 **Pages 16–23**	**Book Talk** • Important Details • Draw Conclusions • Determine Characters' Emotions **Writing:** Personal Response	Make and Confirm Predictions *Hidden Surprises,* p. T21	Cause and Effect *Journeys of Wonder,* pp. T624–T625
Day 4 **Pages 24–31**	**Book Talk** • Make Comparisons • Determine Theme **Writing:** Personal Response	**REREAD** FOCUS STRATEGY *Journeys of Wonder,* p. T263	**CHARACTERS'** FOCUS SKILL **FEELINGS AND** **ACTIONS** *Journeys of Wonder,* pp. T262–T263
Day 5 **Wrap-Up**	**Project** ✓ Write a Book • Inquiry Project **Writing** ✓ Research Report *Journeys of Wonder,* pp. T288–T289 **Language Link** • Sensory Details **Assessment** ✓ Comprehension Test		

*Additional support is provided in *Collections.*
✓ Options for Assessment

Bonesy and Isabel • **249**

Bonesy and Isabel

BOOK TALK

Read pages 2–9. Then meet with your group to discuss and answer the following questions:

1 What is the setting of this story? Describe the place and time.

2 Why do you think the man and woman brought Isabel to Sunbury Road?

3 What does the author mean when he writes that all the people and animals on the farm know different parts of its story?

RESPONSE JOURNAL

Do you think Isabel will be happy in her new home? Explain.

Strategies Good Readers Use

FOCUS STRATEGY **REREAD**

What part of the story might be clearer to you if you reread it? Find that part. Write the page number and explain what you learned by rereading.

SKILLS IN CONTEXT

FOCUS SKILL **CHARACTERS' FEELINGS AND ACTIONS: ACTIONS AND FEELINGS MOBILE**
Sometimes an author tells what characters do, and the reader has to decide what their actions show. Make an actions and feelings mobile to show Isabel's actions and feelings.

What You Need

- **coat hanger**
- **2 small paper plates**
- **blank index cards**
- **2 pieces of ribbon, 30 inches long each**
- **clear tape**
- **stapler with staples**
- **writing materials**

What to Do

1. Write *Actions* on one paper plate and *Feelings* on the other. Tape them side by side on the coat hanger.

2. On index cards, write Isabel's actions. Staple the cards to a ribbon and staple the ribbon to the first paper plate.

3. On more cards, write what her actions show about her feelings. Staple the cards to a ribbon, and staple the ribbon to the second paper plate.

4. Hang up your mobile.

Here is an idea to get you started:
Actions: *comes from El Salvador to the farm*
Feelings: *nervous and curious*

Think Ahead
How do you think Bonesy will be important in the story?

© Harcourt

Bonesy and Isabel

BOOK TALK

Read pages 10–15. Then meet with your group to discuss and answer the following questions:

1. What are Vera and Ivan like? How do you know?

2. How is Bonesy different from the other animals? Explain.

3. How does Isabel feel about Bonesy? How do you know? Give evidence from the story.

RESPONSE JOURNAL

Describe the relationship between Bonesy and Isabel. If you have had a special relationship with an animal, write about it.

Strategies Good Readers Use

CREATE MENTAL IMAGES

☆On page 13, the author says there are "clouds of laughter" at dinnertime. Close your eyes and picture this scene in your mind. What does the image help you see, hear, and feel?

SKILLS IN CONTEXT

MAIN IDEA: MAIN IDEA TRIPTYCH Sometimes an author repeats an idea to help the reader notice and think about it. The words *We care for you* are repeated throughout the book. Make a triptych, or three-part picture, that illustrates the key idea: *We care for you.*

What You Need

- **3 sheets of white paper**
- **writing and drawing tools**
- **3 pieces of poster board, 8.5" x 11"**
- **sturdy tape and glue**
- **scissors**

What to Do

1. Write *We care for you* on two sheets of paper. Read the paragraphs on pages 6 and 14 that include these words. Draw a picture for each to show what the words mean. Write an explanation of each picture.

2. Cut out your drawings and writing. Glue each set on a piece of poster board.

3. Tape the pieces of poster board together where the edges meet.

4. Create the third piece of your triptych when you find the third paragraph with the words *We care for you.*

Here is an idea to get you started:
Draw a picture of Isabel's parents caring for the animals.

Think Ahead What do you think will happen next in the story?

© Harcourt

Bonesy and Isabel

BOOK TALK

Read pages 16–23. Then meet with your group to discuss and answer the following questions:

❶ What clues show that Emmie and Isabel might become friends?

❷ What has happened to Bonesy? How does Isabel know?

❸ How do you know that Isabel, Vera, and Ivan care about each other? Find words on page 23 that show they care.

RESPONSE JOURNAL

What is your response to Bonesy's death? How does it make you feel? Why? What is good about this part of the story?

Strategies Good Readers Use

MAKE AND CONFIRM PREDICTIONS

Making and checking predictions helps you understand what you read. Predict what will happen next. As you read, check your predictions.

SKILLS IN CONTEXT

CAUSE AND EFFECT: CAUSE-AND-EFFECT CHAIN Cause-and-effect relationships show how an event (a cause) makes something happen (an effect). On page 23, Isabel, Vera, and Ivan are a family. Make a paper chain to show how other events lead up to this event. Brainstorm ideas before you start to make your paper chain. List and number the ideas you will include.

What You Need

- strips of paper in two colors
- writing tools
- tape

What to Do

1. Write the first event on a paper strip. Tape the strip into a ring. Keep your writing on the outside.
2. Write the word *So* on a strip of the other color. Loop it through the first strip, word side out. Tape it.
3. Write the next event on a strip of the first color. Add the ring to your chain.
4. Keep repeating Steps 2 and 3.
5. End the chain with a ring that reads *Isabel, Vera, and Ivan are a family.*

Here is an idea to get you started:

Isabel came from El Salvador. (SO) She didn't know much English. (SO)

Think Ahead
What will Isabel and her family do without Bonesy?

Bonesy and Isabel

BOOK TALK

Read pages 24–31. Then meet with your group to discuss and answer the following questions:

❶ What stories have you read that seem similar to *Bonesy and Isabel?* Explain.

❷ What are some themes, or main ideas, in *Bonesy and Isabel?*

❸ Compare pages 9 and 30. How has Isabel's life changed?

Strategies Good Readers Use

FOCUS STRATEGY **REREAD**

What parts of this story have you reread? Why did you reread them? How did rereading help?

RESPONSE JOURNAL

Imagine that a child from another country came to live with your family. Write about what you could do to help the child feel welcome.

SKILLS IN CONTEXT

FOCUS SKILL **CHARACTERS' FEELINGS AND ACTIONS: FLAP PORTRAIT** Characters' feelings and actions can help you understand what the character is like. Make a flap portrait to show what Isabel is like.

What You Need

- drawing paper
- writing and drawing tools
- scissors
- tape or glue

What to Do

1. Fold a piece of paper in half, then quarters, then eighths. Open it up. On one long side, cut each line to the center fold. You should end up with four flaps that fold down over the uncut half of your paper.

2. On each flap, write a word that tells what Isabel is like.

3. Under each flap, write or draw one or more details from the story that show the trait.

4. Draw a picture of Isabel on another paper. Label the picture *Isabel*.

5. Tape your flap chart to the bottom of your picture.

Here is an idea to get you started: *Flap word:* brave. *Examples of bravery: She comes to a new home in a new country. She helps with the horses.*

Wrap-Up

▶ **Project** WRITE A BOOK On the board, write *Bonesy's life was "a long story and a happy story and a story with a quiet ending."* (page 26). Make notes around the quote as students talk about each part: *a long story, a happy story, a quiet ending.* Tell students they will be writing a book about Bonesy's life.

- Organize students into small groups.
- Have them complete the copying master on page 255 to plan what they will do and who will do each part.
- Then have each group write, illustrate, and publish its story of Bonesy's life. Have each group share its finished story with the class.

▶ **Writing** RESEARCH REPORT Have students respond to the following research writing prompt: **Write a research report about stray animals in your community.** Have students use the copying master on page 256 to plan and record interviews. If possible, invite guest speakers into the class. Remind students to focus on research paper conventions. Use *Journeys of Wonder* pages T288–T289 for additional support. Rubrics for evaluating student writing are provided on pages 292–295.

▶ **Language Link** SENSORY DETAILS Have students look on page 24 for details that appeal to their five senses. Have them write the headings *See, Hear, Smell, Touch,* and *Taste* and list the details that fit each heading. Then ask students to write about a special place or event. Suggest that students include details that involve at least three senses.

Inquiry Project

Bonesy and Isabel can be a springboard for inquiry into a variety of topics and ideas. Brainstorm topics students would like to know more about. Then have them choose a topic and organize their inquiry on a K-W-L chart. Students can pool prior knowledge, conduct interviews, and use print and Internet resources to begin their inquiry projects. A sample K-W-L chart is provided.

K What I Know	W What I Want to Find Out	L What I Learned
Isabel came from there.	What is the country like?	hilly, not mountainous
People speak Spanish. (p. 8)	How large is the population?	San Salvador, the capital, is densely populated.
It is far away. (p. 10)	How do people live?	Most land is used for farming.

✔ **Comprehension Test** Test students' comprehension of *Bonesy and Isabel* by having them complete the copying master on page 257.

Name _____

Project Planner

In *Bonesy and Isabel*, the author describes Bonesy's life as "a long story and a happy story and a story with a quiet ending" (page 26). The story provides some information about Bonesy's life. You can add your own ideas to write and illustrate a book that tells the whole story of Bonesy's life.

What You Need
- paper
- writing and drawing tools

☐ **Step 1.** Discuss with your group what tasks will be involved in writing, illustrating, and publishing your book. Divide up the tasks. Decide who will do each part, and write group members' names beside their task(s).

_____

_____

_____

☐ **Step 2.** Talk with your group about what you know about Bonesy's life from reading *Bonesy and Isabel*. Make a circle chart like the one below to record information from the book. Then use the chart to brainstorm ideas and fill in missing parts of his story. You should include the following information:

- Where did Bonesy come from?
- How did Vera and Ivan find him?
- What was Bonesy like before he got old?

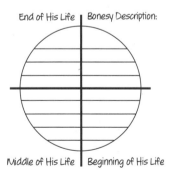

☐ **Step 3.** Work together to write, illustrate, and publish the story of Bonesy's life.

☐ **Step 4.** As a group, share your story with the class. You may want to read it aloud to younger children, too.

Name _____

Research Report

Write a research report about stray animals in your community. Use the
graphic organizer below to list people who would be good sources of information. Then
write some questions. Leave space to record answers during the interview. Use the
answers to write your report.

Prewriting Graphic Organizer

List of People Who Would Know About the Topic: _____

_____

Introduction to the Topic: _____

_____

_____

_____

My Questions:

1. _____

Answer: _____

_____

2. _____

Answer: _____

_____

Note: More questions and answers can be written on the back.

© Harcourt

Name _____

Comprehension Test

Read each question below. Then mark the letter for the answer you have chosen.

1. **Isabel comes to Sunbury Road because**
   - Ⓐ it is summer.
   - Ⓑ Vera and Ivan want a daughter.
   - Ⓒ Bonesy needs a companion.
   - Ⓓ Vera and Ivan need help on the farm.

2. **Why do Vera and Ivan have so many animals?**
   - Ⓕ They take in stray animals.
   - Ⓖ They need the animals to work on the farm.
   - Ⓗ Isabel brings them to the farm.
   - Ⓙ The animals belong to other people.

3. **Which does NOT describe Isabel?**
   - Ⓐ patient
   - Ⓑ helpful
   - Ⓒ gentle
   - Ⓓ rude

4. **How does Isabel learn about the farm?**
   - Ⓕ She asks lots of questions.
   - Ⓖ Vera and Ivan tell her stories.
   - Ⓗ She listens to the animals.
   - Ⓙ She reads books.

5. **Who is Isabel's first friend in her new home?**
   - Ⓐ an old dog named Bonesy
   - Ⓑ a girl named Emmie
   - Ⓒ Vera
   - Ⓓ Ivan

6. **Why does Isabel study English under the dining room table?**
   - Ⓕ She makes too many mistakes.
   - Ⓖ Bonesy is always there to listen.
   - Ⓗ Vera and Ivan tell her to.
   - Ⓙ She doesn't want anyone to know.

7. **What happens to Bonesy?**
   - Ⓐ He dies.
   - Ⓑ He gets sick.
   - Ⓒ He hurts his back legs.
   - Ⓓ He runs away.

8. **What do Vera, Ivan, and Isabel do under the table?**
   - Ⓕ talk about Bonesy's life
   - Ⓖ talk about their guests
   - Ⓗ make plans for the future
   - Ⓙ share their sadness about Bonesy

9. **Which is a main idea in *Bonesy and Isabel*?**
   - Ⓐ Spanish is easier than English.
   - Ⓑ People can share feelings without words.
   - Ⓒ Dogs make the best companions.
   - Ⓓ Animals should live outside.

10. **On a separate sheet of paper, write a short answer in response to the question below.**
    How does Bonesy help Isabel become part of her new family?

Dolphin Adventure

Reading Level

by Wayne Grover

▶ **Theme Connection** As do other selections in "What a Team!" *Dolphin Adventure* spotlights people helping others, the virtue of cooperation, and positive human-animal interaction.

▶ **Summary** While diving on the Florida reef, the author is stunned when a dolphin family approaches him. He quickly realizes the reason for their visit: the baby has a fishhook embedded in its body and is trailing blood. The author establishes the dolphins' trust, calms the baby, and removes the hook with his diving knife. This experience increases his love and profound respect for the undersea world.

▶ **Building Background** Display the book cover, read the title, and tell students that this is a nonfiction informational story whose purpose is to inform the reader. Suggest that students set a purpose for reading *Dolphin Adventure* by making a K-W-L chart about dolphins.

Author Profile

After a long career in the United States Air Force, Wayne Grover became a journalist. He started writing children's books in 1990. An active and outspoken conservationist, he has written, "I write my books and articles to let people know they can make a difference."

Additional Book by the Author
• *Ali and the Golden Eagle*

Vocabulary

Have students use the vocabulary words to complete a chart like the one below. See pages 296–299 for additional vocabulary activities. For definitions of the words, see the Glossary.

Words About Diving Gear	Words About Dolphins	Words About Getting Hurt and Getting Better

Day 1	Day 2	Day 3	Day 4
reefs p. 10 tank p. 10 wet suits p. 11 flippers p. 11 masks p. 11	overboard p. 12 gauges p. 17	clicking p. 19 dolphins p. 20	wound p. 22 fin p. 23 fluke p. 23 communicate p. 27
Day 5	**Day 6**	**Day 7**	**Day 8**
trembling p. 29	surgery p. 33	downcurrent p. 38	survived p. 44 scar p. 45

© Harcourt

	Response	Strategies	Skills
Day 1 Chapter 1	**Book Talk** • Note Details • Make Comparisons • Note Details **Writing:** Express Personal Opinion	**USE TEXT STRUCTURE AND FORMAT** FOCUS STRATEGY *Hidden Surprises,* p. T371	**VOCABULARY IN CONTEXT** FOCUS SKILL *Hidden Surprises,* pp. T370–T371
Day 2 Chapter 2	**Book Talk** • Summarize • Classify • Author's Purpose **Writing:** Express Personal Opinion	Adjust Reading Rate *Hidden Surprises,* p. T209	Figurative Language *Journeys of Wonder,* pp. T152–T153
Day 3 Chapter 3	**Book Talk** • Speculate • Draw Conclusions • Sequence **Writing:** Personal Response	Self-Question *Hidden Surprises,* p. T453	Synonyms and Antonyms *Hidden Surprises,* pp. T524–T525
Day 4 Chapter 4	**Book Talk** • Cause-Effect • Make Comparisons • Classify **Writing:** Identify with Characters	**USE TEXT STRUCTURE AND FORMAT** FOCUS STRATEGY *Hidden Surprises,* p. T371	**VOCABULARY IN CONTEXT** FOCUS SKILL *Hidden Surprises,* pp. T370–T371
Day 5 Chapter 5	**Book Talk** • Interpret Characters' Motivations • Note Details • Make Judgments **Writing:** Personal Response	**USE GRAPHIC AIDS** FOCUS STRATEGY *Hidden Surprises,* p. T409	**MAKE INFERENCES** FOCUS SKILL *Hidden Surprises,* pp. T408–T409
Day 6 Chapter 6	**Book Talk** • Sequence • Make Comparisons • Determine Characters' Emotions **Writing:** Relate to Characters	Summarize *Hidden Surprises,* p. T161	Cause and Effect *Journeys of Wonder,* pp. T624–T625
Day 7 Chapter 7	**Book Talk** • Summarize • Cause-Effect • Distinguish Fact from Opinion **Writing:** Personal Response	Use Reference Sources *Hidden Surprises,* p. T657	Author's Purpose *Hidden Surprises,* pp. T702–T703
Day 8 Chapter 8	**Book Talk** • Make Comparisons • Main Idea • Make Judgments **Writing:** Express Personal Opinion	**USE GRAPHIC AIDS** FOCUS STRATEGY *Hidden Surprises,* p. T409	**MAKE INFERENCES** FOCUS SKILL *Hidden Surprises,* pp. T408–T409
Days 9–10 Wrap-Up	**Project** ✓ Make a Mural • Inquiry Project	**Writing** ✓ News Story *Hidden Surprises,* pp. T392–T393	**Language Link** • Action Words **Assessment** ✓ Comprehension Test

*Additional support is provided in *Collections.*
✓ Options for Assessment

Dolphin Adventure

BOOK TALK

After you read pages 7–11, meet with your group to discuss and answer the following questions:

1 What have you learned so far about the person telling the story?

2 How is the person in the story different from the other divers?

3 What do the divers wear and carry?

RESPONSE JOURNAL

Which part of a diver's gear would you most like to try out? Why?

Strategies Good Readers Use

FOCUS STRATEGY   USE TEXT STRUCTURE AND FORMAT

When you read a chapter book, always read the chapter titles. Write the title of Chapter 1 and tell what it means.

SKILLS IN CONTEXT

FOCUS SKILL   VOCABULARY IN CONTEXT: PLAY A CONTEXT GAME When you do not know what a word means, look carefully at the context–the words and phrases that come before and after it. They will usually give you clues. Make a context game using words from the story.

What You Need

- ten index cards
- writing materials

What to Do

1. Write one of these words or phrases on each card: *Florida, pelicans, inlet, barrier island, Gulf Stream, current, scuba, regulator, sheath,* and *depths.*
2. With a partner, take turns drawing a card.
3. For each card, find the word on pages 7–11. On the card, write two or more context clues that help you know its meaning.
4. Pass the card to your partner. Have your partner read the word and its clues and then give its meaning.

Here is an example to get you started:

phrase: intracoastal waterway (p. 8); context clues: it leads to the open sea, the boat goes down it; meaning: water that boats travel on from inland to the open sea.

Think Ahead
What will happen during the dive?

© Harcourt

Dolphin Adventure

BOOK TALK

After you read pages 12–17, meet with your group to discuss and answer the following questions:

❶ What happens in this chapter?

❷ What kinds of things does the author see?

❸ There is nothing about dolphins in this chapter. Why do you think the author includes it?

RESPONSE JOURNAL

What would you like to see underwater? What might scare you there?

SKILLS IN CONTEXT

FIGURATIVE LANGUAGE: ILLUSTRATE IT Figurative language often uses comparisons to help you imagine something.

What You Need

- **drawing and writing tools**
- **paper or poster board**

What to Do

1. Find a comparison in Chapter 2 that uses *like* or *as*.

2. Make a picture that shows the comparison.

3. Label the picture with the figurative language from *Dolphin Adventure*.

4. Hang your picture in the classroom.

Here is an idea to get you started: *Show lobsters "waving their long feelers like pairs of giant whiskers" by drawing a lobster and showing its feelers moving up and down.*

Think Ahead
When and how will the dolphin adventure begin?

Dolphin Adventure

BOOK TALK

After you read pages 18–21, meet with your group to discuss and answer the following questions:

1 What is the "strange feeling" the author names in the title of this chapter?

2 Why do divers carry float balls?

3 How does the chapter end?

RESPONSE JOURNAL

Imagine yourself swimming all alone far out in the ocean in very deep water. In your journal, describe some of your thoughts and feelings.

SKILLS IN CONTEXT

SYNONYMS AND ANTONYMS: SYNONYM AND ANTONYM MATCHING GAME
A *synonym* is a word that means the same as or almost the same as another word. An *antonym* is a word that means the opposite or almost the opposite of another word.

What You Need

- **twenty-four index cards**
- **writing tools**

What to Do

1. Write each of the following words from Chapter 3 on separate cards: *strange, asked, wanted, laughed,* and *distinct.* Then write a synonym for each word on a separate card. Use your dictionary to help you, if needed.

2. Write each of the following words from Chapter 3 on separate cards: *large, bright, long, stays, right, loud,* and *clear.* Then write an antonym for each word on a separate card. Use your dictionary to help you.

3. Shuffle the cards, lay them face down, and, with a partner, take turns turning over two cards at a time. Each time you make a pair, identify it as a pair of synonyms or antonyms. If you don't make a pair, return the cards face down to the playing surface and let your partner take a turn.

Here is a pair to get you started:
Strange *and* weird *are synonyms.*

Think Ahead
What will the dolphins do?

© Harcourt

Dolphin Adventure

BOOK TALK

After you read pages 22–27, meet with your group to discuss and answer the following questions:

1 Why do the dolphins swim up to the diver?

2 What do the dolphins do that makes them seem human?

3 What challenges does the diver face?

RESPONSE JOURNAL

Tell some of the thoughts and feelings you would have if you were helping an injured dolphin.

Strategies Good Readers Use

FOCUS STRATEGY USE TEXT STRUCTURE AND FORMAT

Write each chapter title so far and list the illustration used with it. Explain how they work together to help tell the story.

SKILLS IN CONTEXT

FOCUS SKILL VOCABULARY IN CONTEXT: FILL IN THE BLANK Context is the words and sentences around an unfamiliar word. You can use context to figure out the meanings of words you do not know.

What You Need

- ten index cards
- writing tools

> Its little _____ rolled in their sockets as it watched me.

> eyes

What to Do

1. Work with a partner to copy 5 sentences from pages 22–24 or 25–27 onto cards. Choose sentences that have some difficult words in them but also have context clues. Leave out one of the key words in each sentence. Write each of those left-out words on a separate card.

2. Keep the cards in separate piles, but mix up each pile and exchange them with another pair who have chosen the other section of pages.

3. Match each word with the sentence it fits in. Tell the context clues that helped you make the match.

4. Have the pair that made the cards check your work.

Here is a sentence you could use, along with the left-out word:

Its little _____ rolled in their sockets as it watched me. [eyes] (The context clues are sockets *and* watched.

Think Ahead
What will happen next? Will sharks come?

© Harcourt

Dolphin Adventure

BOOK TALK

After you read pages 28–32, meet with your group to discuss and answer the following questions:

❶ Why does the author pet the baby dolphin for a few minutes before doing anything else?

❷ What is the greatest danger for the dolphin?

❸ How believable do you find this story so far?

FOCUS STRATEGY USE GRAPHIC AIDS

*E*xplain what the illustration on page 30 shows and how it helps you understand the story.

RESPONSE JOURNAL

List some of the feelings you would have if you were swimming with a dolphin.

SKILLS IN CONTEXT

FOCUS SKILL   MAKE INFERENCES: IDENTIFYING CLUES AND INFERENCES   To make an inference, combine what the story says with what you already know.

What You Need

• three index cards

What to Do

1. Write something that happens in Chapter 5 on one card.

2. On another card, write something you already know that helps you make an inference about what is happening in the story.

3. On the third card, write an inference based on the event and your knowledge.

4. Trade cards with a partner. Have your partner identify which card is which by labeling the back of it as *story event, knowledge,* or *inference.*

5. Check your partner's work.

Here is an example of a story event:
The baby dolphin swims between the mother and father dolphin.
Here is background knowledge you might have: *Animals care for and protect their young, especially when they are in danger.*

Think Ahead What do you think is most likely to happen?

Dolphin Adventure

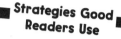

BOOK TALK

After you read pages 33–37, meet with your group to discuss and answer the following questions:

1 After holding the baby on the sea floor, what is the first thing the diver does?

2 Why is what the diver does like surgery?

3 What is the author thinking and feeling as he uses his knife?

> **Strategies Good Readers Use**
>
> ### SUMMARIZE
>
> List the main events that have occurred so far.

RESPONSE JOURNAL

Do you think you would have the courage to do what the author is doing? Explain why or why not.

SKILLS IN CONTEXT

CAUSE AND EFFECT: MAKE A CAUSE-AND-EFFECT CHAIN There are many different causes and effects in Chapter 6. You can identify them by looking for the things that happen as a result of certain actions.

What You Need

- **half-sheets of colored paper**
- **paper fasteners**
- **writing materials**

What to Do

1. Write these actions on separate sheets of colored paper: The author (1) pulls up the line, (2) pulls the line free, (3) touches the hook shaft, (4) runs his finger into the wound, (5) tries to wiggle the hook free, and (6) takes the hook out. Write the effects of these actions, and other causes, on more sheets of paper. You will see that some effects turn into new causes.

2. Put the causes and effects in order.

3. Form a cause-and-effect chain by attaching the sheets with paper fasteners.

4. Display your chain in the classroom.

Here are ideas to get you started:

The author pulls up the line → blood flows out of the baby → the author pulls the line free → the baby cries out in pain

Think Ahead

What problem could result from all the blood?

Dolphin Adventure

BOOK TALK

After you read pages 38–43, meet with your group to discuss and answer the following questions:

1 How do the dolphins protect their baby from the sharks?

2 How does the author stop the baby's bleeding?

3 Can you tell for sure that the dolphin is saying "thank you" to the author? Why or why not?

RESPONSE JOURNAL

What did you learn that you did not already know about dolphins?

Strategies Good Readers Use

USE REFERENCE SOURCES

*L*ook up *dolphin* in an encyclopedia. Read about what their clicking means. Write down what you learn.

SKILLS IN CONTEXT

AUTHOR'S PURPOSE: POINT OUT THE PURPOSES Authors often write to entertain, inform, or persuade. They may, however, write for many other purposes, such as to help people understand ideas and solve problems.

What You Need

- poster board
- writing and drawing materials

What to Do

1. Make a list of reasons why the author wrote this book.
2. Make a large circle on poster board. Divide it into as many parts as the author's purposes.
3. Write a purpose in each part of the circle.
4. If you wish, decorate your poster with dolphins swimming around the circle.
5. Give your work a title.
6. Hang your poster in the classroom.

Here is one purpose: *to give information about dolphins*

Think Ahead
This seems to be the end of the story. What more could happen?

© Harcourt

Dolphin Adventure

BOOK TALK

After you read pages 44–47, meet with your group to discuss and answer the following questions:

1 What selections in *Hidden Surprises* show people and animals together?

2 What is one message the author of *Dolphin Adventure* wants to send?

3 Would you recommend this book to another reader? Why or why not?

> ### Strategies Good Readers Use
>
> **FOCUS STRATEGY** **USE GRAPHIC AIDS**
>
> Find the three illustrations in the book that give the most information. Write the page number of each and tell what it shows.

RESPONSE JOURNAL

Do you like the way this book ends? Tell why or why not.

SKILLS IN CONTEXT

FOCUS SKILL **MAKE INFERENCES: MAKE A POSTER** To make an inference, you follow steps. You find a story event, you think about what you know, and you put both together to form an idea that is not stated in the story.

What You Need

- poster board
- writing tools

What to Do

1. Find an example of an inference you made while reading *Dolphin Adventure*.
2. Write the title *How to Make Inferences* at the top of your poster board.
3. Plan a diagram for the poster that shows steps in the process of making the inference.
4. Copy your diagram onto the poster board.
5. Hang your poster in the classroom.

Here are some inferences you might have made: *The author is a brave person. The author has little or no fear of the undersea world.*

© Harcourt

Wrap-Up

▶ **Project** **MAKE A MURAL** If students have never made a mural, explain what it is. Tell students that they will be making a mural of scenes from *Dolphin Adventure*.
- Have students form small groups.
- Ask students to complete the Project Planner on page 269.
- Provide a large sheet of butcher paper on which to create the mural.
- Provide time for everyone to see, admire, and discuss the work of each group.

▶ **Writing** **NEWS STORY** Have students respond to the following writing prompt: **Write a news story about the author's dolphin adventure**. Have students use the copying master on page 270 to plan a news story. Remind students to focus on clear and accurate word choice. Use *Hidden Surprises* pages T392–T393 for additional support. Rubrics for evaluating student writing can be found on pages 292–295.

▶ **Language Link** **ACTION WORDS** Point out to students that there are many exciting action words in this story. Have students make a list of six or more of them and explain their meanings.

Inquiry Project

Reading *Dolphin Adventure* may stimulate many questions about scuba diving, scuba gear, the lives and habits of dolphins and other undersea life, and the nature of coral reefs. To explore ideas for inquiry, have students create a web like this one:

✔ **Comprehension Test** Test students' comprehension of *Dolphin Adventure* by having them complete the copying master on page 271.

Name _____

Project Planner

There are many details to "see" in your mind's eye as you read *Dolphin Adventure*. Your job in this project is to make a large mural to show them.

☐ **Step 1.** List as many ideas for pictures as you can think of.

_____

_____

_____

_____

_____

What You Need

- a large sheet of paper
- pencils and painting materials
- research materials for pictures of undersea life and diving gear not shown in the book

☐ **Step 2.** Circle your best ideas for pictures you want to be sure to include.

☐ **Step 3.** Organize your mural space as shown below. Write names or sketch ideas where your pictures will appear.

☐ **Step 4.** Start your mural. Draw lightly in pencil first, so you can make changes as needed. Then paint.

☐ **Step 5.** Present your mural to the class.

News Story

Imagine the author calls the local newspaper on the day he helps the
dolphin baby. You are the reporter who comes to interview him. Write a news story about
the author's dolphin adventure. Use the first part of this organizer to record facts. Use the
next part to plan your story.

Prewriting Graphic Organizer

Who: _____

What: _____

_____

_____

Where: _____

When: _____

_____

_____

Why/How: _____

Title: _____

Beginning Sentence to Create Interest: _____

_____

Body: _____

_____

_____

_____

_____

© Harcourt

Name _____

Comprehension Test

Test Prep

Read each question below. Then mark the letter for the answer you have chosen.

1. **Which best describes the diver?**
   - Ⓐ He is diving all alone.
   - Ⓑ He is diving alone, but his friend Amos is in the boat.
   - Ⓒ He stays with other divers.
   - Ⓓ He is hunting fish with other divers.

2. **Which best describes the diver during his first dive?**
   - Ⓕ peaceful, happy, filled with wonder
   - Ⓖ eager to get back to the boat
   - Ⓗ interested in the fish, but worried
   - Ⓙ scared of the morays and sharks

3. **What is the first sign that the dolphins are nearby?**
   - Ⓐ Sharks appear.
   - Ⓑ The water gets suddenly dark.
   - Ⓒ There is a loud clicking noise.
   - Ⓓ A trail of blood appears.

4. **Which best describes dolphins?**
   - Ⓕ never friendly to people
   - Ⓖ not usually friendly to people
   - Ⓗ usually dangerous to people
   - Ⓙ very dangerous to people, but not as dangerous as sharks

5. **Why does the baby dolphin need help immediately?**
   - Ⓐ The fish hook will kill it.
   - Ⓑ The loss of blood will kill it.
   - Ⓒ The blood will draw a shark attack.
   - Ⓓ The plastic line will strangle it.

6. **Why do the dolphins keep leaving?**
   - Ⓕ They are scared.
   - Ⓖ They have to get air.
   - Ⓗ They fight off many, many sharks.
   - Ⓙ They seem to change their mind.

7. **What is the "surgery" in this story?**
   - Ⓐ The author removes a fin.
   - Ⓑ The author cuts a fishing line.
   - Ⓒ The author uses a knife to stop the bleeding.
   - Ⓓ The author removes a hook.

8. **The moment of greatest danger for the author is when**
   - Ⓕ he holds down the baby dolphin.
   - Ⓖ the father dolphin looks him in the eye.
   - Ⓗ the pair of bull sharks appears.
   - Ⓙ he puts his knife in the dolphin.

9. **How does the author know the baby survived?**
   - Ⓐ He sees a baby with a scar two weeks later.
   - Ⓑ Amos sees the baby later.
   - Ⓒ He knows it in his heart.
   - Ⓓ He sees it on a television report.

10. **On a separate sheet of paper, answer the question below.**
    When the author tells the story of what happened, some people may not believe him. Give three reasons.

Horsepower: The Wonder of Draft Horses

Reading Level

by Cris Peterson

Theme Connection
As students read *Horsepower: The Wonder of Draft Horses*, they will learn the history of draft horses and the role these giants play on today's farms. As in "Cocoa Ice," draft horses are important to their owners, who recognize their power and value their ability to work in teams.

Summary
Draft horses were once the working backbone of America—clip-clopping through streets and fields, pulling heavy loads, and ferrying people. Although modern transportation has redefined the role of the draft horse, this breed continues to be important and cherished. Through well-crafted text and striking photographs, young readers will learn about the history and current use of these powerful, intelligent animals, as well as the bond that exists between them and the humans who raise them.

Building Background
Tell students that *Horsepower* is an informational story about a kind of horse known as a draft horse. Explain that the story tells about different breeds of draft horses and the people who take care of them. It also gives facts and information about the history and past uses of draft horses. Invite students to share what they know about taking care of horses. Then have students read to be informed about draft horses and to find out how they are used today.

Author Profile
A member of a dairy farming family in Wisconsin, author Cris Peterson writes a weekly column about children's literature. Her books provide children with an insight into the world of farms and farming. "My writing career," says Peterson, "began when I gave mouth-to-mouth resuscitation to a newborn calf and I knew I had a good story."

Additional Books by the Author
- *Century Farm: One Hundred Years on a Family Farm*
- *Extra Cheese, Please! Mozzarella's Journey from Cow to Pizza*
- *Harvest Year*

Vocabulary

Have students take turns giving an imaginary tour of a farm in which they use the vocabulary words listed below. Students acting as tourists can make comments or ask their tour guides questions that use the vocabulary words. See pages 296–299 for additional vocabulary activities. For definitions of the words, see the Glossary.

This is where we demonstrate how to hitch teams of horses.

Wow! Look at those horses prance!

Day 1	Day 2	Day 3	Day 4
hooves p. 3	harness p. 9	hitch p. 15	produce p. 29
power p. 4	control p. 9	prance p. 17	nicker p. 30
giant p. 6	teams p. 10	raise p. 19	partnership p. 30
	demonstrate p. 12		

	Response	Strategies	Skills
Day 1 Pages 2–7	**Book Talk** • Important Details • Summarize • Author's Viewpoint **Writing:** Personal Response	**USE REFERENCE SOURCES** FOCUS STRATEGY *Journeys of Wonder,* p. T347	**SUMMARIZE** FOCUS SKILL *Journeys of Wonder,* pp. T346–T347
Day 2 Pages 8–13	**Book Talk** • Make Inferences • Summarize • Draw Conclusions **Writing:** Make Judgments	Adjust Reading Rate *Hidden Surprises,* p. T209	Main Idea *Hidden Surprises,* pp. T612–T613
Day 3 Pages 14–21	**Book Talk** • Sequence • Cause-Effect • Draw Conclusions **Writing:** Determine Characters' Emotions	Self-Question *Hidden Surprises,* p. T453	Compare and Contrast *Journeys of Wonder,* pp. T304–T305
Day 4 Pages 22–30	**Book Talk** • Make Comparisons • Theme • Express Personal Opinion **Writing:** Express Personal Opinion	**USE REFERENCE SOURCES** FOCUS STRATEGY *Journeys of Wonder,* p. T347	**SUMMARIZE** FOCUS SKILL *Journeys of Wonder,* pp. T346–T347
Day 5 Wrap-Up	**Project** ✓ Create a Draft Horse Poster • Inquiry Project **Writing** ✓ Research Report *Journeys of Wonder,* pp. T390–T391 **Language Link** • Figurative Language **Assessment** ✓ Comprehension Test		

*Additional support is provided in *Collections.*
✓ Options for Assessment

Horsepower: The Wonder of Draft Horses

BOOK TALK

After you read pages 2–7, meet with your group to discuss and answer the following questions:

1 What details does the author give to help you understand Kate's size?

2 How were horses like Kate once used in America?

3 How do you know that the author admires draft horses?

RESPONSE JOURNAL

How might you feel standing beside a horse like Kate?

Strategies Good Readers Use

FOCUS STRATEGY USE REFERENCE SOURCES

*N*ame two reference sources you could use to better understand the topic of draft horses.

SKILLS IN CONTEXT

FOCUS SKILL SUMMARIZE: GUESS MY PET! When you summarize, you retell ideas in your own words. Knowing how to summarize when you read nonfiction will help you understand and remember the important details that you read about a topic. Imagine that Keane or MacKenzie is playing "Guess My Pet." with a group of friends. Write a passage that one of them could use to play the game. The passage should summarize what Kate is like and why she is so special, without telling that she is a Percheron draft horse.

What You Need

- notebook paper
- writing and drawing tools
- 5" x 7" index card

What to Do

1. Review pages 2–7 of *Horsepower*. Note details that describe Kate.
2. Write your summary on one side of the index card. Include the main ideas and important details about Kate. Follow the same order of details given in the story, but use your own words.
3. Draw a picture of Kate on the other side of the index card.
4. Share your passage and drawing with a partner.

My Pet

Kate

Here is a story detail to help you get started: *Kate's black hooves are the size of dinner plates.*

Think Ahead
How do you think draft horses like Kate are used today?

Horsepower: The Wonder of Draft Horses

BOOK TALK

After you read pages 8–13, meet with your group to discuss and answer the following questions:

1 How does the harness help Keane and MacKenzie control Kate?

2 What are three ways people use draft horses today?

3 What conclusion can you draw about Amish farmers?

RESPONSE JOURNAL

What would be the best part of taking care of Kate? What would be the hardest part?

> **Strategies Good Readers Use**
>
> **ADJUST READING RATE**
>
> *W*rite about a time when you read a passage in a story more slowly to understand information that was difficult or unfamiliar.

SKILLS IN CONTEXT

MAIN IDEA: MAIN IDEA PUZZLES The main idea tells what a paragraph is mostly about. Details tell more about the main idea. Create three jigsaw puzzles that show main ideas and details about draft horses from pages 8–13.

What You Need

- notebook paper
- stiff paper for puzzles
- writing and drawing tools
- scissors

What to Do

1. Look for and jot down the main idea of each paragraph in pages 8–13. Then find and jot down details that tell about each main idea.

2. On stiff paper, draw puzzle pieces. In one piece, write the main idea for page 9. In the other pieces, write details that support the main idea.

3. On the back, illustrate the main idea. Cut the puzzle. Repeat steps 2 and 3 for pages 10 and 12.

4. Mix up all your puzzle pieces. Place them word-side up. Challenge classmates to put the puzzles together. Tell them to look for main ideas and details.

Here is a main idea from page 9 to get you started:

"Instead of a saddle, Kate wears a harness when she works."

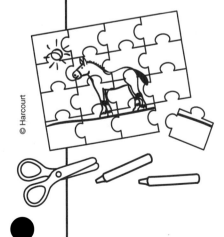

© Harcourt

Think Ahead
What will happen at field day?

Horsepower: The Wonder of Draft Horses

BOOK TALK

After you read pages 14–21, meet with your group to discuss and answer the following questions:

1 What do the owners have to do before their teams are ready for plowing?

2 What may happen if the lead horses are not faster than the wheel horses?

3 When can young draft horses be part of a working team?

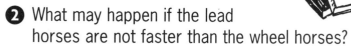

RESPONSE JOURNAL

What do you think the owners are feeling and thinking as they drive their teams on field day?

Strategies Good Readers Use

SELF-QUESTION

Write one question that you asked yourself as you read pages 14–21. How did asking questions help you understand facts and information in the story?

SKILLS IN CONTEXT

COMPARE AND CONTRAST: FIELD DAY MOBILES Comparing and contrasting helps you understand what the author is describing. Make mobiles to compare and contrast Don and Bruce's draft horse teams.

What You Need

- notebook paper
- colored yarn
- hole punch
- construction paper
- large and small horse shapes to trace
- scissors and writing tools

What to Do

1. Review pages 14–21 and jot down details about each team. Circle three details for each team.

2. Trace and cut out two large horse shapes. Write *Don's Team* on one and *Bruce's Team* on the other. Trace and cut out six small horse shapes. Write the details on the smaller shapes.

3. Punch a hole at the top of each shape and thread yarn through the holes. Punch three holes at the bottom of each large shape and attach the details to the correct team.

4. Hang your mobiles side by side.

Here's a detail to get you started:
Bruce raises Belgian draft horses.

Think Ahead
What qualities does a good draft horse have? How are the teams alike? How are they different?

© Harcourt

Horsepower: The Wonder of Draft Horses

BOOK TALK

After you read pages 22–30, meet with your group to discuss and answer the following questions:

1 What story in *Journeys of Wonder* shows how animals and their owners work together?

2 What do you think the author wants you to understand about the people who own draft horses?

3 If you could attend a field day with Keane and MacKenzie, what would you be most excited to see or do? Why?

Strategies Good Readers Use

FOCUS STRATEGY USE REFERENCES SOURCES

*T*ell how you used a dictionary or an encyclopedia to understand a word or idea in this informational story.

RESPONSE JOURNAL

Do you agree with the author that draft horses are "amazing" animals? Why or why not?

SKILLS IN CONTEXT

FOCUS SKILL SUMMARIZE: DRAFT HORSE NEWSLETTER When you summarize, you retell only the most important parts of a story in your own words. Using information in the story, create a newsletter to send to draft horse owners.

What You Need

- **notebook paper**
- **blank white paper**
- **writing materials**

What to Do

1. Revisit pages 14–30 in *Horsepower* to review field day events and to find out how David prepares his horses for showings. Jot down details.

2. Use your notes to write two brief articles. One article should summarize field day events. The other should summarize how David gets ready for showings. Include only the most important details. Add headlines and drawings. Give your newsletter a catchy title and write it at the top.

3. Share your newsletter with classmates.

Here is a sentence to get you started: *"All winter long, Warrior, Patrick, and several other horses go through 'basic training' on a daily schedule."*

"Warrior stands at attention."

© Harcourt

Wrap-Up

▶ Project CREATE A DRAFT HORSE POSTER

Remind students that the author of this informational story points out how and why people have kept draft horses from disappearing. Tell students that they will use information from the story and from additional research to create a poster that tells about and honors draft horses.

- Organize students into small groups.
- Have students discuss both what they have learned about draft horses from the reading and what else they might like to find out.
- Ask students to complete the copying master on page 279 to plan the facts and details they will share with their group.
- Have each group work together to create a poster.

▶ Writing RESEARCH REPORT

Have students respond to the following writing prompt: **Write a draft of a research report on one kind of horse you learn about by looking in reference sources and on the Internet.** Have students use the copying master on page 280 to write their report drafts. Remind students to focus on organization. See *Journeys of Wonder* pages T390–T391 for additional support. Rubrics for evaluating student writing are provided on pages 292–295.

▶ Language Link FIGURATIVE LANGUAGE

Tell students that figurative language is the use of words that say one thing but mean another. Writers of informational stories use figurative language to make their stories more enjoyable and to help readers understand what is happening. Have students create a chart with the headings *What the Words Say* and *What the Words Mean*. Then have them record figurative language from *Horsepower* and explain what it means. Discuss how the use of figurative language makes the story more enjoyable and the ideas clearer.

Inquiry Project

Horsepower can be a rich source of topics and ideas for inquiry. Have students brainstorm topics they would like to know more about and record their ideas in a web like the one shown. Students can use reference books and the Internet to begin their inquiry projects.

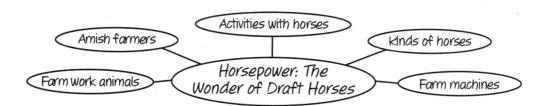

✔ Comprehension Test

Test students' comprehension of *Horsepower* by having them complete the copying master on page 281.

Name _____

Project Planner

Using what you learned from reading *Horsepower*, and from additional research, create a poster that tells about and honors draft horses.

☐ **Step 1.** Discuss with your group what kinds of information your poster might include. Make a list of ideas.

_____

_____

_____

What You Need
- poster board
- writing and drawing materials
- scissors
- old magazines
- reference sources

☐ **Step 2.** Complete the K-W-L chart below to review what you know and develop questions that you would like your research to answer. Discuss the following questions:

- What are the different kinds of draft horses?
- What are the features and traits of draft horses?

| K
What I Know | W
What I Want to Know | L
What I Learned |
|---|---|---|
| | | |
| | | |
| | | |

☐ **Step 3.** Work together to research draft horses. As a group, decide how best to display the information in a poster.

☐ **Step 4.** Create your poster. You might include text about draft horses past and present or show a chart of different kinds of draft horses and their special features.

☐ **Step 5.** As a group, present your poster to the class.

© Harcourt

Name _____

Research Report

Write a draft of a research report on one kind of horse that you learn
about by looking in reference sources and on the Internet. First, take careful notes. Then
use the graphic organizer to help you plan your research report.

Prewriting Graphic Organizer

Title: _____

Introduction: _____

_____

Middle: _____

_____

_____

_____

Conclusion: _____

_____

Drafting Checklist:

☐ Use your outline for ideas.

☐ Write the title of your report.

☐ Write a topic sentence for each paragraph.

☐ Follow your outline to add facts and examples to support your topic
   sentence.

© Harcourt

Name _____

Comprehension Test

Read each question below. Then mark the letter for the answer you have chosen.

1. **Which is a breed of draft horse?**
   - Ⓐ Don
   - Ⓑ Percheron
   - Ⓒ Amish
   - Ⓓ Warrior

2. **Which best describes Kate?**
   - Ⓕ large and powerful
   - Ⓖ smart but wild
   - Ⓗ small and fierce
   - Ⓙ lazy and sweet

3. **Which are parts of a harness?**
   - Ⓐ feather, blanket, saddle
   - Ⓑ armor, plates, nails
   - Ⓒ wagon, plow, hitch
   - Ⓓ collar, hames, traces

4. **Where do draft horse owners gather to show off their teams?**
   - Ⓕ corn fields
   - Ⓖ Amish farms
   - Ⓗ special field days
   - Ⓙ city parades

5. **What makes Bill and Bob good leaders for Don's four-horse team?**
   - Ⓐ They are older and have more experience than the other horses.
   - Ⓑ They are faster than the other horses.
   - Ⓒ They are stronger and more graceful than the other horses.
   - Ⓓ They never need to rest.

6. **What makes Bruce's lead mare different from other lead mares?**
   - Ⓕ Bonnie can pull a four-bottom plow.
   - Ⓖ Bonnie has given birth to many foals.
   - Ⓗ Bonnie is blind.
   - Ⓙ Bonnie is a Belgian draft horse.

7. **How can you tell a Clydesdale from other draft horses?**
   - Ⓐ by its red leather harness
   - Ⓑ by the feathering on its legs
   - Ⓒ by its large smooth hooves
   - Ⓓ by its soft nicker

8. **In halter and hitch competitions, Clydesdales are judged on**
   - Ⓕ how long they can stand still.
   - Ⓖ how much corn they can pull.
   - Ⓗ how quiet they are.
   - Ⓙ how they look and work as a team.

9. **Which sentence is a fact?**
   - Ⓐ It's hard to imagine a time when "horsepower" meant horses working.
   - Ⓑ Kate is a remarkable horse.
   - Ⓒ Twenty-seven million draft horses were America's main source of power.
   - Ⓓ Belgians create an impressive team.

10. **On a separate sheet of paper, write a short answer to this question:**
    What did you learn about draft horses that helps you understand why people want to keep them from disappearing?

～Literature Circle Student Record～

STUDENT'S NAME _____ **DATE** _____

TITLE _____ **AUTHOR** _____

Use the following matrix to rate student behaviors as you observe students in Literature Circles. Use the information to assess skills and to identify areas where students may require additional support.

The Student	Often	Occasionally	Rarely
prepares for discussion			
participates in discussion			
offers quality responses to literature			
uses prior knowledge			
connects selection to real life and to other literature			
appreciates illustrations and uses graphic aids			
demonstrates use of listening skills through interaction and responses			
is willing to consider alternative viewpoints			
is willing to ask questions and seek help from others			
enjoys the literature			
Other Criteria: _____ _____ _____			

© Harcourt

～Literature Circle Bookmarks～

Cut out the bookmarks that go with the type of book you are reading. Use the questions on the book-marks to help you remember things you might want to discuss in your literature circle group. On the backs of the bookmarks, write down your answers to the questions, important page numbers, and any other ideas you would like to discuss with your group.

FICTION

1. Do the characters in your book act like real people? What makes them seem real or not real?

2. What is the setting of your book? How does the author give you information about it?

3. How does the author use action, dialogue, thoughts, or descriptions to create a mood or affect your emotions?

FICTION

1. What do you think might happen next? What clues has the author given you?

2. What is the most important idea in this section? Why?

3. What did you like the most about what you just read? What did you like the least? Why?

NONFICTION

1. How does the author organize the information? How does this organization help you under-stand the text?

2. What main idea or ideas is the author writing about?

3. Is the information enjoyable to read? How does the author get and keep your attention?

NONFICTION

1. What opinions, if any, does the author express?

2. What kinds of graphic aids does the author include? How do they help you understand the text?

3. After reading this section, what are some things you would like to learn more about?

Literature Circle Bookmarks

Notes

_____

_____

_____

Notes

_____

_____

_____

Notes

_____

_____

_____

Notes

_____

_____

_____

© Harcourt

Literature Circle Roles

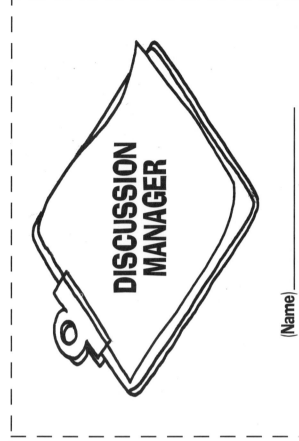

DISCUSSION MANAGER

_____
(Name)

PASSAGE PILOT

_____
(Name)

WORD EXPLORER

_____
(Name)

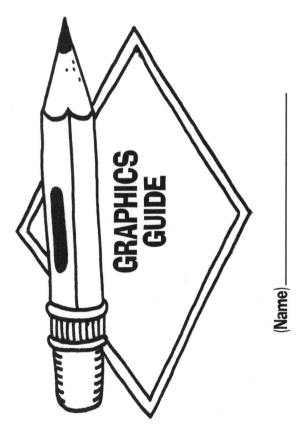

GRAPHICS GUIDE

_____
(Name)

© Harcourt

Literature Circle Roles

PASSAGE PILOT

- Find parts of the text that you think are important or interesting enough to share.
- Plan to read these parts aloud or to have others do so.

DISCUSSION MANAGER

- Make a list of questions to open the discussion.
- Ask about important ideas and about readers' thoughts.
- Involve each member in the discussion.

GRAPHICS GUIDE

- Draw and share a sketch, diagram, or other graphic that shows something about the book or an idea, thought, or feeling you had while reading.
- Explain your graphic.

WORD EXPLORER

- As you read, watch for important or interesting words to point out to your group.
- Help your group members find these words and discuss their meanings.
- Find out meanings of words you don't know.

Literature Circle Roles

SHARING SUPERVISOR

(Name)

SUMMARY STARTER

(Name)

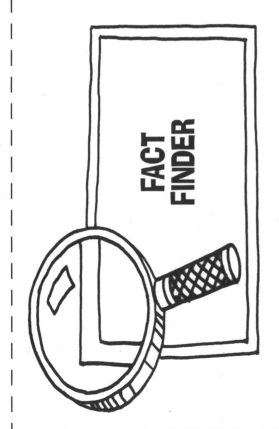

FACT FINDER

(Name)

SETTINGS NAVIGATOR

(Name)

© Harcourt

Literature Circle Roles

SUMMARY STARTER

- Write a short statement to sum up what you read.
- For fiction, tell the most important events of the story.
- For nonfiction, tell the main idea or ideas.
- Lead the group in identifying a one-sentence summary of the text.

SHARING SUPERVISOR

- Lead the group in deciding on a creative way to share what you read.
- Gather the supplies your group needs.
- Make sure the group is ready to present to the class.

SETTINGS NAVIGATOR

- Keep track of the times and places, or settings, mentioned in your book.
- Create a map or diagram to show how the setting changes.

FACT FINDER

- Choose something you read about that either interests or puzzles you.
- Use reference sources to find a piece of information to share about that topic.
- Find information about ideas your group wants to explore further.

~Literature Circle ✓ Checklist ~

Fill out this checklist after each meeting of your Literature Circle. Check **Yes** or **No** for each item. Then write at the bottom what you would like to do better next time. Look at the checklist again before the next meeting of your Literature Circle.

NAME _____ **DATE** _____

TITLE _____ **AUTHOR** _____

WAS I READY FOR LITERATURE CIRCLE?

	Yes	No
Did I bring my book?		
Did I do the reading we agreed upon?		
Did I either write notes for my role or write in my journal?		

DID I TAKE PART IN THE DISCUSSION?

	Yes	No
Did I share my ideas and feelings?		
Did I ask questions about things I didn't understand?		
Did I listen carefully to others?		

WHAT CAN I DO BETTER NEXT TIME?

_____

_____

_____

_____

_____

_____

© Harcourt

Learning Contracts

A learning contract is a written agreement between a student and teacher that sets conditions for independent study. For example, the contract may specify tasks that the student is to complete, terms that the student must abide by, and a date by which the contract is to be completed. Learning contracts give students a taste of independence balanced by a sense of taking responsibility for their own work.

A BALANCED APPROACH

INDEPENDENCE
- work at own pace
- make decisions

RESPONSIBILITY
- observe terms of contract
- complete task on time

LEARNING CONTRACTS

Learning Contracts for Independent Reading

You can use contracts to encourage above-level readers to read more difficult books at their own pace and to share their responses in innovative ways. Keep in mind that even good readers may need some guidance to learn to pace themselves appropriately. To help develop pacing skills, you may want to establish checkpoints at which you review the student's progress, as well as end dates by which the reading and the student's response to the literature should be completed.

A copying master for an independent reading contract can be found on page 291. You can also adapt this contract to use for other types of independent projects.

INDEPENDENT READING CONTRACT

1. I will read this book: _____
      (title)

   by _____
      (author)

2. I will complete the book by this date: _____

3. I will respond to the literature and share it with classmates in the following way:

_____

_____

_____

_____

4. I will complete my response or sharing by this date: _____

5. I agree to work within the following guidelines:

_____

_____

_____

_____

6. I agree to checkpoints that my teacher may list on a separate sheet of paper and attach to this contract.

   Student and teacher agree to all of the terms stated in this contract.

DATE OF SIGNING: _____

SIGNATURE OF STUDENT _____

SIGNATURE OF TEACHER _____

© Harcourt

Writing Rubrics

The rubrics on the following pages give criteria for evaluating students' expressive, informative, and persuasive writing. As you analyze your students' written work and talk to students about their writing, you will want to emphasize the Traits of Good Writing shown in this diagram.

▶ The Traits of Good Writing

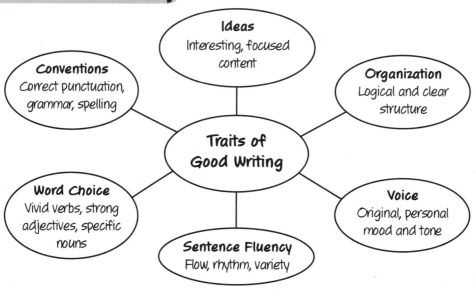

Ideas
Interesting, focused content

Conventions
Correct punctuation, grammar, spelling

Organization
Logical and clear structure

Traits of
Good Writing

Word Choice
Vivid verbs, strong adjectives, specific nouns

Voice
Original, personal mood and tone

Sentence Fluency
Flow, rhythm, variety

▶ Using the Rubrics

FOR ASSESSMENT Use the rubrics to score a student's work by noting which criteria best describe the piece of writing you are evaluating. Students can also use the rubrics to assess their own writing or for peer assessment in pairs or small groups. You may want to have students attach the marked rubric to the piece of writing in their portfolios so they can assess their progress over the course of the school year. You may also use the rubrics to point out strengths and areas for improvement in conferences with students and their family members.

AS TEACHING TOOLS Before students begin each writing assignment, discuss with them the rubric for the type of writing they are about to do. Have them set goals for their writing by focusing on the criteria for excellence, and encourage them to suggest other important criteria to add to the rubric. Then, as students work through the stages of the writing process, have them refer to appropriate points in the rubric to remind them what to include or how to improve their writing.

© Harcourt

Scoring Rubric for Expressive Writing

	Score of 4 ★★★★	Score of 3 ★★★	Score of 2 ★★	Score of 1 ★
Ideas	The paper fits the purpose. The audience would enjoy it.	The paper fits the purpose. The audience would probably enjoy it.	The purpose and audience are not very clear.	It is not possible to identify the purpose and audience.
Organization	There is a clear beginning, middle, and ending.	There is a beginning, middle, and ending, but one section may not be clearly defined.	The beginning, middle, and ending are not clearly defined.	The paper does not have a beginning, middle, or ending.
Word Choice	The paper has rich description, sensory details, and vivid words and phrases.	The paper has some description, a few good details, and some interesting words and phrases.	The paper has only a little description, only a few details, and few colorful words or phrases.	The paper has almost no description or details, and no interesting words or phrases.
Voice	The writing is original and engaging. It is appropriate for the purpose and audience.	The writing is appropriate for the purpose and audience.	Language isn't always appropriate for the audience and lacks originality.	Writer's voice is not evident in the writing.
Sentence Fluency	The sentences are written in a variety of ways.	Some sentences show variety, but many are the same type.	Most of the sentences are written in the same way.	Most sentences are not written correctly.
Conventions	There are very few errors in spelling, grammar and punctuation.	There are a few errors in spelling, grammar and punctuation.	There are many errors in spelling, grammar and punctuation.	There are so many errors that the writing is hard to understand.

Scoring Rubric for Informative Writing

	Score of 4 ★★★★	Score of 3 ★★★	Score of 2 ★★	Score of 1 ★
Ideas	The paper fits the purpose. The audience would understand it.	The paper fits the purpose. The audience would probably understand it.	The purpose and audience are not very clear.	It is not possible to identify the purpose and audience.
Organization	The paper has a clear introduction, a well-organized middle, and a summary or conclusion.	The paper has an introduction, a middle that is organized and mostly in logical order, and a summary or conclusion.	The topic is not introduced clearly. Some details are not in order or drift from the topic. The ending is not clear.	The paper does not have an introduction. Details are poorly organized. There is no summary or conclusion.
Word Choice	The paper has description and rich details, and it uses signal words and phrases appropriately.	The paper has some description and details. Some signal words or phrases are not clear or specific.	The paper has few details, not enough description, and few signal words or phrases.	The paper has almost no description or details, and no signal words or phrases.
Voice	The writing is original and engaging. It is appropriate for the purpose and audience.	The writing is appropriate for the purpose and audience.	The writing isn't always appropriate for the audience and lacks originality.	Writer's voice is not evident in the writing.
Sentence Fluency	The sentences are written in a variety of ways.	Some sentences show variety, but many are the same type.	Most of the sentences are written in the same way.	Most sentences are not written correctly.
Conventions	There are very few errors in spelling, grammar and punctuation.	There are a few errors in spelling, grammar and punctuation.	There are many errors in spelling, grammar and punctuation.	There are so many errors that the writing is hard to understand.

© Harcourt

Scoring Rubric for Persuasive Writing

	Score of 4 ★★★★	Score of 3 ★★★	Score of 2 ★★	Score of 1 ★
Ideas	The paper fits the purpose. It is designed to persuade a specific audience.	The paper fits the purpose. It might persuade the audience it was written for.	The purpose and audience are not very clear.	The paper does not have a clear purpose or identifiable audience.
Organization	The paper clearly states an opinion, gives logical reasons that support it, restates the opinion, and calls for action.	The paper states an opinion and gives reasons that mostly support it. The ending restates the opinion but does not call for action.	The paper states an opinion, but not all supporting reasons are logical or clear. The ending does not restate the opinion.	The paper states an opinion but does not support it. The ideas are poorly organized and drift from the topic.
Support for Ideas	The paper has details and/or examples that add information about the reasons.	The paper has some examples and/or details to add information about the reasons.	The paper has only a few details that add information about the reasons.	The paper has no details or examples.
Word Choice	The paper has colorful and specific words and phrases.	The paper has some vivid or colorful writing.	The paper has very few colorful words or phrases.	The paper has no interesting or emotional words or phrases.
Voice	The writing is original and engaging. It is appropriate for the purpose and audience.	The writing is appropriate for the purpose and audience.	The writing isn't always appropriate for the audience and lacks originality.	Writer's voice is not evident in the writing.
Sentence Fluency	The sentences are written in a variety of ways.	Some sentences show variety, but many do not.	Most sentences are written in the same way.	Most sentences are not written correctly.
Conventions	The paper has very few errors in spelling, grammar and punctuation.	There are a few errors in spelling, grammar and punctuation.	There are many errors in spelling, grammar and punctuation.	There are so many errors that the writing is hard to understand.

Vocabulary Activities

These activities can be used to practice specific vocabulary words from the lesson plans for the Leveled Library books or to extend and enrich your students' vocabularies. Mix and match activities according to your needs.

Vocabulary Password

Team A	Team B
̶H̶H̶T	///

MATERIALS:

- word cards with a vocabulary word on each card
- paper and pencils for keeping score

DIRECTIONS:

1. This game can be played by two teams of two to four players, plus one additional student who acts as Quiz Master.
2. The Quiz Master gives a word card to a player on Team A. The player defines the word without using the word itself. If the other players on Team A guess the word and use it in a sentence, their team gets one point.
3. If Team A cannot guess the word, the Quiz Master gives the same card to a player on Team B. That player gives his or her team a different clue for the word. If Team B guesses correctly and uses the word in a sentence, they get one point. If not, Team A gets another turn, and so on.
4. When the first word is guessed correctly, the Quiz Master begins the second round by giving Team B a new word. Teams continue to take turns, starting each round with a new word.

In a Spin

MATERIALS:

- simple cardboard spinner, as shown

DIRECTIONS:

1. Divide the spinner into sections, and write a vocabulary word in each section.
2. Two to four players take turns spinning the pointer.
3. The player who spins reads aloud the word on which the arrow stops. He or she then gives a definition for the word and uses it in a sentence.

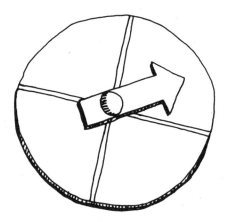

Vocabulary Activities

The Word Bug

MATERIALS:

- slips of paper with vocabulary words
- paper bag or small box
- picture of "Word Bug"
- chalkboard, chalk

DIRECTIONS:

1. Divide students into two teams. Fold the slips of paper with the vocabulary words, and place them in a paper bag or small box. Designate a small area on the chalkboard for each team.
2. The first player on Team A draws a slip of paper from the bag or box, reads the word aloud, and gives its definition. If the definition is correct, the player draws one part of the Word Bug's body on the chalkboard. If the definition is not correct, another team member can provide the correct definition but does not draw a part of the bug's body.
3. The two teams take turns picking words until one team has completed its drawing of the Word Bug.

VARIATION: This game can also be played by pairs of students. Player A picks a slip of paper and reads the word aloud. Player B gives the definition. If the definition is correct, Player B draws one part of the Word Bug. Players take turns until one of them has drawn the complete bug.

Sort Them Out

MATERIALS:

- paper
- pencils

DIRECTIONS:

1. Have students work in pairs or small groups to sort vocabulary words into categories. Categories might be based on similarities or differences in letter or syllable patterns, word meanings, parts of speech, or ways words are used. You may want to extend the activity by having students think of similar words to add to the completed categories.
2. After students have completed their sorts, have them compare and discuss their work with other pairs or groups.

Closed Sort: You provide the categories and model the sorting procedure.

Blind Sort: You provide the categories. Students work in pairs. One calls out a word; the other indicates where it belongs.

Writing Sort: You provide the categories and call out the words. Students write the words in the appropriate categories.

Open Sort: Students create categories based on the words to be sorted.

3. Depending on the words you are using, the skill level of your students, and students' familiarity with word sorts, you might choose any of the options listed.

© Harcourt

Vocabulary Activities

Tell a Story

MATERIALS:
- writing paper
- pencils
- tape recorder
- audiocassette tape

DIRECTIONS:
1. Have students work in small groups to make up brief stories or dialogues that include vocabulary words.
2. Depending on the available words and students' abilities, you may want to assign particular vocabulary words or set a minimum number of vocabulary words that students must use.
3. Students can write their stories or dialogues on paper and then record them. Have students play their tapes for classmates, who listen for the vocabulary words and decide whether they are used correctly.

Across and Down

MATERIALS:
- scrap paper
- pencils
- graph paper

DIRECTIONS:
1. Students work in pairs or small groups to construct puzzles using vocabulary words. Suggest that students look for shared letters and try different combinations on scrap paper until the puzzle looks good to them.
2. Have students copy their completed puzzle on graph paper and number each word in the puzzle.
3. Tell students to write clues for each of the words in the puzzle. A clue might be in the form of a picture, a definition, an antonym, or a sentence with a blank for the target word.
4. Have students exchange and complete each other's puzzles.

1. e x c h a n g e
2.
   o
3. b r e e z y
   r
   e
   c
   t

DOWN
1. not wrong

ACROSS
2. trade
3. A light wind blows on a _____ day.

© Harcourt

Vocabulary Activities

What's My Word?

MATERIALS:
- cards with vocabulary words
- chalkboard, chalk

Burden

DIRECTIONS:

1. Mix the vocabulary cards and place them face down.
2. The first player takes the top card and reads the word silently. He or she can pantomime the word or illustrate it on the board but cannot speak or write.
3. The other students try to guess the word. If they cannot figure it out in several tries, the student with the card can choose a classmate to help him or her communicate the meaning of the vocabulary word.
4. After students have guessed the correct word, another student takes the next card on the pile, and play continues.

Idiom Collecting

MATERIALS:
- chart paper
- markers

Seeing Red

DIRECTIONS:

1. Choose one or more idiomatic expressions that students have come across in their reading. Write the idioms on chart paper, and ask students to illustrate them in both their figurative and literal senses.
2. Use the expression to begin an idiom collection. Encourage students to add and illustrate idioms they encounter in their reading or other media or in their everyday lives.
3. As the collection grows, suggest that students look for ways to categorize the idioms. For example, some expressions refer to colors ("green with envy," "feeling blue"); some mention foods ("take the cake," "butter someone up"), and so on. Students might also categorize idioms that use a particular word ("get cold feet," "give the cold shoulder to," "throw cold water on.")

Using Retelling to Assess Comprehension

▶ Retelling

Retelling is an assessment strategy that may be used to measure a student's strengths and weaknesses in comprehension. Listening to a retelling provides insights into a student's ability to construct meaning, to identify important information, to make inferences, and to organize and summarize information. Specifically, listening to a retelling can help you assess whether the student

- relates the main idea and relevant details in sequence
- provides a summarizing statement
- includes story elements
- uses phrases, language, or vocabulary from the text
- evaluates an author's point of view, purpose, or craft
- stays on topic
- understands relationships in the text
- provides extensions of the text
- relates text to relevant experiences

▶ Oral Retelling

When conducting an oral retelling, ask students to tell the story in their own words. Try not to interrupt. Allow plenty of time for a student to complete an oral retelling, and be sure the student has nothing more to say before ending the session.

For the emerging reader who is reading books with limited text, the retelling may be short and fairly simple: adjust criteria in the attached rubric as necessary. For more complex books, if a student needs prompting, try using generic statements such as "Tell me more," "Keep going," and "You're doing a good job." If you need to elicit more information, prompt the student by asking open-ended questions such as these:

- What was the character's main problem?
- What was your favorite part of the story?
- Where did the story take place?
- Who else was in the story?
- How did the story end?
- What else do you remember from the story?

▶ Written Retelling

When conducting a written retelling, ask students to tell the story in their own words and not to worry about spelling or handwriting. Allow plenty of time for students to finish writing before ending the session.

Use the rubric on the following page to assess oral and written retellings.

~Scoring Rubric for Retellings~

SCORE	CHARACTERISTICS
3	**Proficient: Student retells the text using complex responses that demonstrate a thorough understanding and interpretation of the text.** • relates the main idea and important and supporting details • relates text in sequence • provides a summarizing statement • includes story elements such as setting, characters, plot, problems, and resolutions • uses phrases, language, vocabulary, sentence structure, or literary devices from the text • evaluates the author's point of view, purpose, or craft • stays on topic • discriminates between reality and fantasy, fact and fiction • understands relationships in text such as cause and effect • classifies, groups, compares, or contrasts information • provides extensions of the text by making connections to other texts, relating relevant experiences, or making generalizations
2	**Satisfactory: Student adequately retells the text and demonstrates an understanding of the text.** • relates the main idea and relevant details • relates most of the text in sequence • includes story elements such as setting, characters, main problem, and resolution • uses language or vocabulary from the text • stays on topic • discriminates between reality and fantasy • understands relationships in text such as cause and effect • classifies, groups, compares, or contrasts information • provides some extensions of the text by making connections to other texts or relating relevant experiences
1	**Minimal: Student makes several inaccurate, incomplete, or irrelevant statements or otherwise provides evidence of lack of comprehension.** • misunderstands main idea and omits important details • relates text out of sequence • omits story elements or provides incorrect information about setting, characters, and plot • provides a poorly organized or unclear structure • provides no extensions of the text

～Individual Reading Inventory～

The three Benchmark Books in the Leveled Library are accompanied by a two-page Individual Reading Inventory (IRI) feature in addition to their regular lessons. These IRI features appear on pages 304–309.

What Is an IRI?

An Individual Reading Inventory is an assessment tool for learning about a student's reading strategies and for planning instruction. While a student is reading aloud, the teacher records everything he or she says or does. An IRI has two primary parts: a reading passage and comprehension questions.

Administering the IRI

1. Before the reading, explain the task. Tell the student that he or she will read a passage aloud and then answer four questions.

2. During the reading, unobtrusively record oral miscues on the Individual Reading Inventory Form. Use the Marking Oral Reading Miscues chart to record oral errors and self-corrections.

3. After the reading, ask the student the questions at the bottom of the Individual Reading Inventory Form. Mark correct (+) and incorrect (-) responses.

Miscues

Total the number of miscues and self-corrections. Then follow the steps on the Individual Reading Inventory Summary Form to compute the Error Rate. Look for an Error Rate of 10% or less to confirm instructional reading level and 5% or less to confirm independent reading level.

Error Rate

1. Total the number of miscues.

2. Subtract the total number of self-corrections from the total number of miscues for a subtotal.

3. Divide this subtotal by the word count of the passage.

Fluency

Count the number of words read correctly in one minute. Count repetitions and self-corrections as correctly read words. Look for the following ranges of correctly read words per minute:

- 40–60 by the end of grade one
- 60–90 by the end of grade two
- 80–100 by the end of grade three
- 100–120 by the end of grade four
- 100–130 by the end of grade five
- 120–140 by the end of grade six

Comprehension

Total the number of correct responses to the questions. Look for a score of 75% or higher to confirm instructional reading level. To help evaluate comprehension errors, questions 1 and 2 require literal thinking, and questions 3 and 4 require inferential thinking.

～Marking Oral Reading Miscues～

READING MISCUE	MARKING	SAMPLE
1. Omissions	Circle the word, word part, or phrase omitted.	I will let you (go) in.
2. Insertions	Insert a caret (∧) and write in the inserted word or phrase.	We bought a ∧big parrot.
3. Substitutions	Write the word or phrase the student substitutes above the word or phrase in the text.	the Dad fixed ~~my~~ bike.
4. Mispronunciations	Write the phonetic mispronunciation above the word.	feed Have you ~~fed~~ the dog?
5. Self-corrections	Write the letters SC next to the miscue that is self-corrected.	~~spot~~ sc We took our space.
6. Repetitions	Draw a line under any part of the text that is repeated.	It is your garden <u>garden</u> now.
7. Punctuation	Circle punctuation missed. Write in any punctuation inserted.	Take them home (.) Then come back and you and I will go to town.
8. Hesitations	Place vertical lines at places where the student hesitates excessively.	Pretend / this is mine.

Individual Reading Inventory Form

STUDENT: _____   **DATE:** _____

SELECTION TITLE: *Willie's Not the Hugging Kind*, page 17   **WORD COUNT: 91**

But that was not how Willie felt. More than anything, Willie wanted to be the hugging kind.

Willie watched each morning as his daddy hugged first his mama and then Rose. He remembered how safe and happy he always felt with his daddy's strong arms around him.

He remembered how good it felt to put his arms around his mama. She smelled a little like lemon and a little like the lilac powder in the bathroom. She felt big and a little lumpy. She also felt soft and safe and warm.

Comments: _____

_____

_____

_____

_____

Indicate correct (+) or incorrect (–) response for each question:

1. **What does Willie want more than anything?** (to be the hugging kind)
2. **What does Willie remember each morning as he watches his family hugging?** (how it felt to be hugged)
3. **How are Willie's parents' hugs alike and different?** (Willie's daddy has strong arms. Willie's mama feels soft and warm and smells nice. He felt safe when either of them hugged him.)
4. **How does the author tell you that Willie wants to be hugged by his family?** (The author says that Willie wants to be the hugging kind and describes Willie's memories of being hugged.)

© Harcourt

Individual Reading Inventory Summary Form

STUDENT: _____   GRADE: _____   DATE: _____

PASSAGE: _____   WORD COUNT: _____

1. Miscues

    Total number of miscues _____

        Meaning-based miscues _____

        Graphic/sound-based miscues _____

    Comments and patterns observed: _____

_____

    Total number of self-corrections _____

    Comments and patterns observed: _____

_____

Error Rate

- Subtract the number of self-corrections from the total number of miscues for a subtotal.
- Divide the subtotal by the word count of the passage.

   _____ ÷ _____ = _____

     (SUBTOTAL)   (WORD COUNT)   ERROR RATE

2. Fluency

    Number of words read per minute _____

   _____ ÷ _____ = _____

(NUMBER OF CORRECT   **(WORD COUNT)**   **FLUENCY RATE**
WORDS READ PER MINUTE)

    Comments and patterns observed: _____

_____

3. Comprehension

   _____ ÷ **4 x 100** = _____%

(TOTAL CORRECT ANSWERS)   **COMPREHENSION SCORE**

    Comments and patterns observed: _____

_____

Summary Comments

_____

Willie's Not the Hugging Kind • 305

Individual Reading Inventory Form

STUDENT: _____   DATE: _____

SELECTION TITLE: *Coyote and the Laughing Butterflies,* page 12   WORD COUNT: 102

When Coyote's wife came home, she again found him asleep next to his empty sack. Now she was really mad! She sat down next to him with her empty wooden bowl and sighed very loudly.

Coyote awoke and jumped up all at once, rubbing his eyes with his big paws.

"My wife, I am sure that I went to the lake! My legs are stiff and sore from all this running," he told her.

She just shook her head and said, "Coyote, I'll give you one more chance. I need the salt by tomorrow."

"Tomorrow you will have the salt," Coyote promised.

Comments: _____

_____

_____

_____

_____

Indicate correct (+) or incorrect (–) response for each question:

1. **How does Coyote know he went to the lake?** (His legs are stiff and sore from running.)
2. **When does Coyote's wife need the salt?** (by tomorrow)
3. **Why does Coyote rub his eyes?** (He was sleeping until his wife's loud sigh woke him up.)
4. **How do you know this isn't the first time Coyote has failed to get the salt for his wife?** (The passage says that his wife found him asleep *again* and that she will give him *one more chance.*)

© Harcourt

Individual Reading Inventory Summary Form

STUDENT: _____   GRADE: _____   DATE: _____

PASSAGE: _____   WORD COUNT: _____

1. Miscues

Total number of miscues _____

    Meaning-based miscues _____

    Graphic/sound-based miscues _____

Comments and patterns observed: _____

_____

Total number of self-corrections _____

Comments and patterns observed: _____

_____

Error Rate

- Subtract the number of self-corrections from the total number of miscues for a subtotal.

- Divide the subtotal by the word count of the passage.

_____ ÷ _____ = _____

    (SUBTOTAL)   **(WORD COUNT)**   **ERROR RATE**

2. Fluency

Number of words read per minute _____

_____ ÷ _____ = _____

(NUMBER OF CORRECT   **(WORD COUNT)**   **FLUENCY RATE**
WORDS READ PER MINUTE)

Comments and patterns observed: _____

_____

3. Comprehension

_____ ÷ **4 x 100** = _____%

(TOTAL CORRECT ANSWERS)   **COMPREHENSION SCORE**

Comments and patterns observed: _____

_____

Summary Comments

_____

Individual Reading Inventory Form

STUDENT: _____   **DATE:** _____

SELECTION TITLE: *The Chickenhouse House*, page 33   **WORD COUNT: 104**

Then one day, Grandfather and Grandmother, the aunts and uncles, and a whole lot of neighbors came to help build the house. Wagon after wagon drove into the shade of the cottonwood trees. The men climbed down with their tools in boxes, the women with baskets of food. The women left jars of tea and root beer in the creek to cool. They lugged the baskets to the chickenhouse.

Alena was glad to see her cousins and friends, glad it was house-raising day.

She played ball-and-base and pull-away with the other children. Between games she helped fetch cool drinks for the thirsty working men.

Comments: _____

_____

_____

_____

_____

_____

Indicate correct (+) or incorrect (–) response for each question:

1. **Why is Alena happy on this day?** (She is happy to be with her cousins and friends and happy that it is house-raising day.)
2. **Who comes to help build the house?** (Grandfather, Grandmother, aunts, uncles, and neighbors)
3. **How is the work of the men different from the work of the women?** (The men work on building the house. The women help prepare food and drinks for the men.)
4. **What job does Alena have that day?** (She and the other children fetch cool drinks for the workers.)

Individual Reading Inventory Summary Form

STUDENT: _____   GRADE: _____   DATE: _____

PASSAGE: _____   WORD COUNT: _____

1. Miscues

Total number of miscues _____

    Meaning-based miscues _____

    Graphic/sound-based miscues _____

Comments and patterns observed: _____

_____

Total number of self-corrections _____

Comments and patterns observed: _____

_____

Error Rate

- Subtract the number of self-corrections from the total number of miscues for a subtotal.

- Divide the subtotal by the word count of the passage.

_____ ÷ _____ = _____

    (SUBTOTAL)   **(WORD COUNT)**   **ERROR RATE**

2. Fluency

Number of words read per minute _____

_____ ÷ _____ = _____

(NUMBER OF CORRECT   **(WORD COUNT)**   **FLUENCY RATE**

WORDS READ PER MINUTE)

Comments and patterns observed: _____

_____

3. Comprehension

_____ ÷ **4 x 100** = _____%

(TOTAL CORRECT ANSWERS)   **COMPREHENSION SCORE**

Comments and patterns observed: _____

_____

Summary Comments

_____

Snowshoe Thompson
Page 20
1. He is a young boy who has not seen his father for a while. He wants his father to come home at Christmas.
2. getting a letter to Danny's pa in California
3. He will make snowshoes for crossing the mountains. Then he will take the letter to Danny's dad.

Page 21
1. He says everyone in Norway uses them. He must be from Norway.
2. It shows the time period: people had to make what they needed by themselves. No one could just go to a store and buy skis. The scene shows that Snowshoe Thompson is not only brave but also good with his hands.
3. He is bold. He is good with his hands. He is determined. He is patient with Danny.

Page 22
1. He tries them out.
2. They think he is crazy. They call him names. They predict failure.
3. Possible responses: He could freeze to death; he could get lost; an animal could attack him; he could lose his food and go hungry.

Page 23
1. Responses will vary.
2. It is important to try out new ideas. You must sometimes take a risk to do something good.
3. Responses will vary.

Page 27
1. C 2. J 3. B 4. G 5. C 6. F 7. D 8. G 9. C
10. Responses may vary. Students should summarize the main events of *Snowshoe Thompson* and give some idea of how Danny will portray the events for a listener.

Coyote: A Trickster Tale from the American Southwest
Page 30
1. He means Coyote goes wherever he wants to go.
2. He does not think about what he is doing.
3. They may feel afraid because they know that Coyote is always getting into trouble.

Page 31
1. He always wants what other animals have.

2. He calls Coyote foolish and suggests that the crows have some fun with him.
3. They stick some of their feathers into Coyote's fur.

Page 32
1. All the feathers are from the crows' left wings.
2. They cackle and chuckle at how Coyote behaves.
3. Coyote is getting boastful and rude. He dances out of step and sings off-key.

Page 33
1. It says Coyote's tumbling into the dust made him the color of dust. His tail has a black tip because it was burned as he fell.
2. He runs after the flying crows even though he knows what they have done to him.
3. Responses will vary. Students should give examples of similarities between *Coyote* and one of the stories in *Journeys of Wonder*.

Page 37
1. B 2. F 3. D 4. H 5. B 6. J 7. B 8. J 9. B
10. Students should include specific examples from the book that show what makes Coyote an interesting character.

Two of Everything
Page 40
1. a poor farming man and wife who lived long ago in China
2. in a farming area of China
3. It is ancient. It is large. Mr. Haktak has never come across it before.

Page 41
1. A second hairpin appears in the pot.
2. It makes two of anything that is put into it.
3. They are very excited about it.

Page 42
1. She bends over to hug the pot. When the door opens, Mrs. Haktak loses her balance and falls inside headfirst.
2. There are now two Mrs. Haktaks.
3. They are worried about the pot's special powers. Responses will vary.

Page 43
1. Responses will vary.
2. They thought it was either good or okay. They did not think it was a problem.
3. Responses will vary.

© Harcourt

Page 47
1. A 2. J 3. C 4. G 5. D 6. F 7. C 8. F 9. C
10. They were not unhappy at the beginning of the story, but they seem happier at the end because they have so much.

Booker T. Washington
Page 50
1. They were not free and had to work hard.
2. The girls could go to school and did not have to work, while Booker could not go to school and had to work hard.
3. Their cabin was rundown, they had only burlap clothes, and they did not have enough to eat.

Page 51
1. He may have heard of the city or the President and decided he liked that name.
2. It is likely that the family needed the money Booker could earn.
3. One difference was that he was now free and could dream about a different future. One thing that stayed the same was that he had to work hard.

Page 52
1. The mines were dark, dirty, and unsafe, while Mrs. Ruffin's house was not. Also, Booker could go to school after he finished his work in the house.
2. His mother bought him a speller, and his neighbors gave him whatever they could to help him get to school.
3. She did not know anything about him, and when he came in he was dirty.

Page 53
1. He had good training and teaching experience at Hampton Institute. Also, he believed very strongly in the need for education and hard work.
2. He always had plans for the future and believed that he could change his life. He was always willing to work hard to get what he wanted.
3. Responses will vary. Students should cite examples of the kind of behavior that young readers might imitate.

Page 57
1. B 2. H 3. A 4. J 5. C 6. F 7. B 8. J 9. D
10. Responses will vary. Students should cite examples of Booker's goals (such as learning as much as he could) and of how he reached them (such as by believing in his dream and working hard).

Ibis: A True Whale Story
Page 60
1. She is a baby humpback whale.
2. They have to get used to boats. They have to learn not to be afraid of them.
3. At first Ibis is afraid of the boats, but after she sees the friendly faces of the people in them, she decides she likes the boats.

Page 61
1. She is curious. She is learning to manage for herself, and she is friendly to the people in the boats.
2. The net keeps Ibis from swimming easily. It is around her mouth, so it makes it hard for her to eat, too.
3. Possible responses: Maybe Blizzard will get the other whales to help her. Maybe Ibis will get sick and die. Maybe the people in the boats will rescue Ibis.

Page 62
1. She goes toward the deep ocean.
2. Ibis is very weak. She might die.
3. She does not know what is happening, so she is very scared. This is not something that usually happens to whales.

Page 63
1. Responses will vary.
2. Possible response: People can hurt or help whales. People should learn about whales so both will be able to live together.
3. Responses will vary.

Page 67
1. C 2. F 3. D 4. G 5. C 6. F 7. D 8. G 9. B
10. Responses will vary. Responses might include descriptions of Ibis's feelings and her connection to humans.

The Edible Pyramid
Page 70
1. The Edible Pyramid restaurant
2. The restaurant is shaped like a pyramid. The restaurant has a food pyramid menu.
3. The cat in the tuxedo is the spokesperson; the customers are animals, such as a mouse, a rabbit, and a pelican.

Page 71
1. barley soup, granola, corn grits, millet
2. The rows are divisions of the pyramid. They are also groupings. For example, the first row groups bread, cereal, rice, and pasta; the second row

groups fruits and vegetables.

3. The bottom row is wider than the second row, which means more servings per day. The bottom row also contains different foods than the second row.

Page 72
1. the milk, yogurt, and cheese group and the meat, poultry, fish, dry beans, and nuts group
2. It is poultry, so it is in the meat, poultry, eggs, fish, dry beans, and nuts group.
3. Possible responses: The pictures are interesting and make the book fun to look at. The pictures help you understand what is in each category.

Page 73
1. Responses will vary.
2. She wants you to learn healthful ways to eat. She wants you to learn the food groups and how much you should eat each day from each one.
3. Responses will vary.

Page 77
1. A **2.** J **3.** C **4.** F **5.** D **6.** G **7.** B **8.** H **9.** B
10. Responses will vary. Students should explain that the pyramid is wide at the bottom, or base, and that the group you should eat most from is at the base: the bread group. As you go up the rows, you eat fewer servings. The second row has fruits and vegetables, the third row has meat and milk, and the last row, or top, of the pyramid has fats and sweets, of which you should eat very little.

Making Friends
Page 80
1. Being alone is okay and can even be fun; being lonely is wanting to be with someone but not being able to.
2. He is lonely, and his dad gives him a game. Chaz thinks the game will help him find new friends. When it doesn't, Chaz gets angry at his dad.
3. Possible responses: anger, nastiness, shyness

Page 81
1. Possible responses: good times and bad times; laughing, jokes, bad feelings
2. There is no one way to make friends. Sometimes it is easy, and sometimes it is very hard.
3. Amy feels the way I do. I have had some of the same feelings she has.

Page 82
1. Possible responses: friends you write to, faraway friends, best friends, friends in groups, friends

who are your relatives
2. Your friend can go off with someone else, making you feel left out and jealous. Also, the friendship can change over time.
3. Ashika does not want another friend to come between her and her best friend.

Page 83
1. Responses will vary.
2. It is not easy to make friends; everyone has trouble with it sometimes.
3. Responses will vary.

Page 87
1. C **2.** J **3.** B **4.** F **5.** A **6.** H **7.** D **8.** J **9.** D
10. You should try not to be jealous, accept that friendships change, and tell friends how you feel. Don't expect to make friends by giving away candy or other things, owning the best things, or trying to get back at those who make you feel bad.

Willie's Not the Hugging Kind
Page 90
1. His friend Jo-Jo made him feel it was silly.
2. He thinks it is babyish.
3. Both want to be hugged. Rose accepts hugs, but Willie pretends he doesn't like them.

Page 91
1. pride, fear
2. hugging his mom and dad
3. that Jo-Jo was the one who said hugging was silly, not he

Page 92
1. He means that hugging is like being attacked or that it is wrong. He does not want it to happen to him.
2. He feels frustrated. He feels sad. He feels a little happy just to be hugging *something*.
3. It is sad and lonely. It is not the way life is supposed to be.

Page 93
1. Responses will vary.
2. She wants you to think about how good it is to hug and be hugged back. She wants you to show your feelings and not hide them.
3. Responses will vary.

Page 97
1. D **2.** F **3.** A **4.** G **5.** B **6.** G **7.** C **8.** F **9.** C
10. Responses will vary. They will probably be friends because they still like each other, even if they disagree about hugging.

Frida María

Page 100

1. Details in the pictures and the text set the story long ago in the Southwest.
2. Frida is cheerful and adventurous. She loves horses and her family.
3. Mamá wants Frida to behave like a lady, and Frida wants to ride in a horse race.

Page 101

1. Cook says Frida learns quickly, and she shouts *Ole!* when Frida stops the rat. Mamá says, "No, no, NO! This is not done!"
2. Mamá thinks Frida is too wild. She thinks Frida should just sew, cook, sing, and dance.
3. Frida is sad; she does not notice her sisters' kisses; all she can think of is Mamá and Fiesta; she cannot take a deep breath.

Page 102

1. Frida feels sad. She cannot be herself or use her energy.
2. She just watches everyone having fun because she cannot ride in the race.
3. She cannot help it. She wants to ride so much that she just jumps on when she sees the race.

Page 103

1. Responses will vary.
2. The themes involve being yourself while also being part of a family and community.
3. Frida's biggest success is showing Mamá that she is special, even though she is not the proper señorita Mamá had wanted her to be.

Page 107

1. A 2. J 3. C 4. G 5. A 6. J 7. A 8. G 9. A
10. Responses will vary. Students should include specific examples that show Mamá's opinion of Frida at the beginning of the book and at the end.

Jordi's Star

Page 110

1. Jordi chases his goats over bare rocky hills, lives in a hut, and has to walk to the river for water.
2. He wants to dig a well; no, he doesn't reach water.
3. The storm fills Jordi's hole with rainwater.

Page 111

1. Before he sees the star, he is tired and lonely. Seeing the star fills him with joy and wonder.
2. He is trying to protect the star and make it feel welcome and safe.
3. No. He thinks the star goes to the bottom of the pool to sleep during the day.

Page 112

1. The rain causes the water level to rise inside the wall Jordi has built around the pool, so the pool becomes a pond.
2. He sells goat's milk cheese and asks his clients for cuttings, seedlings, and seeds to add to his garden.
3. He is becoming very happy; his life is easier because he doesn't have to go so far for water.

Page 113

1. Responses will vary.
2. Finding something to love can change a person's life. Land that has been ruined can be restored. Happiness can lead to more happiness. Effort and time can bring beauty to a bare place.
3. Responses will vary. For example, students may like the theme, the setting, or the way the author describes things.

Page 117

1. D 2. F 3. B 4. F 5. C. 6. J 7. C 8. G 9. A
10. Students should include specific reasons from the story that explain how finding the star changes his life.

Cam Jansen and the Triceratops Pops Mystery

Page 120

1. Jennifer has a photographic memory. She is like a camera: she takes pictures in her mind. *Cam* is short for *camera*.
2. The author gives an example of how well Cam can remember what she sees.
3. Cam will discover a mystery and solve it.

Page 121

1. It would be hard to find things at first. It is a big store with lots of people and lots of different departments. Until you get to know the store, it could take a while to find what you want.
2. the floor plan; the map; where everything is located
3. They check the aisle they think it will be in, ask for help, and look where they are told to look.

Page 122

1. He is organized and knows where everything is, but he is not very patient or helpful to his customers.
2. He thinks they were bought quickly.
3. They were stolen. Too many disappeared in just a few minutes.

Page 123

1. The magnetic strips on the CDs sets off the beeper on the security gate.
2. Possible responses: to make the reader laugh, to add interest, and to make fun of the funny names, words, and songs of many singing groups
3. I would not care about the mystery; I would look out the back door; I would tell everything I knew or thought to the security guard.

Page 124

1. It is wet. The man seems to be carrying a watermelon that has already been cut open, which does not make sense.
2. She thinks this may be the way the thief escaped.
3. She is a suspect. She is suspicious because she is wearing a raincoat. The raincoat is a good place to hide stolen CDs.

Page 125

1. Cam is taking a mental picture.
2. They walk out the back entrance and someone closes the door on them. The door locks, and they cannot get back in.
3. She discovers a trail or she discovers evidence.

Page 126

1. He thinks they are just kids who do not know anything. He is busy.
2. Yes. She suggests a believable explanation of what happened.
3. Cam and Eric. They know what to do. The security guard is not using his head the way they are.

Page 127

1. Responses will vary.
2. He thinks she really uses her head and her memory. He thinks she is smart and she knows how to stick with her ideas.
3. Responses will vary.

Page 131

1. A 2. H 3. D 4. J 5. B 6. J 7. C 8. G 9. D
10. Responses will vary. Students may say that Cam uses her photographic memory. She also uses the ability to watch closely and think about what she sees. Both Eric and Cam refuse to give up. They both think fast.

Julian's Glorious Summer
Page 134

1. One "story," or lie, is about not saying Gloria's name; the other is about having to work all summer.
2. He is afraid of bicycles. He does not want to have anything to do with bicycles.
3. Responses will vary.

Page 135

1. This is a way of showing how angry Julian's dad is. His eyes are practically on fire (red) or cold as ice (blue).
2. Julian has gotten himself into a fix. He does not know what to do, so he just lies there. You do not know what will happen next as the chapter closes.
3. Julian will have to work hard all summer; he will admit he lied; he will learn to ride a bike.

Page 136

1. It is funny. It shows the tricks brothers play on each other.
2. She wants him to know that something better will happen. She wants him to think about what happened and try to change it.
3. He is a normal kid. He sometimes tells stories. He is afraid of riding a bike but does not want anyone to know, maybe because he is ashamed or embarrassed. He is a little too proud to say what he is feeling.

Page 137

1. Responses will vary.
2. Julian gets over his fear. He grows up a little. Maybe he even learns something about telling stories. The author wants you to know that you should just admit what you are afraid of.
3. Responses will vary.

Page 141

1. C 2. F 3. B 4. F 5. C 6. G 7. A 8. J 9. C
10. Responses will vary. Students may note that once Julian's mom talks to him and gets him to admit his fear, things change. Students might also reasonably say the turning point happens when Julian's dad gets him the bike. Then Julian almost has to learn to ride it. Julian's summer goes from being full of "suffering" to being glorious. Julian changes from sad to happy.

Coyote and the Laughing Butterflies
Page 144

1. The setting is a grassy mesa surrounded by hills. There is a salt lake about a mile away.
2. Yes; he wants to do nothing but sleep.
3. trees, mud, grass, and animals

© Harcourt

Page 145
1. He is up bright and early the next day and runs even faster this time. He does not even stop to talk to his friend Lizard.
2. Perhaps he has slept instead of doing jobs for her before.
3. Do not take a nap.

Page 146
1. He may want to save time and energy so he does not need to take a nap this time.
2. He feels good about finally completing the task and getting so much salt.
3. Responses will vary.

Page 147
1. Answers will vary.
2. It says that the butterflies laugh so hard at the trick they have played on Coyote that they fly in crazy patterns.
3. Responses will vary.

Page 151
1. A 2. H 3. D 4. H 5. C 6. F 7. C 8. G 9. D
10. Responses will vary. Students should include specific examples from the book that support their assessments of Coyote's character.

My Horse of the North
Page 154
1. Northern Iceland in summer. It is the time when sheep roam in the mountains. *Réttir* will come at summer's end.
2. The sheep are up there. She is dreaming of *réttir*.
3. The mystery makes you want to find out what *réttir* is. Maybe he will tell what it is on the next page.

Page 155
1. He puts the pronunciation in parentheses after the word; he usually gives a definition in the text.
2. The pictures show dapples, gold mane (long neck hair) and tail, and her stripe and snip.
3. He says they are gentle and friendly, a unique breed, and as old as the Vikings.

Page 156
1. Margrét loves Perla; she talks to Perla, and her favorite chore is brushing the horse.
2. They have never ridden in one before.
3. The cows herd themselves. The children must find more challenging animals to practice on.

Page 157
1. They laugh because the idea of herding geese is funny.
2. The pictures show what the geese look like and what they do. They show why herding them is funny.
3. Margrét and Perla do work well together; Margrét knows how to tell Perla what to do, Perla responds to Margrét, and they succeed in herding the geese.

Page 158
1. Margrét's mother makes sweaters of the wool. They may sell wool, sweaters, or meat from the sheep for a living.
2. They work together to herd the geese.
3. They can stop, ride fast, and turn the horses to herd animals.

Page 159
1. They have successfully tested their skills with the rams.
2. The words *the big roundup* tell what *réttir* is. Responses will vary.
3. The *réttir* brings the sheep down from the mountains to be protected and fed in barns during the winter.

Page 160
1. surprised, because she gasps; confident, because she feels ready
2. They are ready to herd the sheep; they direct them and keep them going. If they had not practiced, Margrét might fall off or they might not have been able to herd the sheep.
3. Responses will vary.

Page 161
1. Responses will vary.
2. Possible responses: Practice helps people accomplish their dreams. Children can be important helpers in a family business. *Réttir* is an important annual event in Iceland.
3. The author had to learn about Iceland and visit or live there to take the pictures. He had to know about horses and be good at writing and photography.

Page 165
1. C 2. G 3. C 4. J 5. A 6. G 7. D 8. H 9. A
10. Responses will vary. Students should explain what réttir is, when and why it is held, and how the sheep are brought down from the mountains.

Mama Provi and the Pot of Rice
Page 168
1. Lucy spends the night twice a month. She and Mama Provi play games, listen to records, share stories, and have meals together.
2. She grew up in a big family and learned to cook for a dozen people.
3. It is her special dish, and she is making it to take to Lucy, who cannot visit because she has chicken pox.

Page 169
1. She is going to the eighth floor to visit Lucy.
2. She stops to rest, smells delicious food, and knocks on her neighbors' doors to exchange her rice for their special dishes.
3. She is thoughtful and generous because she goes to see Lucy and shares her special dish. She does not think twice about knocking; she has a good sense of smell.

Page 170
1. Mrs. Landers called her to say Mama Provi was coming up.
2. Mrs. Woo gives tea but does not take any rice.
3. They are friendly and generous. They like Mama Provi.

Page 171
1. Responses will vary.
2. It is good to be friends with your neighbors. People have different talents. When people share their talents, everyone benefits.
3. The author might live in an apartment building, have friendly neighbors, or know someone like Mama Provi.

Page 175
1. C 2. G 3. B 4. F 5. D 6. J 7. B 8. J 9. D
10. Students should include specific examples that show that Mama Provi reached her goal of cheering up Lucy.

What Do Authors Do?
Page 178
1. One plans to write a chapter book about his dog. The other plans to write a picture book about her cat.
2. Rufus is the dog that belongs to the man. Max is the cat that belongs to the woman.
3. The authors watch their pets from their windows. Rufus appears to be chasing Max.

Page 179
1. They make lists or outlines. Sometimes they sketch in order to get ideas.
2. The authors need more information, so they begin to search for it and ask questions.
3. You could group the characters as two authors and two pets, or you could group the man and the dog, and the woman and the cat.

Page 180
1. getting ideas, prewriting, gathering information, drafting, revising; responses will vary.
2. Some writing is not good enough. It is not interesting, does not stay focused on the story, or is not clear.
3. They read one another's writing and make suggestions for improving it. They also tell what is good about the writing.

Page 181
1. They get writer's block; the process can take a year or more; they get rejection letters. They solve these problems by sticking to their goals and revising their work.
2. Sometimes the rejection letters make the authors cry.
3. Writers just keep working, working, working. They have to make a lot of changes. They have to have faith in their work.

Page 182
1. The editor may ask for changes.
2. They might change the ending, the beginning, or a particular chapter. Responses will vary.
3. The writing process is complicated. It takes a lot of work and involves a lot of steps, people, and changes.

Page 183
1. Designers decide how the book will look.
2. Authors don't have much say. They have more say if they also do the illustrations. Otherwise, the designer and the illustrator take over.
3. Illustrations are very important in books for children. They have to be exciting. They have to match the story exactly.

Page 184
1. All the pages are printed at once on giant sheets of paper that are put through printing presses.
2. It means secured to the cover.
3. It can take a year or many years. Usually it takes at least a year, because the printing part alone can take 8 months.

Page 185
1. Responses will vary.
2. The author wants her readers to know the many

things writers go through to write a book. Her main idea is that writing a book takes a lot of hard work and involves many steps.

3. Responses will vary.

Page 189
1. C **2.** H **3.** A **4.** J **5.** B **6.** F **7.** C **8.** J **9.** D
10. Responses should address aspects of being an author that are described in the book.

Earth: Our Planet in Space
Page 192
1. All people live on Earth.
2. A layer of air (the atmosphere) separates Earth from space.
3. The dark places are seas, and the gray places are land. The white places are clouds or snow.

Page 193
1. A planet is "a large world that travels around the sun." (page 4)
2. The sun is a million times bigger; light comes from the sun.
3. Uranus, Neptune, and Pluto are missing. For some reason (size? distance?) they were not included among the eight photographs used to make the picture.

Page 194
1. People long ago could not get into space to see Earth; on Earth, the horizon looks flat, except for land features such as hills.
2. Earth is (nearly) round, like a ball; it spins like a top.
3. As Earth spins, the part away from the sun is in darkness (night) and the part facing the sun has light (day). Whatever part is in darkness is always turning toward light, and vice versa.

Page 195
1. Students have traveled around the sun as many times as their age.
2. Earth and the sun are about 93 million miles apart; this makes Earth the right temperature to support life.
3. If Earth's orbit changed, temperatures would get colder or hotter. If the change were great enough, life would be altered and perhaps ended.

Page 196
1. Earth's tilt and orbit cause the changing seasons.
2. Seasons change least at the equator because the middle is least affected by Earth's tilt.
3. Days are longer on the part of Earth tilted toward the sun (summer), shorter where Earth is tilted away from the sun (winter).

Page 197
1. Earth's atmosphere is essential to life; it regulates temperature and contains water, dust, and gases.
2. The magnetic field protects, or shields, Earth from radiation, which could kill everything.
3. An aurora is colored lights that are visible in the night sky. The lights are caused by Earth's magnetic field.

Page 198
1. Oceans cover nearly three-quarters of Earth. This is important because changes in the ocean can affect all of Earth.
2. Sometimes mountains are pushed up. Water and weather erosion, on the other hand, wear away rock and earth; erosion usually occurs slowly. (Other natural forces, such as earthquakes, work faster.)
3. These photos were taken from space or from an airplane. They show Earth from above, and so show more than a land photo would.

Page 199
1. Responses will vary.
2. Earth is a special and unique planet. Earth is the only planet that supports life. Natural and human forces change Earth's surface. Most of what people do cannot be seen from space.
3. Responses will vary.

Page 203
1. C **2.** G **3.** A **4.** J **5.** A **6.** G **7.** D **8.** F **9.** A
10. Students should use examples from the book to tell how Earth's atmosphere, magnetic field, and distance from the sun allow it to support life.

The Chickenhouse House
Page 206
1. fall; grass as high as the horses' backs; not a bush or shrub on the land; only a few cottonwood trees along a creek
2. They have moved to a new farm. The chickenhouse is the only building that Father has had time to build.
3. She finds it dim, bare, and too small.

Page 207
1. Everything feels strange; the night sounds are different.
2. Grandfather and Uncle Clark come to help Father build a shed for the animals.
3. Alena misses her grandparents and living in their house. She leans her head against the cow and

asks it if it misses Grandfather's barn.

Page 208
1. At first she thought it was dim and too little; now she thinks it is nice to sit inside and listen to the rain.
2. She may be jealous.
3. The house is too full of people, voices, and smells. Emily and William are mean to her.

Page 209
1. Details include sleet and snow, howling wind, and blizzard.
2. William shakes out the contents right away; Alena hugs hers to her chest and waits to open it. Alena is patient; she treasures special moments.
3. The author probably believes that holidays are times when families should stop and enjoy each other's company. Mother and Father sit together and have coffee; Alena is content to sit on Father's lap. Earlier the whole family gathered at Grandfather's for Thanksgiving Day dinner.

Page 210
1. Mother's voice comes in little jerks; she pushes back her hair, which people often do when they have been working hard.
2. He has to plow the fields and plant seeds for crops of oats and corn.
3. She may know that once a bird smells the scent of humans on its nest, it will abandon the nest and the eggs in it.

Page 211
1. The cellar must stay cool in order to keep the family's stored food fresh.
2. Friends and relatives arrive to help Father frame, side, and roof the house. The women bring food to share at a picnic.
3. She is probably relieved because she has gotten used to living in the chickenhouse house, and now she does not want to move out.

Page 212
1. When Alena sits on her sofa, her toes touch the floor instead of dangling like they used to do. This shows that Alena is taller and her legs are longer.
2. She means that Alena feels strange and uncomfortable.
3. Alena cannot sleep, even though she is tired. She goes out to the chickenhouse and falls asleep on the floor.

Page 213
1. The people in "Cloudy with a Chance of Meatballs" live in a place where all the food they need falls from the sky. The family in "The Crowded House" live in a tiny cottage that gets even more crowded when they bring animals into the house to live with them.
2. People should appreciate that they have a family and a place to live.
3. It shows the kinds of chores children had to do, the clothes they wore, and the games they played.

Page 217
1. B 2. F 3. D 4. H 5. D 6. G 7. A 8. J 9. B
10. She may mean that she had to get used to living in the chickenhouse, but when she did, she really liked it; getting used to any new home takes time.

Aldo Ice Cream
Page 220
1. Aldo is funny; he lies on the ground to look at ants. He notices things, like the ants. He is imaginative, because he imagines what it is like to be an ant or a fish.
2. Aldo wants to learn to swim, to teach DeDe's dog tricks, and to try all the ice cream flavors at a shop in his town. To do these things, he is taking swimming lessons, has taught the dog to shake and play dead, and has tried some flavors.
3. He asks questions about the people and wants to help them be happier. He also wants to visit them again.

Page 221
1. Possible responses: The quarter-a-day plan is silly, because Aldo has no way to make a quarter a day. He has to pay back the quarters he borrows.
2. Mr. Puccini begins to talk, because Aldo asks him about his fish.
3. The cats-on-wheels plan is funny; it is not very safe or nice for the cat, but it does cheer up Mrs. Nardo.

Page 222
1. He finds an advertisement for the Grubby-Sneaker Contest.
2. If Aldo wins the contest, his mother will give him the money she would have spent on shoes to add to his ice-cream machine fund.
3. Trevor's sneakers are grubbier than Aldo's, so Trevor might win the contest.

Page 223

1. "The Three Little Javelinas" is similar because it is about three siblings, and there are three children in Aldo's family. The javelinas help each other the way Aldo helps Karen get her ice-cream maker.
2. Friends and family members can help each other out and do things together that they could not do alone.
3. Possible responses: I thought it was great that Aldo won and got the ice-cream machine. It was nice of him to take ice cream to everyone. DeDe was smart to think of getting Trevor disqualified.

Page 227

1. C 2. J 3. A 4. H 5. A 6. G 7. C 8. H 9. B
10. Responses may vary. Students should write as Mr. Puccini or Mrs. Nardo. They should explain how they met Aldo and tell what they think of him and why.

The Wave
Page 230

1. their rice fields
2. He is older and wiser. He lives much farther up the mountain. He seems to watch, while the others seem more active. He is more like a leader; the people are more like followers.
3. Possible response: A big earthquake will hurt the village.

Page 231

1. Ojiisan is wiser. He has heard about tidal waves before, but the villagers seem to have never heard of them.
2. He sets fire to his own rice fields.
3. He is sad to lose his fields, but he knows he is doing the right thing. He feels the responsibility of being a leader. He feels good that he can save the villagers.

Page 232

1. all the people of the village
2. Yes, because he was able to save the villagers.
3. The tidal wave strikes the shore.

Page 233

1. Responses will vary.
2. Sometimes you have to act quickly and give up your own interests to save other people.
3. Responses will vary.

Page 237

1. B 2. J 3. C 4. F 5. B 6. H 7. A 8. J 9. B

10. Responses will vary. Students may say that tidal waves come after an earthquake. They may also say that before a tidal wave comes, the sea pulls away from the land. Tidal waves are like walls or cliffs of water. They smash down on the land, wrecking what they hit. Tidal waves can kill everyone on shore.

Ramona Quimby, Age 8
Page 240

1. She is like most eight-year-olds. She thinks a lot about what people say and do. She thinks fast with Yard Ape. She likes school. She has a family that loves her.
2. Ramona has to be nice to Willa Jean. Otherwise, her parents might not be able to leave her at the Kemp's. She feels that if she does the wrong thing, her mom will not be able to work full time and her dad will not be able to go to school.
3. She tells about the bus and a kid on the bus who kicks Ramona's seat and steals her eraser. She tells about some things that happen on first days, like needing to learn names.

Page 241

1. embarrassment, fitting in, wanting her teacher to like her
2. There is not a lot of money to spend; they are trying to save money.
3. They put some funny things together, like chicken, yogurt, and chili powder. They make a big mess. They cannot really cook.

Page 242

1. She throws up in the classroom.
2. Possible responses: She is sick; she feels sorry for herself; she is worried about her mom having to leave work; she is embarrassed; her mother's kindness makes her feel tender and sad.
3. Possible responses: She will have some kind of new disaster; she will do something different from what everyone else does; she will do a great job.

Page 243

1. Responses will vary.
2. She thinks that family, knowing how to get along, and being yourself are all important.
3. Responses will vary.

Page 247

1. C 2. H 3. C 4. G 5. C 6. F 7. C 8. G 9. A
10. Responses will vary. Ramona and Beezus are both from the same family, are both beginner cooks, and seem to like to read and be good

© Harcourt

students. Ramona and Beezus are different ages and go to different schools. They have different friends. Beezus does not have to be responsible for Willa Jean.

Bonesy and Isabel
Page 250
1. The setting is Sunbury Road, a farm, in summer.
2. They have adopted her from El Salvador to give her a safe home.
3. Isabel learns about life on the farm as she explores the house and spends time with the people and animals.

Page 251
1. They are kind and caring. They show this by taking care of the animals and by bringing Isabel to live with them.
2. The other animals live outside. Bonesy lives inside because he is old.
3. Isabel loves Bonesy. She feeds him treats, pets him, and studies her English with him under the table. Her actions say *I care for you.*

Page 252
1. They are a family of three, like Isabel's family; the parents are good friends; Emmie repeats *El Salvador* to make Isabel smile again.
2. Bonesy has died: He doesn't respond to Isabel; she can't feel his breath.
3. Vera puts her arm around Isabel. Ivan joins "the family circle" under the table. They share their sadness with "no translation other than their tears."

Page 253
1. "Leah's Pony" is similar to *Bonesy and Isabel*. The main characters are both girls. They each have a special animal. They each lose the animal—Leah sells her pony for a while, and Bonesy dies. Both girls are sad, both get happier, and both help their families.
2. People in families take care of each other. Feelings don't always need words. Everything has a story.
3. On page 9, Isabel listens to the animals' stories. On page 30, she tells Bonesy's story to the animals. She knows more English. She is part of the story of the farm and the family.

Page 257
1. B 2. F 3. D 4. H 5. A 6. G 7. A 8. J 9. B
10. Responses should explain that Bonesy is Isabel's first friend in her new home. When Bonesy dies, Isabel, Vera, and Ivan share feelings of love and sadness, and that makes them a family.

Dolphin Adventure
Page 260
1. He is in Florida on a diving boat, has a friend named Amos, has been diving with the same friends for years, and loves the beauty of the sea.
2. The other divers are there to hunt and carry spear guns. He is there for pleasure and carries only a diving knife.
3. The divers wear wet suits, masks, flippers, and a tank of air. They each carry a diving knife.

Page 261
1. All the divers go into the water. The person telling the story sees many beautiful things underwater, stays there for more than 35 minutes, and then goes back to the boat, feeling he has had a perfect dive.
2. He sees "wonders" and beautiful things. He sees all kinds of fishes. He sees schools of fish, barracudas, lobsters, eels, and sharks.
3. The author wants you to know about the beauty of the sea and all its wonders. He wants to show his own love for the sea and its wonderful creatures.

Page 262
1. a feeling that something is going to happen
2. The floats stay on the top of the water, to tell people in boats that a diver is below the surface.
3. The dolphins are swimming toward the diver.

Page 263
1. The baby is wounded, so the dolphins need help.
2. They are intelligent, they have close family ties. They seem to have human expressions on their faces. They communicate in some ways.
3. danger from dolphins and from sharks

Page 264
1. He is trying to make the dolphin calm down and trust him.
2. a shark attack
3. Responses will vary.

Page 265
1. He cuts the fishing line.
2. He is cutting; he uses a knife to remove an object from the body.
3. He is worried about hurting the baby; that a shark will attack if he does not succeed; and that he will not be able to get the hook out.

Page 266
1. They attack the sharks.
2. He holds his hand tightly on the wound for a long time.
3. No. That is an opinion of the author. The dolphin's behavior does seem like a human way of saying thank you, though.

Page 267
1. Responses will vary.
2. Possible response: People should enjoy and respect underwater life.
3. Responses will vary.

Page 271
1. B 2. F 3. C 4. G 5. C 6. G 7. D 8. H 9. A
10. Responses will vary. Students may note that the story says that dolphins do not usually go up to people. They may doubt that the "father" dolphin looked the diver in the eye or that he nudged or "thanked" him. They may find it hard to believe that the author saw the same baby two weeks later, or that he could identify the scar from a boat that was probably far away.

Horsepower: The Wonder of Draft Horses
Page 274
1. huge black hooves; tall as a basketball player; weighs as much as a classroom of first graders
2. to pull people in carriages; milk wagons; and plows
3. She says they are remarkable; she says you can sense their intelligence.

Page 275
1. They pull on straps and lines connected to the harness to drive Kate.
2. Some farmers use them to pull plows; they march in city parades; some Amish farmers use them for all their field work.
3. Amish farmers use old-fashioned farm equipment. They do not use tractors.

Page 276
1. They have to spend time harnessing and hitching the team.
2. The traces will get loose; the driver may not be able to control the team.
3. after they learn to lead and be tied, and when they are big enough

Page 277
1. Responses will vary.
2. The people who own draft horses are proud of them; they work hard to train them; they enjoy showing them and getting together with other draft horse owners.
3. Responses will vary. Students should refer to an event in the story and give reasons for their choice.

Page 281
1. B 2. F 3. D 4. H 5. A 6. H 7. B 8. J 9. C
10. Draft horses are beautiful, powerful, intelligent animals. They have a long history. They were once very important for producing food and moving people from place to place.

Glossary

A

a·ban·don [ə·ban'dən] *v.* **a·ban·doned** To leave; desert; forsake.

ac·quire [ə·kwīr'] *v.* To get; obtain.

a·fraid [ə·frād'] *adj.* Full of fear or dread.

af·ter·math [af'tər·math] *n.* A result or consequence.

aisle [īl] *n.* A passageway in a building.

a·larm [ə·lärm'] *n.* A device, such as a bell or siren, that gives a signal or sound to warn others of danger.

an·ces·tor [an'ses·tər] *n.* **an·ces·tors** A family member who lived long ago.

an·cient [ān'shənt] *adj.* From a long ago time.

anx·ious [angk'shəs] *adj.* Worried; uneasy.

a·part·ment build·ing [ə·pärt'mənt bil'ding] *n.* A structure with apartments, or groups of rooms to live in.

ap·pe·tiz·ing [ap'ə·tī·zing] *adj.* Pleasing to eat.

ar·gu·ment [är'gyə·mənt] *n.* **ar·gu·ments** An angry discussion or disagreement.

a·ro·ma [ə·rō'mə] *n.* A pleasant smell.

ar·thri·tis [är·thrī'tis] *n.* A disease that causes pain in the joints.

as·tro·naut [as'trə·nôt'] *n.* A person who travels in space.

at·mos·phere [at'məs·fir] *n.* The air surrounding Earth.

au·ro·ra [ô'·rôr'ə] *n.* Colored lights seen in the night sky.

au·thor [ô·thər] *n.* **au·thors** A person who has written something, such as a book, story, or article.

au·to·graph [ô'tə·graf'] *v.* To write one's name.

B

bal·ance [bal'əns] *n.* The ability to keep one's body in a desired position without falling.

bare [bâr] *adj.* Empty.

bay [bā] *n.* A body of water partly surrounded by land; an inlet of the sea or of a lake.

be·have [bi·hāv'] *v.* To act properly.

bi·cy·cle [bī'sik·əl] *n.* A vehicle with two large wheels, one behind the other. A rider moves it by foot pedals and steers it with handlebars.

blaze [blāz] *n.* A bright, glowing flame; fire.

bleat [blēt] *v.* To utter the cry of a sheep, goat, or calf.

bliz·zard [bliz'ərd] *n.* A heavy snowstorm with strong, freezing wind.

blos·som [blos'əm] *n.* **blos·soms** A flower, especially of a plant or tree that bears fruit.

boast·ful [bōst'ful] *adj.* Likely to brag.

boil [boil] *v.* **boiled** To heat a liquid until bubbles form and rise to the surface as steam.

boot [boot] *n.* **boots** A shoe that covers the foot and part of the leg.

breathe [brēth] *v.* To draw air into and let it out of the lungs.

breed [brēd] *n.* A particular kind of animal or plant.

brim [brim] *v.* **brim·ming** To be filled to the top.

brisk·ly [brisk'lē] *adv.* Quickly.

build·ing [bil'ding] *n.* A structure built for shelter or storage, as a house or barn.

bump [bump] *v.* **bumped** To hit against or knock; **bump into** To meet by chance.

bur·lap [bûr'lap] *adj.* Made out of burlap, a coarse material used for making such items as bags or wrappings.

bur·y [ber'ē] *v.* **bur·y·ing** To hide or cover from view.

but·ter [but'ər] *n.* The yellowish fat that becomes separated from milk during churning. It is used as a spread and in cooking.

cack·le [kak'əl] *v.* **cack·led** To make a short, shrill laugh.

cac·tus [kak'təs] *n.* A desert plant that is covered with spines or prickles.

caf·e·te·ri·a [kaf'ə·tir'ē·ə] *n.* A restaurant in which people select food from a counter and then carry it to tables to eat.

calm [käm] *adj.* Quiet; peaceful; still.

car·pen·ter [kär'pən·tər] *n.* A worker who uses wood to make buildings, ships, or other structures.

cel·e·brate [sel'ə·brāt'] *v.* To observe or honor in a special manner.

cel·lar [sel'ər] *n.* A room or several rooms underground, usually beneath a building.

change [chānj] *v.* To make or become different.

change [chānj] *n.* **chang·es** The act or result of making something different.

chant [chant] *v.* **chant·ing** To sing on just a few notes.

chick·en [chik'ən] *n.* A large barnyard bird that people use as food.

chick·en pox [chik'ən poks] *n.* A contagious disease, especially of children, in which blisters form on the skin, causing intense itching.

chuck·le [chuk'əl] *v.* **chuck·led** To laugh softly.

clear [klir] *v.* **cleared** To become free of clouds or fog.

click [klik] *v.* **clicking** To make or cause to make a short, sharp sound.

cli·ent [klī'ənt] *n.* **cli·ents** A customer.

coin [koin] *n.* **coins** A piece of metal stamped by the government for use as money.

com·mer·cial [kə·mûr'shəl] *n.* **com·mer·cials** An advertisement.

com·mun·i·cate [kə·myōō'nə·kāt'] *v.* To give and receive thoughts, information, or messages.

com·pan·ion [kəm·pan'yən] *n.* Comrade.

con·trol [kən·trōl'] *v.* To direct or manage.

cor·rec·tion [kə·rek'shən] *n.* **cor·rec·tions** A change that is made to improve something.

co·zy [kō'zē] *adj.* Warm and comfortable.

crea·ture [krē'chər] *n.* **crea·tures** A living animal or human.

crime [krīm] *n.* An action that is against the law.

cringe [krinj] *v.* **cringed** To shrink in fear.

crow [krō] *n.* **crows** A large black bird with a harsh cawing voice.

cu·ri·ous [kyōōr'ē·əs] *adj.* Eager to know or learn more.

© Harcourt

a add	e end	o odd	o͞o pool	oi oil	t͟h this		a in *above*
ā ace	ē equal	ō open	u up	ou pout	zh vision		e in *sicken*
â care	i it	ô order	û burn	ng ring		ə =	i in *possible*
ä palm	ī ice	o͝o took	yo͞o fuse	th thin			o in *melon*
							u in *circus*

debt [det] *n.* That which a person owes to another person.

dec·o·ra·tion [dek'ə·rā'shən] *n.* **dec·o·ra·tions** Something used for making fancier or more beautiful.

ded·i·ca·tion [ded'ə·kā'shən] *n.* The words dedicating a book to someone.

de·li·cious [di·lish'əs] *adj.* Highly pleasing to the taste; extremely good to eat.

de·mand [di·mand'] *v.* **de·mand·ed** To ask for boldly.

dem·on·strate [dem'ən·strāt'] *v.* To show how something works.

de·part·ment [di·pärt'mənt] *n.* **de·part·ments** A separate part or division.

de·sign [di·zīn'] *v.* To draw plans or sketches for.

de·ter·mined [di·tûr'mind] *adj.* Firmly intending to do something.

dis·o·bey [dis'ə·bā'] *v.* **dis·o·beyed** To refuse or fail to do what is asked.

dis·play [dis·plā'] *v.* **dis·played** To show in a way that attracts notice; exhibit.

dis·qual·i·fy [dis·kwol'ə·fī'] *v.* **dis·qual·i·fied** To declare to be unfit, as to receive a prize.

dis·tance [dis'təns] *n.* The space between two points.

dol·phin [dol'fin] *n.* **dol·phins** A saltwater mammal, related to the whale but smaller, having a long snout.

dou·ble [dub'əl] *v.* To make or become twice as much or twice as great.

dough [dō] *n.* A thick, soft mixture of ingredients, such as is used to make bread.

down·cur·rent [doun·kûr'ənt] *adj.* In the direction of the flow of water.

draft [draft] *n.* **drafts** A current of air.

earth·quake [ûrth'kwāk'] *n.* A shaking or vibration of a part of the earth's surface.

ebb [eb] *v.* **ebbed** To flow out or recede, as the ocean tide.

ed·i·tor [ed'i·tər] *n.* **ed·i·tors** A person who edits, or arranges, corrects, or prepares for publication.

el·e·va·tor [el'ə·vā'tər] *n.* A platform that is raised and lowered to carry passengers or goods up and down inside a building.

en·chant·ing [in·chant'ing] *adj.* Charming; delightful.

en·gine [en'jin] *n.* **en·gines** A machine that uses energy, such as that produced by burning fuel, to do work.

e·quiv·a·lent [i·kwiv'ə·lənt] *adj.* Equal.

e·rode [i·rōd'] *v.* **e·rod·ed** To wear away.

es·ti·mate [es'tə·māt'] *v.* To make a close guess about.

ev·i·dence [ev'ə·dəns] *n.* Something that proves what has happened.

ex·cite·ment [ik·sīt'mənt] *n.* A strong feeling of happiness.

ex·plore [ik·splôr'] *v.* To travel in a new place in order to learn or discover or try new things.

ex·trav·a·gant [ik·strav'ə·gənt] *adj.* Spending too much; wasteful.

fad [fad] *n.* Something that is very popular for a short time.

© Harcourt

fa·vor·ite [fā′vər·it] *adj.* Best loved.

feast [fēst] *n.* A great meal with a lot of food.

feel [fēl] *v.* To seem to be.

feel·ing [fē′ling] *n.* **feel·ings** An emotion.

fend·er [fen′dər] *n.* **fend·ers** A metal part over a wheel.

fes·ti·val [fes′tə·vəl] *n.* A time or occasion for rejoicing or feasting.

fetch [fech] *v.* To go to get, get and bring back.

fi·es·ta [fē·es′tə] *n.* A Spanish word for a celebration or festival.

fin [fin] *n.* A fanlike or winglike part of a fish, whale, seal, or other water animal.

finish line [fin′ish līn] *n.* A line marking the end of a race.

fish·ing [fish′ing] *n.* The catching of fish, either for a living or for pleasure.

flame [flām] *n.* **flames** The burning gas rising from a fire, usually in glowing orange or yellow tongues.

flam·ing [flā′ming] *adj.* Glowing or flaring up like flames.

flip·per [flip′ər] *n.* **flip·pers** Finlike footgear worn by divers to aid in swimming.

flock [flok] *n.* A group of animals of the same kind.

fluke [flōōk] *n.* Part of the tail of a water animal.

flut·ter [flut′ər] *v.* To flap the wings without really flying; fly clumsily.

fly·er [flī′ər] *n.* A leaflet or handbill.

for·give [fər·giv′] *v.* To stop blaming or being angry with.

frame [frām] *n.* A structure inside something that gives support and shape to the thing built around it.

friend [frend] *n.* **friends** A person one knows well, and likes.

frus·tra·tion [frus·trā′shən] *n.* A feeling of disappointment.

fund [fund] *n.* A sum of money set aside for a purpose.

fur·nace [fûr′nis] *n.* A structure in which a fire burns so to heat a building or to melt metals.

gal·lop [gal′əp] *v.* To run at the fastest gait of a four-footed animal.

gar·den [gär′dən] *n.* A plot of land where flowers, vegetables, or other plants are grown.

gauge [gāj] *n.* **gauges** An instrument used for measuring.

gen·er·ous [jen′ər·əs] *adj.* Large and abundant.

gi·ant [jī′ənt] *adj.* Huge or great.

gig·gle [gig′əl] *n.* **gig·gles** A silly or nervous laugh that has high, fluttering sounds.

glide [glīd] *v.* To move smoothly and without effort.

gloo·my [glōō′mē] *adj.* Sad; dejected.

glo·ri·ous [glôr′ē·əs] *adj.* Very pleasant; delightful.

grand·daugh·ter [gran(d)′dô′tər] *n.* A daughter of one's son or daughter.

green·er·y [grē′nər·ē] *n.* Green plants.

greet [grēt] *v.* To show friendly recognition to, as when meeting someone.

a	add	e	end	o	odd	o͞o	pool	oi	oil	t͟h	this			a in *above*
ā	ace	ē	equal	ō	open	u	up	ou	pout	zh	vision			e in *sicken*
â	care	i	it	ô	order	û	burn	ng	ring			ə =		i in *possible*
ä	palm	ī	ice	o͝o	took	yo͞o	fuse	th	thin					o in *melon*
														u in *circus*

groom [gro͞om] v. **groom·ing** To feed, clean, and brush.

group [gro͞op] n. **groups** A number of persons or things.

guard [gärd] n. A person or group that watches over or keeps from harm.

guitar [gi·tär′] n. A stringed musical instrument played by plucking the strings with the fingers or a pick.

hand·ker·chief [hang′kər·chif] n. A square piece of cloth used for wiping the face or nose.

han·dle·bar [han′dəl·bär] n. **han·dle·bars** A curved bar for steering, as on a bicycle.

hap·pi·ness [hap′ē·nis] n. A feeling of being pleased or contented.

hap·py [hap′ē] adj. Enjoying or showing pleasure; joyous.

har·ness [här′nis] n. Leather straps or bands used to connect a horse or mule to a cart, plow, or other piece of equipment.

har·vest [här′vist] n. The gathering and bringing in of a crop.

head·first [hed′fûrst′] adv. With the head first.

hel·per [help′ər] n. Someone who helps or assists.

herd [hûrd] v. To gather animals together into a large group.

his·tor·y [his′tə·rē] n. The study of records of past events.

hitch [hich] v. To fasten or tie.

home·work [hōm′wûrk′] n. Work done at home, especially schoolwork.

home·y [hō′mē] adj. Homelike.

hon·est [on′ist] adj. Acting honorably and justly; not lying, stealing, or cheating.

hoof [ho͝of or ho͞of] n. **hooves** [ho͝ovs or ho͞ovs] The hard covering on the foot of certain animals, such as horses, cattle, and pigs.

hope [hōp] v. **hop·ing** To want and expect.

hor·i·zon [hə·rī′zən] n. The line where the earth and sky seem to meet.

horse race [hôrs rās] n. A race held to determine the fastest horse.

hug [hug] n. **hug·ging** To clasp in the arms.

hur·ri·cane [hûr′ə·kān] n. A storm with heavy rains and strong, whirling winds.

hus·band [huz′bənd] n. A married man.

hut [hut] n. A small, simple house or cabin.

ich·thy·ol·o·gy [ik′thē·ol′ə·jē] n. The study of fish.

icy [ī′sē] adj. Cold, like ice.

i·de·a [ī·dē′ə] n. **i·de·as** A thought in the mind; a way of seeing or understanding things.

i·den·ti·cal [ī·den′ti·kəl] adj. Exactly alike.

il·lus·tra·tor [il′ə·strā·tər] n. **il·lus·tra·tors** An artist who makes drawings for books.

im·me·di·ate·ly [i·mē′dē·it·lē] adv. Right away; now.

im·mense [i·mens′] adj. Very large; huge.

in·for·ma·tion [in·fər·mā′shən] n. Facts about a subject.

in·sti·tute [in′stə·to͞ot] n. An organization, school, or society devoted to a special study or cause.

in·vi·ta·tion [in′və·tā′shən] n. **in·vi·ta·tions** A request that asks someone to come to a place or do something.

© Harcourt

jour·ney [jûr′nē] *n.* A trip taken from one place to another.

ker·chief [kûr′chif] *n.* A square piece of cloth.

ki·wi [kē′wē] *n.* The sweet, edible fruit of an Asian vine, having a fuzzy brown rind.

knap·sack [nap′sak′] *n.* A large bag for supplies, worn strapped to the back.

Lab·ra·dor re·triev·er [la′brə·dôr ri·trē′vər] *n.* A compact, strongly built dog with short fur.

la·dy·like [lā′dē·līk] *adj.* Having good manners, as expected of a woman of wealth or important position.

lan·guage [lang′gwij] *n.* Any means of expressing ideas or emotions.

laugh [laf] *v.* **laugh·ing** To make sounds and show movements of the mouth, eyes, and face that show joy.

lay·er [lā′ər] *n.* A single thickness or covering.

lazily [lāz′ə·lē] *adv.* Slowly; sluggishly.

leap [lēp] *v.* **leapt** [lept] To jump.

lin·en [lin′ən] *n.* **lin·ens** Cloth made of flax fibers.

list [list] *n.* **lists** A series of items, often written in a certain order.

load [lōd] *v.* **load·ing** To put in or on something for carrying.

lone·ly [lōn′lē] *adj.* **1** Feeling alone and longing for the presence of friends. **2** Deserted, as of a place.

lounge [lounj] *v.* **loung·ing** To pass time in a lazy manner.

mag·net [mag′nit] *n.* An object that creates a magnetic field, or moving electric charge, around itself.

mail·bag [māl′bag] *n.* A soft container in which a letter carrier takes mail for delivery.

mall [môl] *n.* A huge structure containing many stores; a shopping center.

mane [mān] *n.* The long hair growing on the neck of some animals, such as the horse and lion.

mar·ga·rine [mär′jə·rin] *n.* A substitute for butter, made of vegetable oils and other ingredients.

mask [mask] *n.* **masks** A covering used to hide or protect all or part of the face.

mat·tress [mat′rəs] *n.* A large pad made of a strong fabric and filled with cotton, foam rubber, or springs, used on a bed.

mead·ow [med′ō] *n.* **mead·ows** A field of grass that is used for hay or grazing.

meal [mēl] *n.* **meals** The food served or eaten at a certain time of day.

meas·ure [mezh′ər] *v.* To find out the size, weight, or time of.

me·chan·ic [mə·kan′ik] *n.* A person who is skilled in the making, using, or fixing of tools or machines.

men·u [men′yoo] *n.* A list of the foods provided for a meal.

© Harcourt

a	add	e	end	o	odd	oo	pool	oi	oil	th	this	
ā	ace	ē	equal	ō	open	u	up	ou	pout	zh	vision	
â	care	i	it	ô	order	û	burn	ng	ring			ə =
ä	palm	ī	ice	oŏ	took	yoo	fuse	th	thin			

ə = { *a* in *above*; *e* in *sicken*; *i* in *possible*; *o* in *melon*; *u* in *circus* }

me·sa [mā′sə] *n.* A hill with a flat top and steep sides, common in the southwestern U.S.

mill [mill] *n.* A machine or device for grinding or crushing.

mois·ture [mois′chər] *n.* Water in very small drops causing dampness.

mor·ti·fy [môr′tə·fī′] *v.* **mor·ti·fied** To humiliate.

moun·tain [moun′tən] *n.* **moun·tains** A mass of land, higher than a hill, rising far above its surroundings.

mourn·ful [môrn′fəl] *adj.* **mourn·ful·ly** *adv.* Showing or causing grief; sorrowful.

mug [mug] *v.* **mug·ging** To attack and rob.

mule [myo͞ol] *n.* **mules** The offspring of a donkey and a horse.

mut·ter [mut′ər] *v.* **mut·tered** To complain; grumble.

mys·ter·y [mis′tər·ē] *n.* Something that is not known, understood, or explained.

Ne·va·da [nə·vad′ə *or* nə·vä′də] A state in the western U.S.

nev·er·the·less [nev′ər·thə·les′] *adv.* All the same.

nick·er [ni′kər] *n.* Neigh; whinny.

Nor·way [nôr′wā′] A Scandinavian country of northern Europe, west of Sweden.

nudge [nuj] *v.* **nudged** To touch or push gently.

nui·sance [n(y)o͞o′səns] *n.* Anything that annoys or bothers.

o·cean [ō′shən] *n.* The great body of salt water that covers about 70 percent of the earth's surface.

or·bit [ôr′bit] *n.* The path taken by a body in space as it moves around something.

or·der [ôr′dər] *n.* A demand or request to buy, sell, or supply something.

o·ver·board [ō′vər·bôrd′] *adv.* Over the side of a ship into water.

pan·ic [pan′ik] *v.* Sudden, overwhelming fear.

part·ner·ship [pärt′nər·ship] *n.* Two or more people working together.

pas·ture [pas′chər] *n.* Ground covered with grass and other plants that horses, cattle, or sheep can eat.

pa·tient [pā′shənt] *n.* A person who is being treated for illness or injury.

ped·al [ped′əl] *n.* **ped·als** A lever pushed by the foot to operate or control something.

pho·to·graph [fō′tə·graf′] *n.* A picture made with a camera.

play·ground [plā′ground′] *n.* An area, often next to a school, for children to play in.

plow [plou] *v.* To use a plow, a large tool used for preparing soil for planting.

pole [pōl] *n.* A long, thin wooden or metal stick.

pot [pot] *n.* A usually round, deep container used for cooking, growing plants, or other household purposes.

pour [pôr] *v.* **poured** To flow or cause to flow in a continuous stream.

pow·er [pou′ər] *n.* A form of energy for doing work.

prair·ie [prâr′ē] *n.* A large region of flat, grassy land.

prance [prans] *v.* To move with high steps.

prin·ci·pal [prin′sə·pəl] *n.* The leader of a school.

print·er [prin′tər] *n.* **print·ers** A person who uses machines to produce printed material.

pri·vate [prī′vit] *adj.* Away from public view; hidden.

pro·claim [prō·klām′] *v.* **pro·claimed** To make known; declare.

pro·duce [prə·d(y)o͞os′] *v.* To bring into being.

pro·nounce [prə·nouns′] *v.* **pro·nounced** To make the sound or sounds of.

prop·er [prop′ər] *adj.* Suitable; fitting; appropriate.

pub·lish·er [pub′lish·ər] *n.* **pub·lish·ers** A person or company that produces books, magazines, newspapers, or similar materials.

pyr·a·mid [pir′ə·mid] *n.* A figure having a flat base and three or more sides. All the sides are triangles that meet in a point at the top.

quartz [kwôrtz] *n.* A hard, glasslike mineral.

quilt [kwilt] *n.* **quilts** A bed covering made of small pieces sewn together by hand.

ra·di·a·tion [rā′dē·ā′shən] *n.* The sending out of energy.

rain·coat [rān′kōt] *n.* A coat, usually waterproof, to be worn in rainy weather.

raise [rāz] *v.* To grow or breed.

rai·sin [rā′zən] *n.* A sweet grape dried in the sun or in an oven.

re·duce [ri·do͞os′] *v.* **re·duced** To make less in size or amount.

reef [rēf] *n.* **reefs** A ridge of sand, rocks, or coral at or near the surface of the ocean.

re·flect [ri·flekt′] *v.* **re·flect·ing** To throw back an image of.

reg·i·ster [rej′is·tər] *n.* A device for counting or recording.

rein [rān] *n.* **reins** A strap placed on a horse to control it while it is being ridden or driven.

re·jec·tion [ri·jek′shən] *n.* The act of rejecting, or refusing to take.

res·i·dent [rez′ə·dənt] *adj.* Living in a place.

re·view [ri·vyo͞o′] *n.* **re·views** An article or essay discussing something, such as a book, movie, or play.

re·ward [ri·wôrd′] *n.* Something given or done in return, such as a gift or prize for merit, service, or achievement.

ridge [rij] *n.* A long, narrow hill.

round·up [round′up′] *n.* A bringing together of cattle.

rouse [rouz] *v.* To wake up.

run [run] *v.* **run·ning** To move quickly.

safe [sāf] *adj.* Free from danger.

salt mine [sôlt mīn] *n.* A place where salt is collected.

scar [skär] *n.* The mark left in the skin after the healing of a wound, burn, or sore.

© Harcourt

a add	e end	o odd	o͞o pool	oi oil	th this		a in *above*
ā ace	ē equal	ō open	u up	ou pout	zh vision		e in *sicken*
â care	i it	ô order	û burn	ng ring		ə =	i in *possible*
ä palm	ī ice	o͝o took	yo͞o fuse	th thin			o in *melon*
							u in *circus*

sea [sē] *n.* The large body of salt water that covers most of the earth's surface.

se·cur·i·ty [si•kyo͝or′ə•tē] *n.* A person or thing that makes one feel safe.

seed [sēd] *n.* The embryo of a plant and the food for its early growth. It is enclosed in a case or covering and is able to grow into a young plant under the right conditions.

seed·ling [sēd′ling] *n.* **seed·lings** A young tree or plant, grown from a seed.

serv·ing [sûr′ving] *n.* **serv·ings** A portion of food.

set·tle [set′(ə)l] *v.* **set·tled** Make a home.

share [shâr] *v.* To give out; to offer.

shed [shed] *n.* A small, low building, often with an open front or sides .

shore·line [shôr′līn] *n.* The line where land meets the water.

shov·el [shuv′əl] *n.* A tool with a handle and a somewhat flattened scoop, used for lifting or moving things.

shy [shī] *adj.* Bashful or uncomfortable with people.

sigh [sī] *v.* **sighed** To let out a deep, loud breath.

si·lence [sī′ləns] *n.* Absence of sound.

sketch [skech] *n.* **sketch·es** A rough, unfinished drawing giving a general impression without full details.

ski [skē] *n.* **skis** One of a pair of long runners of wood, metal, or plastic that are attached to the soles of boots for gliding over snow.

slope [slōp] *n.* **slopes** A piece of hillside that slants.

smooth [smo͞oth] *adj.* Having a surface without any roughness or unevenness.

snow [snō] *n.* Frozen water vapor in the air which falls to the ground as small white flakes.

snow·shoe [snō′sho͞o] *n.* A network of leather thongs or strips, used for walking in deep snow.

soar [sôr] *v.* **soared** To rise high into the air.

sob [sob] *n.* **sobs** The sound of weeping with catches of the breath.

So·lar Sys·tem [sō′lər sis′təm] The sun and the planets that revolve around it.

som·ber [som′bər] *adj.* Gloomy; solemn.

spell [spel] *n.* **spells** A period of time.

spell·er [spel′ər] *n.* A book of exercises in spelling words.

spoke [spōk] *n.* **spokes** One of the rods or bars that connect the rim of a wheel to the hub.

squeeze [skwēz] *v.* **squeez·ing** To press hard upon.

stage·coach [stāj′kōch′] *n.* A large coach pulled by horses and having a regular route from town to town for carrying passengers, mail, and packages.

steel [stēl] *n.* A tough and widely used metal made of a mixture of iron, carbon, and sometimes other metals.

stock·ing [stok′ing] *n.* A covering for the foot and leg.

store [stôr] *n.* A place where merchandise of any kind is kept for sale; shop.

storm [stôrm] *n.* A condition of weather, often having strong winds along with rain, snow, thunder, or lightning.

stran·ger [strān′jər] *n.* A person who is not known.

stray [strā] *v.* To wander away.

sub·ject [sub′jikt] *n.* **subjects** A branch of learning or course of study.

suf·fer·ing [suf′ər•ing] *n.* Pain, distress, anguish, or misery.

© Harcourt

sug·ges·tion [sə(g)·jes′chən] *n.* **sug·ges·tions** Something suggested, or proposed.

sun·glas·ses [sun·glas′iz] *n.* Spectacles to protect the eyes from the glare of the sun, usually made with colored glass or plastic.

sur·face [sûr′fis] *n.* The outer part of any solid body, or the upper level of a liquid.

surgery [sûr′jər·ē] *n.* An operation involving the repair or removal of diseased or injured organs or parts of the body.

sur·round [sə·round′] *v.* **sur·round·ed** To enclose on all sides; envelop; encircle.

sur·vive [sər·vīv′] *v.* **sur·vived** To remain alive or in existence.

tale [tāl] *n.* **tales** A story.

tan·gle [tang′əl] *v.* **tan·gled** To trap or hold as in a snare.

tank [tangk] *n.* A container used to store something.

team [tēm] *n.* **teams** A set of two or more animals harnessed together.

tem·per·a·ture [tem′pər·ə·chər *or* tem′prə·chər] *n.* The degree of heat or cold.

thief [thēf] *n.* A person who steals, especially secretly and without using violence.

thought·ful [thôt′fəl] *adj.* Considerate; kind.

threat [thret] *n.* **threats** A warning or promise that one intends to hurt or punish another person or thing.

tid·al wave [tī′dəl wāv] *n.* A huge ocean wave caused by an undersea volcanic eruption or an undersea earthquake.

tilt [tilt] *v.* **tilt·ed** To tip at an angle.

top [top] *n.* A cone-shaped toy with a point on which it is made to spin.

torch [tôrch] *n.* A source of light, such as a burning stick of wood that can be carried in the hand.

trans·la·tion [trans·lā′shən] *n.* Something that has been translated, or changed into another language.

trem·bling [trem′bling] *n.* The act of shaking, as with agitation, fear, weakness, or cold.

tre·men·dous [tri·men′dəs] *adj.* Large; enormous.

trim [trim] *n.* Decoration; ornament.

trot [trot] *v.* To move at a rapid but not too fast pace.

trust [trust] *v.* To believe in the honesty of another person; to rely on.

tug [tug] *v.* **tug·ging** To pull at with effort.

twice [twīs] *adv.* Two times as much; doubly.

twi·light [twī′līt′] *n.* The light in the sky just after sunset or before sunrise.

twitch [twich] *v.* **twitched** To move with a sharp, quick jerk.

ty·phoon [tī·fōōn′] *n.* A violent hurricane originating over tropical waters in the western Pacific and the China Seas.

un·bro·ken [un·brō′kən] *adj.* Not broken; whole.

un·pack [un·pak′] *v.* To remove things from their containers.

© Harcourt

a	add	e	end	o	odd	o͞o	pool	oi	oil	th	this
ā	ace	ē	equal	ō	open	u	up	ou	pout	zh	vision
â	care	i	it	ô	order	û	burn	ng	ring		
ä	palm	ī	ice	o͝o	took	yo͞o	fuse	th	thin		

ə = { a in *above*; e in *sicken*; i in *possible*; o in *melon*; u in *circus* }

V

val·ley [val′ē] *n.* A low area on the earth's surface, such as between hills or mountains.

van·ish [van′ish] *v.* **van·ished** To disappear suddenly from sight.

va·ri·e·ty [və•rī′ə•tē] *n.* A collection of different things; assortment.

veg·e·tar·i·an [vej′ə•târ′ē•ən] *n.* A person who eats mostly fruits and vegetables and no meat.

Vi·king [vī′king] *n.* **Vi·kings** A Scandinavian warrior who raided the coast of Europe from the eighth to the tenth centuries.

vil·lage [vil′ij] *n.* A collection of houses in the country smaller than a town.

W

wag·on [wag′ən] *n.* A large vehicle pulled by animals.

ware·house [wâr′hous′] *n.* **ware·hous·es** A large building for storing goods or merchandise.

warm [wôrm] *adj.* Comfortably hot.

watch [woch] **watch·ing** *v.* To observe.

wa·ter lev·el [wô′tər lev′əl] *n.* The height of the surface of a body of water.

wa·ter·mel·on [wô′tər•mel′ən *or* wot′ər•mel′ən] *n.* A large fruit with a thick skin, many seeds, and a very juicy pink pulp.

wave [wāv] *n.* **waves** A disturbance consisting of a peak followed by a dip that travels across the surface of a liquid.

well [wel] *n.* A hole dug into the earth to reach a resource, such as water.

wet suit [wet sōōt] *n.* **wet suits** A suit worn by divers that traps a thin layer of water next to their skin to hold in their body heat.

whale [(h)wāl] *n.* **whales** A mammal that lives in the ocean and resembles a gigantic fish.

wife [wīf] *n.* A married woman.

wil·low [wil′ō] *n.* **wil·lows** A type of tree or shrub with branches that hang down and long narrow leaves.

wince [wins] *v.* **winced** To shrink or draw back from pain; flinch.

wool [wŏŏl] *n.* The soft, curly hair of sheep.

work [wûrk] *v.* To put out effort to accomplish something; labor.

work lamp [wûrk lamp] *n.* A small light or lantern on a hat worn by a miner.

wound [wōōnd] *n.* A hurt or injury caused by something piercing, cutting, or tearing through the skin.

wrench [rench] *v.* **wrenched** To twist or pull with force.

Z

zig·zag [zig′zag] *v.* **zig·zag·ging** To move in a zigzag, a series of short, sharp turns.

© Harcourt